Athletes Remembered

Mexicano/Latino Professional Football Players
1929-1970

Errata

Page

47, rt. col., l. 3; 175   Read Theresa Chávez for Trecia Chávez

103   George Mira photo credit: University of Miami Sports Information

130   Jim Plunkett photo credit: John Sandhaus

141, 142   Transpose photo captions

169, lft. col., l. 24   Read Ray Romero for Ric Romero

Bilingual Press/Editorial Bilingüe

General Editor

Gary D. Keller

Managing Editor

Karen S. Van Hooft

Associate Editors

Karen M. Akins

Barbara H. Firoozye

Assistant Editor

Linda St. George Thurston

Editorial Consultant

Janet Woolum

Address:

Bilingual Review/Press

Hispanic Research Center

Arizona State University

P.O. Box 872702

Tempe, Arizona 85287-2702

(602) 965-3867

Athletes Remembered

Mexicano/Latino Professional Football Players
1929-1970

Mario Longoria

Bilingual Press/Editorial Bilingüe
Tempe, Arizona

ISBN 0-927534-63-0

Library of Congress Cataloging-in-Publication Data

Longoria, Mario.
    Athletes Remembered : Mexicano/Latino professional football
players, 1929–1970 / Mario Longoria.
        p.   cm.
    Includes bibliographical references (p.   ).
    ISBN 0-927534-63-0 (alk. paper)
    1. Hispanic American football players—Biography. 2. Latin
Americans—Biography. I. Title.
GV939.A1L66 1997
796.332'092'2—dc20
[B]   96–43251
                                                                   CIP

PRINTED IN THE UNITED STATES OF AMERICA

Cover design, interior by John Wincek, Aerocraft Charter Art Service
Football cards on front and back covers courtesy of The Topps Company, New York

Acknowledgments

The author wishes to thank the following organizations for permission to use player photographs:
Atlanta Falcons, Chicago Bears, Cincinnati Bengals, Dallas Cowboys, Drake University Athletics,
Louisiana State University Office of Public Relations, Miami Dolphins, Oregon State University Sports
Information, Philadelphia Eagles, Phoenix Cardinals, Pro Football Hall of Fame, Purdue University
Athletics, St. Louis Rams, Saint Mary's College of California, San Diego State University Department of
Athletics, San Jose State University Sports Information, Stanford University Department of Athletics,
Sul Ross State University News and Information, Texas A&M University at Kingsville Sports
Information, Texas Christian University Sports Information, Texas Tech University Sports News,
Tulane University Athletics, University of Alabama Department of Athletics, University of Arizona
Sports Information, University of California-Berkeley Sports Information, UCLA Sports Information,
University of Illinois at Urbana-Champaign Sports Information, University of Nebraska at Omaha
Sports Information, and University of Texas at Austin Sports Information.

To my parents,
Santos and Susana;
their love and inspiration
I can never repay.

Contents

Preface

When I first asked my close friends how many Latinos had played professional football over the years, the responses were few. We came up with a list of only ten players, most of them current at the time we pondered this question.

Somehow this did not seem to be accurate. There had to be others, so I decided to do a little research. I began with the city library, where I found an old dusty edition of Roger Treat's *Encyclopedia of Football* in the reference section. This book contained a wealth of information on the old NFL, including profiles of the numerous teams, and, importantly, team rosters of the players. From these rosters I began to identify the Spanish surnames and was amazed at the number of names I found. My next task, which at first appeared simple enough, was to begin gathering information on these players and to determine if, indeed, they were of Mexicano/Latino background.

No sooner did I start this arduous task than it became a crusade. The more I inquired, the more I found. My initial search for a few names became a passionate quest to uncover a lost history.

Years later, after hundreds of letters and a multitude of telephone calls to colleges and universities, alumni associations, U.S. and Canadian professional football teams, sportswriters, and the players themselves, my efforts began to pay off. My research revealed 98 Latinos who have played pro football since 1929. I was awed not only by the numbers but also by the stories these players told about their careers and experiences. Notwithstanding, the project began to overwhelm me, and, upon the advice of Joe Horrigan, curator at the Pro Football Hall of Fame in Canton, Ohio, I decided to end this history of Latinos in pro football in 1970. This year is symbolic because it marks the end of the old era in the NFL and the beginning of a new one.

In 1970 changing circumstances brought together the American Football (AFL) and National Football Leagues (NFL), but it was no easy matter to consolidate the two leagues into one. In 1966 the AFL rivaled the NFL in money and players. That year both leagues spent a total of $7 million to sign collegiate draftees.

The NFL was reported to sign 75 percent of their draftees while the AFL managed to sign almost half of their choices.

The money war continued to escalate. The AFL began to raid NFL teams, taking star players and creating serious business concerns for the established NFL. Not only did the NFL owners have to pay higher prices for the collegians, but they were also forced to increase the salaries of their veteran players to keep them from being lured to the AFL.

One notable Mexicano player caught in this rivalry was Joe Kapp. He was playing in Canada in 1966 but wanted to return stateside to play pro football. Kapp and the Houston Oilers of the AFL began contract negotiations. The Oilers wanted him to begin as their quarterback in 1968. Their offer was lucrative, and, if Kapp could secure an early release from his Canadian contract, there would be a bonus. Once the NFL found out, the front office intervened to nullify the Kapp-Houston agreement. They did this on the basis that Joe Kapp was still the property of the Washington Redskins, who had drafted him in 1959 and had not released him. There was also a standing agreement between the Canadian Football League and the NFL prohibiting tampering with each others players. This would be only a temporary set-back for Kapp.

Meanwhile, in secret meetings, Lamar Hunt of Kansas City and Tex Schramm of Dallas discussed the possibility of a merger of the two leagues. As a result of their efforts, what initially was thought impossible was realized on June 8, 1966, when NFL commissioner Pete Rozelle announced a merger of the two leagues that would become official in 1970.

Under the agreement, the AFL and NFL would combine to form an expanded league of 28 teams by 1970. All existing franchises would be retained and no franchise would be transferred. The teams played separate schedules through 1969, and both leagues agreed to play a yearly championship game beginning January 1967. Today this game is known as the Super Bowl. In 1967 the two leagues held the very first singular draft of collegiate talent, ending a six-year period of competing drafts by the two leagues. In that historical collegiate draft there were three Latinos: Alfredo Ávila was selected by the Washington Redskins and Bruce Cortez and Jim García were taken by the New Orleans Saints.

Amidst all the changes in 1967, Kapp did manage to jump leagues, but not to the Houston Oilers. Instead, Kapp signed a three-year contract with the Minnesota Vikings, where he settled in to lead the team to Super Bowl IV. Kapp's career epitomizes the changing face of pro football in this pivotal year with which *Athletes Remembered* ends.

Acknowledgments

This writer wishes to thank the many people I spoke to over the years about Mexicanos/ Latinos in professional football. What began as a curious interest became a passion and turned into a massive research project that took more than 14 years to complete.

I especially wish to thank Joe Horrigan, curator/ researcher at the Pro Football Hall of Fame, for all his assistance, guidance, and professionalism. Mr. Horrigan's help was truly invaluable to all my efforts.

Others of special importance and recognition are Coach Clem Clower of Salem College, Salem, West Virginia, and T. Edward Davis, former coach and Director of Athletics at Salem College for the years 1923–1941. These two gentlemen enabled me to locate the first and foremost player, Jesse Rodríguez. Also, thanks to Palmira Rodríguez from Fairmont, West Virginia, who provided me with an address for her other famous brother, Kelly Rodríguez. To her and the others, I am deeply indebted for their help.

Also, many thanks to the following professionals and private citizens who contributed to the making of the manuscript:

Dr. Rodolfo Acuña, California State University, Northridge.

Lillian Arbenz, Canadian Football League Hall of Fame & Museum.

Al Corona, *San Francisco Examiner,* friend of Gonzalo Morales.

Cam Cowie, Public Relations, Saskatchewan Roughriders Football Club.

Frank Del Olmo, Editor, *Los Angeles Times.*

Brother L. Dennis, Archivist, Saint Mary's College, Moraga, California.

William Dermody, Public Affairs Officer, U. S. Navy, Great Lakes, Illinois.

Stephen L. Douglas, Director of College Relations, West Virginia Wesleyan College, Buckhannon, West Virginia.

Gilbert Durán, Artist, San Antonio, Texas.

Lawrence Fan, Sports Information Director, San Jose State University.

Louise Froggett, Assistant Curator, Canadian Football League Hall of Fame & Museum.

Jim Gallagher, Director of Public Relations, Philadelphia Eagles.

Victoria Gates, Statistician, Canadian Football League office.

Art Goldchien, friend and teammate of Jesse Rodríguez at Salem College.

Jerry E. Green, Sports Information Office, New Mexico Military Institute.

Carlos Guerra, Columnist, *San Antonio Express-News,* San Antonio, Texas.

Sean Hallinan, Public Relations, National Football League Office.

Tim Hansen, Public Relations, Calgary Stampeders Football Club.

Catalina Hernández, A & A Secretarial Service.

Tony Hernández, *ProMex Sports Publication,* San Antonio, Texas.

Ron Howard, Public Relations, National Football League Office.

Lillian Hum, Public Relations, British Columbia Lions Football Club.

Tom Hurney, Past President of the Touchdown Club of Washington, DC.

Kristan Johnson, Sports Information, University of Illinois.

Josh Keller, Public Relations, British Columbia Lions Football Club.

Rebecca Koontz, M.L.S., Williamsville, New York.

Dave Kuhn, Sports Information Office, San Diego State University.

Gil Hernández-Lafferty, Director of Marketing, Los Angeles Raiders.

Susan Loney, Canadian Football League Information Office.

Ron Manz, Media/Public Relations Coordinator, Calgary Stampeders Football Club.

Patrick McCaskey, Director of Community Involvement, Chicago Bears.

Chick McElrone, Public Relations, Philadelphia Eagles.

Mark A. Meighen, Public Relations, Buffalo Bills.

Danny Montoya, Researcher, Los Angeles, California.

Nick Pappas, Sports Information Office, University of Southern California.

Carlos Reyes, University of Wisconsin-Madison.

Tom Rice, Alumni Association, University of San Francisco.

Larry Robertson, Information Officer, Canadian Football League Office.

Pat Rogers, Public Relations, San Diego Chargers Football Club.

Rubén Román, American Laminating Company, San Antonio, Texas.

Kippie T. Romero, Account Executive and daughter of Ray Romero.

Dr. Ricardo Romo, Vice Provost, University of Texas at Austin.

Edward D. Sáenz, son of Edwin M. Sáenz, Santa Monica, California.

Barbara M. Soper, Assistant Librarian, Buffalo and Erie County Public Library, Buffalo, New York.

Dorothy J. Stechman, Library Assistant, California Polytechnic State University, San Luis Obispo.

John Strey, Sports Information Director, Palo Mar College, San Marcos, California.

Charles M. Taylor, Public Relations Director, Washington Redskins.

Robert Weaver, Sports Information Office, Tulane University.

Jeffrey Wells, Sports Information, University of New Mexico.

Dave Williams, Marketing Manager, Edmonton Eskimos Football Club.

The Lords of Brentwood, San Antonio, Texas.

Lastly, a heartfelt thanks and "un fuerte abrazo" to the players themselves. This is their history and I thank them for being the men and athletes they are.

All-Time NFL Mexicano/Latino Pro Football Players' Roster-Teams, 1929-1968

Name	Year(s)	Teams Played
Jesse Rodríguez	1929	Buffalo Bisons
Kelly Rodríguez	1930	Frankford Yellowjackets/
		Minneapolis Redjackets
	1931	Frankford Yellowjackets
Waldo Don Carlos	1931	Green Bay Packers
Joe Aguirre	1941, 1943-45	Washington Redskins
	1946-49	Los Angeles Dons (AAFC)
Peter Pérez	1945	Chicago Bears
Edwin Sáenz	1946-51	Washington Redskins
John C. Sánchez	1947	Chicago Rockets (AAFC)/Detroit Lions
	1947-49	Washington Redskins
	1949-50	New York Giants
Gonzalo Morales	1947-48	Pittsburgh Steelers
Daniel Garza	1949	New York Yankees (AAFC)
	1951	New York Yanks
Ray Romero	1951	Philadelphia Eagles
Joe Arenas	1951-57	San Francisco 49ers
Eugene Brito	1951-53	Washington Redskins
	1955-58	Washington Redskins
	1959-60	Los Angeles Rams
George Maderos	1955-56	San Francisco 49ers
Rick Casares	1955-64	Chicago Bears
	1965	Washington Redskins
	1966	Miami Dolphins

All-Time NFL Mexicano/Latino Pro Football Players' Roster-Teams, 1929-1968, continued

Robert Luna	1955	San Francisco 49ers
	1959	Pittsburgh Steelers
Alex Bravo	1957-58	Los Angeles Rams
	1960-61	Oakland Raiders
Vernon Valdez	1960	Los Angeles Rams
	1961	Buffalo Bills
	1962	Oakland Raiders
Danny Villanueva	1960-64	Los Angeles Rams
	1965-67	Dallas Cowboys
Tom Flores	1960-61, 1963-66	Oakland Raiders
	1967-68	Buffalo Bills
	1969-70	Kansas City Chiefs
	1971	Buffalo Bills (asst. coach)
	1972-78	Oakland Raiders (asst. coach)
	1979-80	Oakland Raiders (head coach)
	1981-88	Los Angeles Raiders (head coach)
	1992-94	Seattle Seahawks (head coach)
Robert Coronado	1961	Pittsburgh Steelers
Henry Rivera	1962	Oakland Raiders
	1963	Buffalo Bills
Chon Gallegos	1962	Oakland Raiders
Herman Urenda	1963	Oakland Raiders
Joe Hernández	1964	Washington Redskins
Mario Méndez	1964	San Diego Chargers
George Mira	1964-68	San Francisco 49ers
	1969	Philadelphia Eagles
	1970	Baltimore Colts (taxi squad)
	1971	Miami Dolphins
	1974	Birmingham Americans (WFL)
	1975	Jacksonville Express (WFL)
James García	1965	Cleveland Browns
	1966	New York Giants
	1967	New Orleans Saints
	1968	Atlanta Falcons
Joe Kapp	1967-69	Minnesota Vikings
	1970	New England Patriots
Emilio Vállez	1968-69	Chicago Bears
Manny Fernández	1968-76	Miami Dolphins

All-Time CFL Mexicano/Latino Pro Football Players' Roster-Teams, 1948-1971

Name	Year(s)	Teams Played
John Aguirre	1948-50	Calgary Stampeders
Joe Aguirre	1950-51	Winnipeg Bluebombers
	1952	Edmonton Eskimos
	1953-55	Saskatchewan Roughriders
Eugene Brito	1954	Calgary Stampeders
Primo Villanueva	1955-58	British Columbia Lions
Vincent González	1956	Hamilton Tiger-Cats
Alan Valdez(s)	1956-57	Calgary Stampeders
Alex Bravo	1956	Saskatchewan Roughriders
Joe Kapp	1959-61	Calgary Stampeders
	1962-66	British Columbia Lions
Willie Crafts	1961-62	Edmonton Eskimos
Sam Fernández	1962	Hamilton Tiger-Cats
José Hernández	1962	Toronto Argonauts
	1963	Edmonton Eskimos
	1967-70	Edmonton Eskimos
Gus Gonzales	1963	Toronto Argonauts
	1965	Montreal Alouettes
Terry Fernández	1965	Montreal Alouettes
Al Gonzales	1968	Saskatchewan Roughriders
Skip Díaz	1968	British Columbia Lions
Greg Pérez	1970	Calgary Stampeders
	1971	Hamilton Tiger-Cats
George Mira	1972-73	Montreal Alouettes
	1977	Toronto Argonauts

Introduction

The history of Latinos in professional football begins in 1929 with the Rodríguez brothers, Jesse and Kelly, a pair of very talented athletes born in Spain whose family migrated to West Virginia. There the two brothers learned and became skillful at football. In college they played against one another and were recognized as star players by their peers and colleges. Both were running backs and punters whose talents took them to the pros.

In 1929 Jesse Rodríguez signed with the Buffalo Bisons. Once Jesse donned the orange and black of the Bison team it marked the beginning of the Latino presence in the NFL. It would be a tough year, for October witnessed the sudden collapse of the stock market. The NFL felt the effects of the Great Depression as its teams struggled to attract attendance to the games and make their payrolls. Jesse began his career as a professional football player giving pre-game punting exhibitions to attract spectators. With such demonstrations the players could make a name for themselves while helping their team financially.

Jesse played both offense and defense but his claim to fame was his punting. In a conversation with me, the 81-year-old Spanish gentleman mentioned that he finished his only year in the NFL with a remarkable 72 yards-per-punt average. Unfortunately for Jesse, punting statistics were not officially kept by the league back then. I searched the 1929 Buffalo newspaper for statistics to support his claim, but there were no stats to be found. The newspaper game accounts did, however, attest to his punting for incredible distances at Buffalo.

After the 1929 season, Jesse returned to West Virginia, and the Buffalo Bisons disbanded due to financial problems. Although Jesse retired from pro ball, his brother Kelly became was a triple threat athlete who did one better than Bo Jackson or Deion Sanders. He played on two pro football teams in the same season, whereas Jackson and Sanders played on two pro teams but in different sports. Kelly played for the Frankford Yellowjackets and the Minneapolis Redjackets in 1930.

In the 1940s Mexicanos/Latinos were well represented in the NFL as running backs, ends, and linemen. At the outbreak of World War II, they interrupted their careers to serve in the military. They joined the Merchant Marines, Navy, Coast Guard, Army, and Marines. Their tours of duty took them to Europe and such places as Okinawa and Iwo Jima, but they would return from the war to resume their collegiate or pro football careers. It was in this decade that the first Latino draft choice, Joe Aguirre, made All Pro, and Eddie Sáenz led the NFL in kick-off return yardage, thus making their mark in the history of pro football.

The 1950s began with the merger of the All American Football Conference (AAFC) and the NFL. The AAFC operated from 1946 to 1949 and prospered. They had a better attendance record than the NFL and posed a serious threat to the status of the older league; however, the AAFC suffered setbacks in 1948 and 1949, and the NFL regained it prominence. Talks between the two leagues began, and the NFL assimilated three of the seven AAFC teams—the Cleveland Browns, the San Francisco 49ers, and the Baltimore Colts. The remaining AAFC players were placed in a special allocation draft from which the existing NFL teams could select players.

Latino players Joe Aguirre, John C. Sánchez, and Dan Garza all played on AAFC teams. After the merger, all three continued their pro careers in the NFL and the Canadian Football League. The 1950s also produced a crop of Latino running backs. Lupe Joe Arenas and Rick Casares led the NFL in kick-off return and rushing yardage in 1953 and 1956 respectively. A Latino player was selected to play defense on the All Pro team four consecutive years. In Canada, two other Latino running backs etched their names in the CFL record book.

Not all contributions were made on the playing field. In 1952 Mexicano Willie García issued football uniforms instead of wearing them. García, who was from Dallas, Texas, served as the equipment manager for the very first Texas NFL franchise, the Dallas Texans. The team was a wandering franchise that came to Dallas from New York, where they were known as the Yanks. The hope of establishing pro football in the Lone Star State turned to disappointment. The Texans lasted one season, winning only a single game, and then disbanded. Throughout the not-so-spectacular 1952 season, Willie García outfitted his players.

In the 1960s the effect of the Civil Rights movement began to be felt as pro teams signed Black players. Kenny Washington, Woody Strode, Marion Motley, and Bill Willis entered pro football in 1946, a year before Jackie Robinson broke into major league baseball. Like Robinson, these players also endured abuse and discrimination, but they never received the publicity he attracted.

In 1962, the Washington Redskins, the last NFL team to integrate, made history by drafting Heisman

Trophy winner Ernie Davis from Syracuse. They traded Davis to Cleveland for two other Black players, Bobby Mitchell and Leroy Jackson. Ironically, the Redskin's did not realize that one of their three Black draft choices was a U.S.-born Mexicano. He was halfback Joe Hernández from Arizona, whom they selected in the second round and mistakenly thought to be Black.

Latinos rarely received the fame and reverence usually associated with pro football players. Instead, they shared with their Black teammates many of the same experiences of discrimination. Some of the players talked to me about their experiences. For others, I was able to document the treatment they received.

Eddie Sáenz, who played with the Washington Redskins for six seasons, had to contend with the nickname "Tortilla," given to him by the Redskins front office. Whether or not the nickname was meant to be derogatory, Sáenz hated it. The Redskins media guides list the nickname in Sáenz's player information.

Ray Romero, as well as many other players, recalled incidents of racial discrimination off the playing field. Although such incidents angered him for awhile, Romero turned the negative memories into a positive one by becoming a teacher and motivator of young people. When he played for the Philadelphia Eagles in 1951, he showed he was just as good as anyone.

Joe Kapp was given a series of racially based nicknames throughout his career. He has been called "Big Mex," "Mexican Joe," the "Mexican Messiah," "Super Mex," and "El Cid." "El Cid" was given to Kapp while he played with the Minnesota Vikings. When he first heard the name, it reminded him of the movie and the scene where they strapped Charlton Heston into the saddle so he could lead the Spanish into battle and scare the enemy, even though he was dead. In 1970 Kapp told *Sports Illustrated* he took the name as a compliment to him for his ability to finish games even though he was injured. The other nicknames seem to emerge whenever Kapp was wrapped in contract controversy, and everywhere Kapp went to play or coach football there was controversy. Not one to step back from any confrontation, Kapp always met his critics head-on, and most of the time, emerged the winner.

For Al Gonzales, racism reared its ugly head when he was appointed athletic director of New Mexico State University. No sooner was the ink dry on the contract than Gonzales began receiving hate mail slurring his heritage and family. Since Gonzales had dealt with this kind of attitude all his life, he cautiously ignored it. He said that as quickly as the hate mail began it ended because there was no basis for it. He was the first Mexicano to hold that position at New Mexico State, and after twelve years, he's still there.

Of special mention is the Joe Arenas story. He was a member of the renowned 49ers backfield which included quarterback Y. A. Tittle and running backs Hugh McElhenny and Joe Perry. All but Joe Arenas are Hall of Famers. One wonders why the renowned "Fabulous Four" is minus one in Canton, Ohio. This exclusion is a gross injustice to a great athlete. Arenas's pro football record speaks for itself and deserves nothing less than Hall of Fame status.

These incidents are only part of the story because *Athletes Remembered* is more about success than disappointment. This book is the first of its kind anywhere—a sports history with Mexicano/Latino heroes who represent the second largest minority in the United States. It is time for the accomplishments of these players to be remembered and honored.

Mario Longoria
San Antonio, Texas

The First Latinos in Pro Football

Jesse Rodríguez

The history of Latinos in professional football begins with Jesse Rodríguez, an extraordinary man, whose personal legacy was decency and respect. He was admired by all who knew and heard of him. As an athlete, his desire and intensity to succeed in football earned him an honored place in pro football history.

Rodríguez, a Spaniard, broke ground in 1929 as the first Latino to play in the National Football League. His experience is not only important to the story of professional football, but to Latino sportspeople everywhere.

Rodríguez was born on August 4, 1901, in Aviles, Spain, where the Rodríguez family owned and managed a lime and brick factory. When Rodríguez was 11 years old, the family migrated to the United States and made their home near Clarksburg, West Virginia.

Rodríguez attended Victory High School in Clarksburg, and became the first student of Victory High School to be selected to the West Virginia High School All-State Football Team. As a result of his skills on the playing field, he was actively recruited by several West Virginia colleges.

With help from fellow alumni and West Virginia Senator Jennings Randolph, Rodríguez entered Salem (West Virginia) College in the fall of 1925 to begin his collegiate football career. Early into his first season

Rodríguez replaced the starting fullback on offense and also played linebacker on defense. Later he became the team's regular kicker.

One of Rodríguez's teammates at Salem College, Art Goldchien, recalls his friend, "Jesse was considered one of the finest football players in the state, both at Victory High School in Clarksburg and later at Salem College, where I came to know him when we played on that team. He was one of the finest punters I have ever seen, including today's pros who specialize in punting."

In fact, his trademark was in his powerful leg, which could kick a football incredible distances. Rodríguez remembered when he booted a 95-yard punt, 85 feet in the air. "I was seven yards deep in the end zone," he recalled, "in a game when Salem College was playing Marietta College of Ohio. I took my usual three steps and booted the ball. It went to [Salem's] 5 yard line. We won the game 12-0."

His punting ability quickly became renowned in collegiate football circles. Former University of Michigan football star and noted collegiate punter Todd Rockwell and the Salem coach decided to put Rodríguez to the test by arranging a kicking duel. "We lined up and kicked and each time they measured," recalled Rodríguez. After the contest Rockwell told

Rodríguez, "There's no one in the U.S. who can beat you; when you out punt me by 10-15 yards without the roll, you're the best." When asked who won, Rodríguez hesitated then almost apologetically said, "I beat him, but he didn't want it emphasized."

Sports reporter Bruce Harton wrote about young Rodríguez. He said, "When his educated toe sends the leather oval sailing into the air for a distance to his old, but praised record, he gives his head a determined shake and resolves to do better. A great change has come over this sterling athlete from Clarksburg. Last season, Jesse was accepted readily as one of the very finest punters and general all-around football men in West Virginia Conference teams."

During the 1927 season, Rodríguez contributed to the Salem Tigers' success: Against Broaddus College, Rodríguez won the game for Salem by scoring two touchdowns after thrilling runs. He towered above all other players as he knifed through the Broaddus line at will for large gains. Before the first quarter ended, Rodríguez made a thrilling 30-yard run to place the ball in scoring territory and, after two line plays, punched the leather over for the score . . . the second and last tally broke through the Broaddus defense for a 45-yard touchdown run. Against Wilmington College of Ohio, Rodríguez's placement kick gave Salem the one-point margin of victory, Salem 7 Wilmington 6.

Rodríguez's most significant game of the 1927 season was against the rival West Virginia Wesleyan Bobcats. The highly publicized game featured both Rodríguez and his younger brother Kelly, who was a running back with the Bobcats.

The *Clarksburg Exponent* headline read, "Here today, Rodríguez's, Kelly and Jesse, Two Brothers Pitted One against the Other, Score Both Touchdowns of Game."

The memorable game was played on October 7, 1927, at Clarksburg, West Virginia. The Wesleyan Bobcats scored first, Kelly Rodríguez made the touchdown, and Louis Kolopus kicked the extra point. When the Salem Tigers took the offense, Jesse Rodríguez rushed for the touchdown, but the extra point was blocked.

The game turned into a punting duel between the brothers with the honors about even. Late in the game, with the Bobcats controlling the football, Kelly rushed through the Tigers' defensive line. Jesse recalls that someone had knocked him down, and from ground level he saw his brother racing toward the goal line. Determined to stop him, Jesse jumped up and caught Kelly before he reached the goal line, and the game ended with a Bobcat victory 7-6.

In 1928, Jesse Rodríguez continued to be a dominant football player at Salem College. The *Clarksburg*

Exponent describes the game against Bethany College, "The toe of Jesse Rodríguez served the Salem team well. Time after time the Spanish youth got off kicks which caught the Bethany secondary defense napping and as a consequence the greater part of the game was played with Bethany up against the goal posts. He clearly out kicked Bethany's punter by 15 yards on every exchange of punts."

Additionally, Rodríguez, who had been playing a great defensive game as linebacker, scooped up a Bethany fumble and dashed 70 yards for a touchdown. He also kicked 4 of 5 extra points to seal the Salem victory 34-0. In the Marietta College of Ohio game, Salem's first touchdown came as a result of a brilliant aerial attack during which quarterback Rodríguez fired a 20-yard pass to teammate Batson, who sidestepped and dodged an additional 10 yards to score.

Rodríguez himself scored in the final quarter when he carried the ball through the Marietta line for 20 yards and from there bucked the Marietta line three times for a touchdown. In addition to being a fine ball carrier and passer, Rodríguez contributed considerably to the game with his splendid punting. (His kicks invariably carried more distance than the Marietta backs could cover, making Marietta's defensive game dangerous for them all the time.) Final score: Salem 12 Marietta 0.

In the four years Jesse played with the Salem College Tigers (1925-1928) the team posted a record of 20 wins, 9 losses, and 2 ties in West Virginia Intercollegiate Athletic Conference (WVIAC) play. In 1928, the WVIAC selected its first all-conference team; Rodríguez received Honorable Mention on the WVIAC Team.

After graduating from Salem College with an AB degree, Rodríguez was approached by Jim Durfee, a referee who had worked many of the Salem College games.* Durfee asked Rodríguez if he had considered playing professional football. Rodríguez responded in the affirmative and later received an invitation to play for the Buffalo Bisons Football Club of New York.

Rodríguez signed to play fullback and kicker for the Buffalo Bisons for the 1929 season. That year the Buffalo team was comprised of all first-year, inexperienced players. To attract more spectators, prior to the start of each game, Rodríguez gave an exhibition on barefoot kicking.

*Jim Durfee refereed both collegiate and pro football games. Because the NFL was not as organized as it is today with their own scouts, they relied on reporters, game officials, and others to spot pro football talent and share information with them.

Durfee was not officially tied to the Bisons, but it appears his opinion of Jesse's pro capability was their motive for contacting him.

Jesse Rodríguez

Rushing

Year	Team	Games	No.	Yds.	Avg.	TDs
1929	Buffalo Bisons	5	5	13	2.6	0

Pass Receptions

Year	Team	Games	No.	Yds.	Avg.	TDs
1929	Buffalo Bisons	4	1	5	5.0	0

Source: David S. Neft, Richard M. Cohen, and Rick Korch, *The Football Encyclopedia: The Complete Year-By-Year History of Professional Football from 1892 to the Present* (New York: St. Martin's Press, 1994), 83.

A 1929 *Buffalo Courier Express* article tells the story of Rodríguez's exploits in the Buffalo Bisons' first game of the season against the Chicago Cardinals: "Jesse Rodríguez, halfback of the Buffalo team will give an exhibition of barefoot kicking, a department in which he excels. Fans in attendance will be really surprised by the distance that Rodríguez can send the pigskin."

Another newspaper article, this one from Rodríguez's hometown of Clarksburg, West Virginia, recounts that "a curious grin spread across Rodríguez's face when he reminisced about the time he used to give football kicking exhibitions with the Buffalo team, billed as the barefooted wonder from West Virginia."

Rodríguez recalled that before each game he would take off his shoes and kick some for the crowd. "They thought nobody here in West Virginia wore shoes in those days. Actually, I could kick better without shoes. You get a better spiral. Your shoe does not interfere. With a shoe on, sometimes your toe sticks up too high to punt well; you have to touch the ball at impact just right."

That first year the Buffalo Bisons posted 1 win, 7 losses, and 1 tie in National Football League (NFL) play. In the season opener against the Chicago Cardinals, Rodríguez stifled the Cardinal attack with his punts throughout the game. In one instance, the Cardinals backs ploughed their way to the Buffalo 2-yard line, only to lose a fumble on the one yard line. With their backs against their own goal, the Bisons sent Rodríguez in to punt them out of danger. In the third quarter, the Bisons again were backed up and Rodríguez booted a long spiral to Cardinals player Chief Elkins, who fumbled the football when tackled by Voss. The Bisons recovered the ball on the Cardinals' 25-yard line. This time, the Bisons had to settle for a field goal, only to lose the game 9-3.

In the games against the Frankford Yellowjackets, Rodríguez started at halfback, but once again it was his punting that helped the Bisons. The *Buffalo Courier Express* attests to Rodríguez's punting, "Rodríguez punting and the dogged resistance shown by the Bisons' battered line when backed up to their own goalpost were the redeeming features from a local standpoint. With the Yellowjackets threatening the local goal . . . the Bison forward wall stiffened and finally took the ball on downs. Rodríguez immediately punting them out of danger. Early in the second period, Weimer made one of the prettiest plays of the game when he sped down the field under a Rodríguez punt, smashed his way through two blockers, tackled the ballcarrier and flopped him to the turf with a sickening thud."

Against the Chicago Bears, Rodríguez played the tackle position, substituting for player-coach Al Jolley. As Jack Laing wrote, "The Chicago Bears, with Red Grange, Paddy Driscoll, and Joey Sternaman, made their first appearance at Bison stadium. Senn scored both Chicago touchdowns while Grange, 'The Galloping Ghost,' played an important part in the scoring.

"The Bisons with a bolstered and revamped backfield showed a much better offensive punch but fumbling again ruined their chances to score."

The Bisons fumbled twice near the Chicago goal line and lost the game by a score of 16-0. The Bisons showed improvement and played the Providence Steamrollers to a tie. In this game, Rodríguez returned to the fullback position as Buffalo came from behind to tie the 1928 defending world pro football champions 7-7. On November 24, 1929, the last game of the season, Buffalo defeated the Chicago Bears 19-7 at Wrigley Field in Chicago to post their only NFL win that season.

Rodríguez finished the season in what he estimated to be an impressive 72 yards per punt average. However, disappointed with the Buffalo team, he packed his bags and returned to West Virginia. Nevertheless, he concluded his brief career with the distinction of being the first Latino in professional football.

Following his football career, Rodríguez worked at the Union Carbide Company of West Virginia for a number of years, but a heart condition forced him into early retirement. His friend and former teammate, Art Goldchien, says, "After his retirement from participating in football, Rodríguez would take time to visit various schools and attempt to teach young players how to properly kick a football. He did this because of his love for the game and his interest in the young." Rodríguez worked with kickers from Salem College and local high schools.

In 1964, Rodríguez spoke about football then and now in a *Clarksburg Exponent* interview. "They're smarter now than they used to be. It used to be the power; now it's quickness and smartness. It used to be all power plays, now it's trick plays, pass plays, and they work . . . We use to punt in the old days on any down, not just the fourth."

When asked about some of the great ball players whom he played against in the bygone era, he recalls one in particular, "Kelly Rodríguez, my brother, who made all-state and played professionally with Philadelphia and Boston. He got better as he went along . . . he was good!"

In 1974, Jesse Rodríguez was named to the All-Time West Virginia Intercollegiate Athletic Conference Team for the years 1925-65. His brother Kelly also was named to the team.

Goldchien remembers: "The last time we spent time to reminisce, he was the same Jesse as I have always known him to be. He still had his desire, his intensity, and his ability to cooperate with others. I'm sure this was passed on down to others as an inspiration to them. Winning to him was as important as to anyone engaged in athletics, but he won by adhering to his ideals. After all, participating in athletics is best when following the Golden Rule. He had respect for his opponents and gained their respect in return."

Rodríguez died October 12, 1983, in Clarksburg, West Virginia. Goldchien sums up what many people felt about Jesse Rodríguez: "Jesse passed away, leaving a void, but one must remember there are those who gained from being associated with him, young and old."

The Spanish Armada
Kelly Rodríguez

The other half of the Rodríguez professional football duo is Jesse's brother Kelly Rodríguez. He was so well-known as a superlative football talent that his reputation preceded him wherever he went. His accomplishments were incredible, and upon entering the college and pro ranks, fans were treated to the thrilling and exciting Rodríguez brand of football.

His early start in football was described in the 1935 *Boston Redskins Press Guide:* "From way over yonder in Aviles, Spain, came the infant Kelly Rodríguez, who bloomed into manhood in West Virginia and subsequently carved his niche in football's hall of fame. This fiery fellow, born August 9, 1907, is 5'10" tall, weighs 185 pounds and has black hair and brown eyes. Ever since he tackled the gridiron sport as a prep athlete, he has been listed as a halfback or fullback. Rodríguez graduated from West Virginia Wesleyan in 1930 and belongs to the Kappa Alpha Fraternity. His brother Jesse played professionally with the Buffalo Bisons in 1929 and that season Kelly was earning honors galore as the most valuable performer on the Wesleyan Team."

From the very beginning, Rodríguez reached for the stars and became an All-State selection at Victory High School in Clarksburg, West Virginia. With his illustrious prep football career concluded, the much sought after Rodríguez attended West Virginia Wesleyan College from 1926 to 1930. He became an immediate success, with overpowering football talent that earned him the nickname "Spanish Armada." An all-around player, Rodríguez played on offense and defense and did all the punting for the Wesleyan Bobcats. Rodríguez's fierce competitiveness became his trademark, and his gridiron exploits became legendary in the history of West Virginia collegiate football.

In 1926, Rodríguez's freshman season, the Wesleyan Bobcats won 4 and lost 6 in a very tough schedule. The victories came over Salem College 15-0; Bethany 19-7; Broaddus 13-0; and Davis & Elkins

College 9-7. In the 1927 season opener, the Wesleyan Bobcats lost to West Virginia University 27-7, and except for the passing of Mickey McClung and the running of Forest Bachtel and Rodríguez, Wesleyan did not show much power. However, in this his sophomore season, Rodríguez came into his own.

Rodríguez took over the team's leadership and was the signal caller on both offense and defense. The season's highlight occurred on October 7, 1927, when the Wesleyan Bobcats played the Salem Tigers. The highly publicized game featured both Kelly and his brother Jesse. Kelly scored first on a pass interception, then Jesse rushed for Salem's only touchdown. The game was hotly contested between the brothers. In the end, the Wesleyan Bobcats defeated the Salem Tigers 7-6, when Salem's extra point conversion failed.

During the 1928 collegiate season, Rodríguez scored 10 touchdowns to lead the team offensively. West Virginia sportswriter Kent Kessler writes about Rodríguez's performance against Xavier College of Cincinnati, Ohio, to illustrate the great football season Rodríguez experienced in 1928: "Xavier had lost only one game and was expected to beat Wesleyan with ease; however, Kelly Rodríguez showed Cincinnati the best football player it saw all season. Rodríguez, a triple-threat man and almost as spectacularly invincible on defense as offense . . . shone like a star in a game that produced some of the very best football ever seen at Corcoran field, Ohio . . . Kelly scored one touchdown and one point after touchdown" (Wesleyan 19-Xavier 7). John J. Carrol, a friend of Rodríguez, had this to say about the Xavier game: "Your play in 1928 was the greatest he had ever witnessed. Said if you were with Ohio State or any other big schools, you would have been an All-American."

Other game accounts for the 1928 season (included in *Hail West Virginians!*) evidenced Rodríguez's spectacular gridiron efforts. "The West Virginia Wesleyan Bobcats steamrolled their way to victory over Fairmont State College, 43-0. Rodríguez intercepted a Fairmont pass on the 44 yard marker and raced the distance for the score. The Spanish lad made good the only try for the extra point. Against New York University in a losing effort, Kelly Rodríguez, the Irish-Spanish West Virginian, was almost his team's whole offense. Rodríguez threw a long forward pass to teammate McClung, then McClung threw one to Rodríguez. This drive took Wesleyan 70 yards for its lone touchdown. Rodríguez made the extra point" (NYU 26-Wesleyan 7).

"At Concord State College, West Virginia Wesleyan found some real opposition, but won 18-0. Rodríguez, the fullback, was the outstanding star. He made the Bobcat's first two touchdowns. Both in the first period. The work of Rodríguez was marked by beautiful interference and good broken field running."

"In the Georgetown game, West Virginia Wesleyan came here today with a strong line but Georgetown depended chiefly on forward passes to win an easy victory, 34-7. . .Wesleyan tallied near the end when Rodríguez, fullback, picked up a fumble and ran fifty yards. He also kicked the extra point."

"Then came Waynesburg College. West Virginia Wesleyan soundly trounced the Waynesburg College Yellowjackets 34-0. A beautifully executed lateral pass to Batchel to Paul Watson to Rodríguez was good for 76 yards and a touchdown. The Wesleyan's second score came on the third play of the second quarter . . . Rodríguez got five and on the next play galloped around left end for a touchdown."

Against Navy, the *Clarksburg Telegram* reports, "A rampant Navy team . . . ripped their way through Wesleyan for a 37-0 victory, out of the Wesleyan defeat looms Rodríguez, who throughout the afternoon in the kicking game, gained more ground with his big toe than all the rest of the backs did by carrying the ball."

Next on the schedule was Salem College. This game, like in the previous season, pitted Rodríguez against his brother Jesse. However, this time the game became a punting duel between the brothers, with Kelly's left-footed boots carrying a little farther than Jesse's. Aside from the brother match-up, Wesleyan fought up and down a mud-soaked gridiron and defeated Salem College 12-0. In the game Kelly Rodríguez intercepted a forward pass and followed his catch with a 40-yard broken field run for one of Wesleyan's two touchdowns.

In the season finale, Rodríguez and company took on the "Thundering Herd" from Marshall College. In the first quarter play, Rodríguez slipped through left tackle for a 26-yard touchdown run. Rodríguez kicked the extra point and Wesleyan led Marshall 7-0. However, the momentum switched over to Marshall in the second half, and they went on to win the game 13-7.

1928 was a great season for Rodríguez. He led Wesleyan in scoring with 70 points—10 touchdowns, and 10 extra points—and was selected first team All-West Virginia Intercollegiate Athletic Conference Team.

The 1929 edition of the Wesleyan Bobcats opened the collegiate season with a victory over Concord College. Rodríguez picked up where he left off the previous season by scoring the first Wesleyan touchdown of the season. A fighting Bobcat team out played the highly touted Mountain Lions team from Concord College, beating them 39-0. Rodríguez also kicked 3 points after touchdown in their winning effort.

That year, Rodríguez and teammate Cliff Battles led the Wesleyan team offensively. The 1929 Wesleyan team had a good season in spite of its five losses. Wesleyan beat Concord 39-0, Salem College 47-0, Bethany 52-0, and Marshall 28-0. Rodríguez finished the season with 4 touchdowns and 3 extra points.

Kelly Rodríguez

Pass Receptions

Year	Team	Games	No.	Yds.	Avg.	TDs
1930	Frankford Yellowjackets	13	4	27	6.7	1

Rushing

Year	Team	Games	No.	Yds.	Avg.	TDs
1930	Frankford Yellowjackets	13	34	105	3.1	0
	Minneapolis Redjackets	2	8	5	0.5	0
		15	42	110	1.8	0

Kickoff Returns

Year	Team	Games	No.	Yds.	Avg.	TDs
1930	Frankford Yellowjackets	7	1	50	50.0	0

Punt Returns

Year	Team	Games	No.	Yds.	Avg.	TDs
1930	Frankford Yellowjackets	14	2	41	20.5	0

Passing

Year	Team	Games	Atts.	Comp.	Yds.	%	Int.	TDs
1930	Frankford Yellowjackets	13	41	12	94	34.1	9	0
	Minneapolis Redjackets	1	1	1	16	100.0	0	0
		14	42	13	110	32.3	9	0

Punts

Year	Team	Games	No.	Yds.	Avg.
1930	Frankford Yellowjackets	13	23	954	41.4
	Minneapolis Redjackets	2	11	440	40.0
		15	34	1,394	41.0

Source: Frankford Yellowjackets Game Programs: September 27, 28, 1930; October 4, 12, 26, 1930; November 9, 15, 1930. This information provided by Joe Horrigan, Curator, Pro Football Hall of Fame, Canton, Ohio.

Also, the Minneapolis Redjackets statistics came from David S. Neft, Richard M. Cohen, and Rick Korch, *The Football Encyclopedia: The Complete Year-By-Year History of Professional Football from 1892 to the Present* (New York: St. Martin's Press, 1994), 87, 107, 108, 110.

At the end of a great collegiate football career, Rodríguez had been twice selected to the All-West Virginia Intercollegiate Athletic Conference First Teams (1928 and 1929). Additionally, he received Honorable Mention on several All-Eastern Teams.

In 1930, upon graduation from Wesleyan, Rodríguez signed to play professional football with both the Frankford Yellowjackets of Philadelphia and the Minneapolis Redjackets of the NFL.

Rodríguez's first year with the Frankford team was a frustrating one. In the 1930 campaign, Frankford won 4, lost 11, and tied 1. Rodríguez played a utility role in the Yellowjacket's backfield. In the first exhibition game, against Clifton Heights, Rodríguez played quarterback and threw a touchdown pass to Royce Goodbread for the third score of the game. Frankford won the game 33-6.

In the regular season opener against the Staten Island Stapletons, Rodríguez flung a 19-yard touchdown pass to Cookie Tackwell for the only touchdown of the contest as Frankford won 7-3. In addition to these quarterback chores, Rodríguez also punted and rushed for yardage.

In the game against the Newark Tornadoes on October 4, 1930, Rodríguez played all of the backfield positions and punted six times for the Yellowjackets. In the next two contests, against the Chicago Bears and the Providence Steam Rollers, Rodríguez played punter and quarterback. And in the November 15 game against the Portsmouth Spartans, Rodríguez netted one punt for 56 yards and rushed for another 62 yards.

The highlight of Rodríguez's rookie pro season was the second Green Bay Packers game. Although the Packers avenged their earlier loss to Frankford by beating them 25-7, Rodríguez had his best game of the season. He tallied on a 3-yard touchdown pass from Art Pharmer to account for the only Frankford score. In the punting department, Rodríguez powered a punt for 74 yards.

In Frankford, one of the oldest districts in Philadelphia, the Yellowjackets played all their home games on Saturday, because Pennsylvania State "Blue Laws" did not allow them to play on Sunday. So after the November 2 schedule of games, Rodríguez along with several other Frankford teammates, were asked to play for the Minneapolis Redjackets on days when only one team was scheduled. Due to player shortages, the Yellowjackets and Redjackets pooled their players to assist each other in finishing out their schedules. Although this was contrary to league rules, the NFL office permitted this arrangement in hopes of improving league competition. In the two games with the Minneapolis Redjackets, Rodríguez played running back, quarterback, and punter.

Rodríguez remained with the Frankford Yellowjackets through the 1931 season. That year the Yellowjackets played only eight NFL games and did not finish the season. Rodríguez recalls the game against the Bears, "When playing against the Chicago Bears, I played 60 minutes with two cracked ribs, backing up the line against the great Red Grange and doing a good job of containing him."

Shortly thereafter, Rodríguez retired from professional football and returned to West Virginia. "While playing pro ball I was under great pressure from my father-in-law to quit and go into business with him. He owned the greatest fleet of trucks in West Virginia and was a contract hauler for the A&P Tea Company. They served 144 stores in West Virginia, Pennsylvania, and Maryland. But I stayed with the Yellowjackets until they dissolved their franchise, then I retired," comments Rodríguez about his initial retirement.

In 1935, at the earnest request of former collegiate teammate Cliff Battles, Rodríguez came out of retirement and signed a contract to play for the Boston Redskins of the NFL. That year Rodríguez played sparingly and left the Redskins early in the season. In 1936, Rodríguez received another offer to play football, this time in the California Professional Football League on the West Coast. But he declined the offer and retired permanently from pro football.

Upon declining the offer to play professional football in California, Rodríguez concluded a remarkable and illustrious career. He returned to West Virginia to work in the family trucking business.

In 1974 Rodríguez was honored for his collegiate football playing in being named to the All-Time West Virginia Intercollegiate Athletic Conference Team for the years 1925-65. His brother Jesse Rodríguez was also named to the team.

About his brother, Rodríguez had this to say, "In my opinion, Jesse was the greatest punter in football." As brothers they respected each other's talents and excelled not only in football, but in the game of life. They were indeed extraordinary individuals who pioneered the Latino presence in professional football, and all Latinos can take great pride in their accomplishments.

The Champion
Waldo E. Don Carlos

Waldo E. Don Carlos, a descendant of Spanish conquistadors, was a fierce competitor who played for the Drake University Bulldogs of the Missouri Valley Conference. In the pros he played for the Green Bay Packers in 1931, during the "Iron Man" era in the NFL, becoming the first Latino professional football champion.

Waldo E. Don Carlos was born on October 16, 1909, in Greenfield, Iowa. According to Don Carlos, his family came to this country in 1750, settling first on the Carolina coast, then migrating west to Greenfield, Iowa, around 1878 and several years later to Des Moines, Iowa. Don Carlos claims that the family can be traced back to a son of Don Carlos, heir to the Spanish throne in the early 1700s. Because the ascendancy to the throne was never realized, the family migrated to the New World.

Centuries later in Des Moines, New World descendant Waldo Don Carlos attended Theodore Roosevelt High School, where he and his teammates captured both the city and state football championships. As a prep athlete, he learned techniques for winning that followed him to college, pro football, and his law career.

In 1927 Don Carlos entered Drake University, where he studied law and played football whenever his studies permitted. Back then, freshmen at Drake did not play varsity football, so Don Carlos the athlete waited until his sophomore year to come into his own. He joined the football team in 1928, which turned out to be one the best seasons in school history.

Drake opened the 1928 season against Simpson College, a game of historical significance because it was the first night game played west of the Mississippi—huge floodlights illuminated the stadium. With Don Carlos playing center on offense and backing up the line on defense, Drake disrupted Simpson's passing attack and defeated them 40-6. Drake then beat Marquette and Grinnell and went on to face Notre Dame. The Irish played splendidly, handing Drake its only loss of the season, 32-6. Although outplayed, Drake was not outfought, and Don Carlos stood out in general line play. For the next two seasons that Drake played Notre Dame, Don Carlos turned in stellar performances against the Fighting Irish.

The 1929 campaign began with victories over Simpson College, Oklahoma A & M, and Washington.

Drake tied Grinnell and lost to Missouri, Temple, and Notre Dame for a season record of 5 wins, 3 losses, and 1 tie. In their annual Notre Dame clash, the Bulldogs led 7-6 for the first three quarters, but in the fourth quarter Notre Dame scored two touchdowns to eliminate Drake's hopes of a win. Don Carlos remembers the game: "We led Notre Dame the first three quarters 7 to 6. Finally they won with a score of 19 to 7. Our squad consisted of 28 men, and Notre Dame had a hundred or so dressed for the game."

In Don Carlos's senior year (1930), Drake continued to dominate the Missouri Valley Conference, winning the conference championship for the third consecutive year. He played superbly against the University of Oregon Webfoot in a losing effort and turned in a solid performance in their victory over Iowa State.

As in previous games against Notre Dame, he left an unforgettable impression of his aggressive style of play. Drake's 1931 college yearbook *The QUAX* notes, "Don Carlos has been styled by the *Notre Dame Football Review* as the sparkplug of a fighting Drake line that held Notre Dame at bay. Tim Moynihan, Notre Dame center, who has met some of the best pivot men in the country says, 'Don Carlos is the best center I played against all year.'" At season's end, Don Carlos was picked for Knute Rockne's All Western Team and for the second consecutive year was All Missouri Valley Conference selection.

His highly successful collegiate career springboarded Don Carlos into pro football for a single season. The NFL collegiate draft did not exist until 1936. Instead, coaches or team representatives contacted prospects and enticed them to play in the pros. Don Carlos received contract offers from the Green Bay Packers and the Portsmouth Spartans, who later moved to Detroit and became the Lions. He chose Green Bay partly because Earl "Curly" Lambeau, the Packers' coach, had attended Notre Dame. He recounts his early pro football days with Green Bay: "We started play or practice early in August. We didn't have a regular stadium to play or practice in at the time. There was only one coach and we practiced only running plays. In our only scrimmage before our first game, over 5,000 people came out to watch us play. Wisconsin really supported the team.

"We had Cal Hubbard as a tackle on our team, the biggest man at 265 pounds. Bo Molenda of Michigan was our fullback. Vern Lewellen of Nebraska was a halfback. He could punt a ball 70 yards and come very close to his target. Mike Michalske of Penn State played left guard. Johnny "Blood" McNally was a great left end, and Tom Nash of Georgia was right end. We also had a halfback by the name of Arnie Herber who

could throw a pass seventy yards." Curly Lambeau, Johnny "Blood" McNally, Robert "Cal" Hubbard, Mike Michalske and Arnie Herber are all members of the Pro Football Hall of Fame. Don Carlos was among the best in the history of the NFL.

It was a rewarding pro football experience for Don Carlos. He received offers from two teams, both of which later in the season finished one and two in league standings. The Packers were the defending NFL champions and began their 1931 season with a 26-0 victory over the Cleveland Indians. For the next 8 games the Packers were invincible and raced from one victory to another. Their toughest challengers were the Portsmouth Spartans, but they did not play each other that season.

Their winning streak ended as Ernie Nevers lead the Cardinals to an upset victory, 21-13. Nevers threw two touchdown passes and kicked two extra points to hand Green Bay its first defeat of the season.

With the following game, the Packers regained their momentum to beat New York 14-10. Elsewhere in the league, Ernie Nevers helped the Packers' cause by leading the Cardinals in a second consecutive upset, a 20-19 triumph over the Portsmouth Spartans. This put the Packers ahead of the Spartans in the win-loss record.

Green Bay won their next two games but lost the season finale to the Chicago Bears 7-6. This gave them a 12-2 season record compared with Portsmouth's 11-3. The 1931 campaign concluded on a schedule dispute. In *The Football Encyclopedia: The Complete Year-by-Year History of Professional Football from 1892 to the Present,* David Neft describes what happened: "Portsmouth could tie for the title with a victory over the Packers in a game they said they had scheduled for December 13 at Portsmouth. To their surprise, Green Bay refused to play.

"The game they explained, was not on the official league schedule but had only been tentatively scheduled after the official schedule had been drawn. As such, either party had a right to cancel it. NFL president Joe Carr agreed with the Packers, giving Green Bay its third straight championship."

Needless to say, it was a well-deserved title few could argue with. Throughout the season Don Carlos had alternated at the center position, which thus earned him the distinction of being the very first Latino on an NFL championship team in the history of the sport.

Regrettably, the 1931 NFL season was the only pro campaign for Don Carlos. Throughout his football career he had not experienced a losing season, and even though Green Bay continued their winning tradition, the talented Don Carlos was now committed to study law at Drake University. Anxious to make up time, he attended summer school in 1932 and graduated with a law degree in 1933. That season the Chicago Bears won the NFL Championship while Green Bay finished third in the Western Division.

Don Carlos went on to practice law in Greenfield, Iowa, for the next 50 years, interrupted only by World War II, when he became a lieutenant in the U.S. Navy and served as a communications officer aboard the battleship U.S.S. Pennsylvania. Recalling his tour of duty, he says, "The Pennsylvania was to be the flagship for the planned invasion of Japan. However, while in Buckner Bay, Okinawa, the ship was hit by an aerial bomb that blew a hole in our hull about 60 feet by 40 feet, and our quarterdeck was flushed with water in about 30 minutes. There were about 1,200 ships in the bay at the time and the repair ships were alongside very quickly and kept us afloat. I believe this was on August 9, 1945, and the war ended on August 12, 1945."

With the war over and victory achieved, Don Carlos returned to family and friends in Iowa and continued his law career. He served on the Board of Governors of the Iowa State Bar Association and as county attorney of Adair County. He was a member of the Iowa Trial Lawyers Association and Fellow of the Probate Organization for the United States. After having distinguished himself in his chosen career, he retired from the profession on July 1, 1984. Today, Don Carlos and his wife Dorothy reside in the community of Sun City West, Arizona.

The Forties

Joe Aguirre
First Latino Draft Choice and All-Pro

With ancestry in northern Spain and birthright in the United States, Joe Aguirre was born on October 17, 1918, in Rock Springs, Wyoming. As a high school player, the tall and talented Aguirre was regarded by many as an athlete of promise. Upon finishing his prep days in Rock Springs in 1937, Aguirre went west to play college ball at St. Mary's College of California. While at St. Mary's he perfected his football skills under coach "Slip" Madigan.

In 1938, Aguirre's sophomore year, the St. Mary's Gaels won 6 of 9 games. Their wins included a victory over the Texas Tech Raiders in the Cotton Bowl by the score of 20-13. Aguirre continued to develop during the 1939 season. The biggest win for the Gaels that year was a 40-7 win over Loyola University.

By his senior year Aguirre had developed into an exceptional receiver, and he could also kick field goals and extra points with proficiency. In the 8 games they played that season, Aguirre's best performances came against Loyola and Fordham. Against Fordham, Aguirre's 30-yard field goal gave St. Mary's a 9-6 win. At season's end, Aguirre's gridiron efforts brought him an All-American Honorable Mention selection.

In 1941 Aguirre made history as the first Latino chosen in the draft when the Washington Redskins of the NFL selected him in the 9th round.

The 1941 draft was an important one for the Redskins, selecting not only Aguirre, but also ends Ed Cifers from the University of Tennessee, Al Krueger from Southern California, tackle Ed Beiner of Notre Dame, Fred Davis from the University of Alabama, and running back Cecil Hare from Washington State. These men would comprise one of the best teams Washington ever had.

From the beginning, Aguirre showed promise. "For the first two weeks of training," wrote *Washington Star* sports columnist Bill Dismar on September 11, 1941, a week before Aguirre's first professional game, "big Joe Aguirre of St. Mary's of California and equally husky Sam Goldman of Howard College of Alabama stood head and shoulders above the rest figuratively as well as literally. Each weighs in the low 220s, stands 6 feet 3½ and is strong and rugged."

Aguirre and the other rookies melded well with the team's veterans, and the Redskins led the NFL' s Eastern Division for 1941 with an impressive 5-1 record. Aguirre's greatest moment in that season came when he kicked a 36-yard field goal to beat the Brooklyn Dodgers 3-0.

But then came December 7, 1941, and the U.S. entry into World War II. Aguirre left the Redskins to serve in the Merchant Marines from December 1942 to November 1943.

When Aguirre returned to professional football and to the Redskins, he returned to a championship team that had won the NFL East-West play-off in 1942 and that for the third time in four years, were playing the Chicago Bears for the NFL championship. One year away from the game had not lessened Aguirre's skills. He caught a 25-yard touchdown pass from Sammy Baugh and kicked the extra point to make his presence known. His kicking and pass-receiving abilities began to play an important part in the Redskins' victories.

In 1944 Aguirre became the first Latino American named to the NFL All-Pro Team. During his all-pro season with the Redskins, Aguirre caught 34 passes for 410 yards and scored 4 touchdowns.

The 1945 season was a very successful campaign for Aguirre and Washington. Quarterback Sammy Baugh set an NFL record with an incredible 70.3 percent completion rate. The Redskins won 8 and lost 2. Aguirre proved his importance to the Redskins as a kicker when, in the Chicago Cardinals game, he booted a 19-yard field goal, with 25 seconds left, to break the tie and give Washington the victory over the Cardinals 24-21.

But it is the 1945 NFL championship game—unfortunately for Aguirre—that is best remembered among those years of Redskins victories.

The heartbreaking game came on December 16. The Redskins, who led the NFL Eastern Division and were favored to win by three points, faced the Western Division victors the Cleveland Rams. (The following year the Rams moved to Los Angeles.) The game took place at the Rams' stadium in Cleveland.

Bad omens followed the Redskins from the start. Superstitious players on the team later recalled that the Redskins departure date from Washington was December 13 and that the Redskins had left from Track 13 at Union Station. Then as the players waited to board their assigned coaches, they saw a casket wheeled by. Minutes later, two large bundles of Christmas mail fell from a wagon to the sidewalk, narrowly missing two of the Redskins. When the train arrived in Cleveland, it was 13 minutes late.

The day of the game, the weather was bitterly cold, -7°F, with a strong, gusting wind that kept blowing all day long. "It was so cold," wrote one sports writer, "that the hot broth served in the glass-enclosed press coop turned to jellied consommé from cup to lip." It was so cold that the brass instruments of the famous Redskins marching band froze up and couldn't be played, no matter how hard the band members worked at warming them up.

For days the field had been covered with 9,000 bales of straw and tarpaulins to keep it from freezing, but to no avail. On the day of the game the field was frozen and frozen solid.

A brief disagreement ensued between Redskins Coach Dud DeGroot and Cleveland Coach Adam Walsh over cleated football shoes. Although both coaches agreed to wear cleated shoes, the Redskins brought along sneakers in case the field was frozen solid. Cleated shoes, they feared, would prove disastrous on a frozen field.

But the sneakers were never used. "We don't have any sneakers," Walsh complained to DeGroot. "I guess we can't afford them and if you use them and we don't, then you get an unfair advantage. I'd appreciate it if we could play this game on even terms."

DeGroot conceded and ordered his team to practice in their cleated shoes.

"If we had worn them [sneakers] in the game," said one team member afterwards, "there's no question that we would have been a more effective team. We would have beaten Cleveland."

Early in the first quarter, the Rams blocked a punt and forced the Redskins back to their own goal line. Sammy Baugh—the most famous Redskin of his time—dropped back in punt formation deep in his end zone, but instead of kicking, he executed a fake and passed toward Wayne Millner. The football, however, did not reach Millner. Instead, it slipped from Baugh's hands, hit the Redskin goalpost and rebounded into the end zone for an automatic safety for the Rams.

In the second quarter, halfback Frank Filchock threw a 26-yard touchdown for the Redskins. Aguirre converted the extra point to put the Redskins in the lead for the first time in the game, 7-2. In the same quarter, the Rams added a touchdown and a conversion to their score, to make it 9-7 at the half. In the third quarter, both teams scored again, bringing the game to 15-14. But then came the heartbreaker.

With Cleveland ahead, Washington moved into position for a last valiant effort—a field goal from 31 yards with 6:16 remaining in the fourth quarter. Baugh held the football on the frozen ground while Aguirre kicked. The field goal was long enough, but a sudden gust of cold winter wind blew it off target.

Al Costello of the *Washington Post* described the events in these words: "As the ball sailed high everybody held their breath as referee Ronald Gibbs hesitated momentarily before waving the 'No Good' signal. The leather was only a few feet to the right."

The Redskins lost the championship 15-14 and the winner's prize of $164,542.80 went to the Rams. The game marked the end of an era for the Redskins. It would be 25 years before Washington had a championship once again—a team that could compare with the Redskins of the first half of the 1940s.

Aguirre led the NFL that year in the number of completed field goals (7) for the entire season. The following year, 1946, he left the Redskins and the National Football League to play ball with the Los Angeles Dons of the newly formed All-American Football Conference (AAFC).

During his first season with the Dons, Aguirre established an all-time single point after touchdown record for a single game with 8 conversions, when his team crushed the Buffalo Bisons, 62-14. Additionally, in another game against the Bisons, Aguirre had a clutch pass reception for 67 yards and a touchdown in the final minutes of play, to tie Buffalo 21-21. And in the Cleveland Brown's game, big Joe Aguirre booted an 11-yard field goal in the last 20 seconds to give the Dons a 17-16 victory over the league-leading Browns

Joe Aguirre

Pass Receptions

Year/s	Team	No.	Yds.	Avg.	TDs
1943	Washington Redskins	37	420	11.3	7
1944	Washington Redskins	34	410	12.0	4[1]
1946-49	Los Angeles Dons (AAFC)	63	1040	16.5	16[2]
1950	Winnipeg Blue Bombers (CFL)	17	292	17.1	2
1951	Winnipeg Blue Bombers	2	12	6.0	0
1952	Edmonton Eskimos (CFL)	38	549	14.4	5
1953	Saskatchewan Roughriders	3	43	14.3	0
1954	Saskatchewan Roughriders	2	32	16.0	0[3]
		196	2,798	14.2	34

Kickoffs

Year/s	Teams	No.	Yds.
1951-54	Winnipeg Blue Bombers	114	6,258[4]
	Edmonton Eskimos		
	Saskatchewan Roughriders		

Punt Returns

Year	Team	No.	Yds.	Avg.
1952	Edmonton Eskimos	2	57	28.5[5]

Scoring

Year/s	Team/s	PATs	FG	TDs	Total Pts.
1941	Washington Redskins	8	2	2	26
1943	Washington Redskins	-	-	7	42
1944	Washington Redskins	15	4	4	51
1945	Washington Redskins	23	7	0	44[6]
1946-49	Los Angeles Dons (AAFC)	33	5	16	144[7]
1950	Winnipeg Blue Bombers	32	5	2	59
1951	Winnipeg Blue Bombers	20	1	0	23
1952	Edmonton Eskimos (CFL)	30	1	5	63
1953	Saskatchewan Roughriders	1	0	0	1
1954	Saskatchewan Roughriders	28	19	0	85
1955	Saskatchewan Roughriders	31	14	0	73[8]
		221	58	36	611

Notes

1 *Washington Redskins 1986 Press Guide,* 212.

2 Roger Treat, *The Encyclopedia of Football* (London: A.S. Barnes and Company, 1979), 711.

3 "Canadian Football League Individual Statistical Record for Joe Aguirre."

4 Ibid.

5 Ibid.

6 *1986 Press Guide,* 214.

7 Treat, 711.

8 "Statistical Record for Joe Aguirre."

of the AAFC. For his outstanding play during the year, Aguirre was named to the AAFC All-Pro Second Team.

When the AAFC merged with the NFL in 1949, Aguirre accepted an offer to play in the Canadian Football League (CFL). The 1950 season found him with the Winnipeg Blue Bombers, where he led the CFL Western Conference in scoring with 59 points and was named to the CFL Western Conference All-Star Team.

Aguirre then joined the Edmonton Eskimos for two seasons and wrote himself into Edmonton's career statistics. On September 1, 1952, in the game against the Calgary Stampeders, he caught 8 passes for 204 yards to rank him fifth in Edmonton Eskimo all-time statistics for pass reception yards in a single game. The following year he signed on as a player-coach with the Saskatchewan Roughriders and played his final three seasons in pro football. In 1954, with a season total of 85 points, he led the CFL Western Conference in scoring one last time before finishing his career in 1955. The history-making Latino played a combined total of 14 years in professional football.

For Aguirre it was a long road from the football field of St. Mary's College to his retirement from pro football in Saskatchewan, Canada. Everywhere he played he was a star, but no one could tell by his demeanor. To those who knew him, he was a quiet man who nevertheless brought a lot of excitement to football. Although a master of the game, he has not been duly acknowledged, but some day, Big Joe Aguirre, the Latino football hero, will gain the recognition he assuredly deserves.

Chicago Guard Peter Pérez

Peter J. Pérez played only one year of professional football in the National Football League, but it was a historic one. World War II had come to an end as the German armies surrendered to Allied Forces in May of 1945, and the Japanese surrendered aboard the *USS Missouri* in Tokyo harbor on September 2, 1945. Pérez played against the likes of Bob Waterfield, the sensational rookie quarterback for the Cleveland Rams and the league's Most Valuable Player, Honduras-born Steve Van Buren of the Philadelphia Eagles, who captured his first of four career rushing titles, and Redskin and fellow Latino Joe Aguirre, who led the NFL in field goals, hitting 7 of 13 attempts. In retrospect, it was a remarkable experience for the 5 foot 10 inch Mexicano athlete.

Pérez was born on April 23, 1924, in Aurora, Illinois. His parents had migrated from the silver mining area of Zacatecas, Mexico, to the United States and Illinois in the early 1900s. The Pérez family settled in Aurora, Illinois, where Peter attended Marmion Military Academy. He played outstanding prep football at Marmion and, with help from his coach Hank Fallon, obtained a football scholarship to the University of Illinois. Pérez moved to Champaign to play collegiate football with the "Fighting Illini," coached by the renowned Ray Eliot.

In his first and only year, 1943, Pérez started at the offensive tackle position. That season, the Illinois team upset the University of Wisconsin 25-7, defeated the University of Pittsburgh by the score of 33-25, and shut out the University of Iowa 19-0. When asked about his collegiate football days at Illinois, Pérez recalls his efforts against Pittsburgh and the heart-breaking loss to Ohio State. He remembers the Ohio State game was bitterly played to a 26-26 tie and then won by the Ohio State Buckeyes on a field goal after regulation time had expired. The *New York Times* described how the Buckeyes won the game: "With the score deadlocked at 26-26, Ohio had blasted its way to the Illinois 15-yard line, only to lose the ball on a fumble. Two plays later Illinois fumbled and Ohio regained the football. Two seconds remained to play and Ohio State attempted a pass play which went incomplete as the game ended. The teams then raced to the dressing rooms and the fans filed from the stadium thinking the game was over. However, Illinois had been penalized for being offside and the teams were ordered back for one more play. Twelve minutes had elapsed as the teams lined up for the last play. Ohio State substitute quarterback John Stungis then kicked a 25-yard field goal to beat Illinois 29-26."

With the war still raging, Pérez left the university after the 1943 season to join the military. However, a perforated eardrum kept him out of the service. Instead, he served with the Merchant Marines in the European theater of operations and returned home after his tour.

In 1945 Pérez signed to play professional football with the Chicago Bears of the NFL, after his college coach Ray Eliot wrote a letter of recommendation to the Bears. Pérez started as offensive guard for the Bears in games against the Green Bay Packers, Cleveland Rams, and the Chicago Cardinals. That year, the Bears, coached by Hartley Anderson and Luke Johnson, posted a win over the Packers 28-24; defeated the Pittsburgh Steelers 28-7; and beat the cross-town rival Chicago Cardinals 28-20. The Bears' last 2 wins can be attributed to the return of Coach George Halas. Coach/owner Halas returned to the Bears in November 1945 after his tour of duty with the U.S. Navy.

Pérez had played the majority of the 1945 season with the Bears and then been released. Interestingly,

Pérez received $150 per game and was paid for the entire season. After his NFL experience, Pérez played pro football in the East Coast League from 1946 to 1949.

The East Coast League comprised minor league professional teams, which supplied players to the NFL teams. Pérez was a player-coach with the Akron Bears and the Bethlehem Bulldogs. Other teams in the East Coast League included teams from Paterson/Newark, New Jersey; Wilkes-Barre, Pennsylvania; and Richmond, Indiana. The teams played against one another and also played exhibition games against the NFL teams, such as the Chicago Bears, New York Giants, Buffalo Bills, and Philadelphia Eagles.

In 1949 Pérez left professional football and returned to Aurora, Illinois. He married and pursued a career in law enforcement. At age 59 Pérez retired from the Aurora Police Department and went to work for the Kane County sheriff's office in the juvenile department. Pérez and his wife María had five sons and one daughter. Their two eldest sons, Pedro and Paul, played collegiate football at Eastern Illinois University and the University of Wisconsin, respectively. The third son, Mike, is an Aurora city police officer. Their fourth son, Matthew, and daughter Marcía reside in Aurora, and their fifth son, Pat, lives in California.

Reflecting on his collegiate and pro football careers, Pérez relates two important observations. "In those times, Mexicanos/Latinos were a rarity in football," he notes. When Pérez was playing, the only other Latino in the NFL was Joe Aguirre, who played with the Redskins. But Eddie Sáenz, Gonzalo Morales, John Sánchez, and Dan Garza quickly followed his lead. Secondly, Pérez says, "If I had to change or do anything different, I would return to the University of Illinois and finish my college education." He cites education as being so important to succeed in whatever endeavors one chooses to undertake.

Although Pérez played a lone season with the Chicago Bears, he has no regrets about his short NFL career. As a member of the Chicago Bears player alumni, Pérez makes it a point to attend their alumni functions in Chicago each year. These functions are exciting, he says, and it does this old timer good to reminisce about his once being a blocking lineman for Bears Hall of Famer Sid Luckman. But this is only for a little while; the rest of the time, his family have his attention, because in retirement, this is what he enjoys.

Eddie Sáenz
NFL Kickoff Return Leader

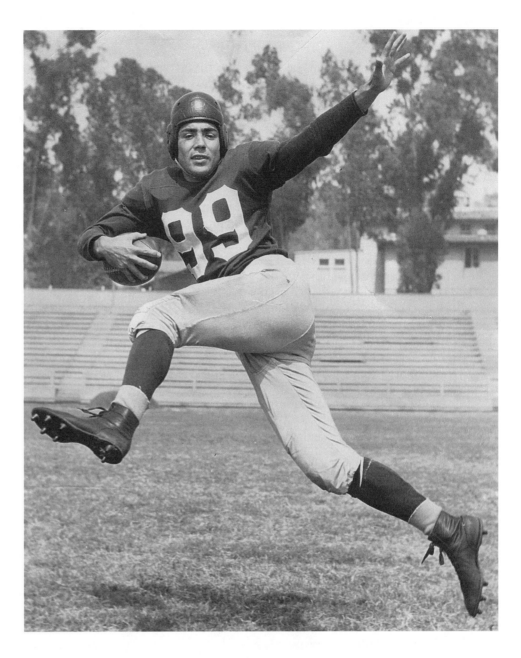

His name was Edwin Matthew Sáenz, born September 21, 1922, in Santa Monica, California. But to friends and fans in Los Angeles he was Eddie Sáenz, youngest of the five Sáenz brothers. Like their father Cy, a local boxing promoter and owner of the Culver City Boxing Arena, the Sáenz brothers were well known for their athletic prowess.

Not surprisingly, all the brothers were boxers at one time or another. Gabriel was something of a local favorite in the boxing arena's weekly amateur fights. Manuel fought as a lightweight. Ernie went on to become school boxing champ in college at Santa Barbara. Daniel saw the most action in the ring and was the only one of the Sáenz brothers to fight professionally. And of course, there was Eddie.

The Sáenz brothers didn't limit themselves to the ring. Gabriel went to California Polytechnic University

and excelled as the college's starting quarterback. Manuel, the wiry lightweight, showed his reach, reaction, and wallop as one of the all-time great volleyball players of Southern California. An AAU All-American, Manuel was chosen by the Helms Athletic Foundation as "Most Outstanding Volleyball Player of the Half Century." And like Gabriel, Ernie was a star quarterback at both Santa Monica College and Santa Barbara State University.

And then there was Eddie.

Eddie Sáenz took to football with the vengeance and heart of a boxer. Sáenz began his collegiate football career at Loyola University of Los Angeles, where he played for the Loyola Lions for the years 1940-42. The war was on, and in 1942 Sáenz entered a U.S. Naval Reserve program. Assigned to the University of Southern California (USC) for training in 1943, Sáenz's football skills did not leave him, and he picked up where he left off at Loyola. Playing for USC, Sáenz led the Trojans through battle after battle as their leading rusher. He helped USC win the Pacific Coast Conference Championship with spectacular performances against UCLA, St. Mary's College of California, University of San Francisco, and California. Against UCLA Sáenz romped 86 yards for a score and then returned a UCLA punt 40 yards for a touchdown. In the St. Mary's game he returned an interception 39 yards to set up a Trojan score. And against the University of San Francisco he sped 43 yards for a touchdown. Sáenz also sparked the USC offensive drive with runs that led the Trojans to an eventual score in the game against California.

The victories earned the team a berth in the 1944 Rose Bowl. Sáenz's seeming unstoppability sent the Washington Huskies into a flaming downward spiral that in the end tallied USC 29, University of Washington 0. Sáenz's participation in the 1944 Rose Bowl earned him the distinction of being the first Mexicano to play in the football classic.

Sáenz's football career was interrupted at a critical time by the war effort. Shortly after his Rose Bowl heroics, Sáenz joined the Navy and was sent to Illinois to train at the Great Lakes Naval Training Center. But this time training would not be for the grueling demands of the gridiron. The Great Lakes would be a temporary home for Eddie the sailor.

Sáenz's reputation as a football player preceded him to the center. Shortly after arriving he began training, both for naval service and the center's football team. During that time, some military installations fielded football teams that played competitive collegiate schedules.

Sáenz's teammates at Great Lakes included Paul E. Brown and Ara Parseghian. Brown later would become owner and coach of the Cleveland Browns of the NFL—for those who wondered where the team got its name—and would later coach the Cincinnati Bengals. Parseghian would go on to become the legendary coach of the University of Notre Dame.

When the 1944 season opened against Fort Sheridan, Sáenz was nursing an ankle injury. Though his mentors used him sparingly, Sáenz drew first blood of the season, scampering around left end for an 11-yard touchdown run. As his injuries healed he saw more action. Against Western Michigan Sáenz scored another touchdown, this one on a short dive into the end zone that delighted fans who had heard of this young Mexican American's California glories. The game was a prelude to the upcoming game against the Wisconsin Badgers.

When the Bluejackets—as the training center's team was called—came on the field, Sáenz led the pack. Sáenz had a exceptional game against the Badgers. The *New York Times* reported the game saying, "Great Lakes roared back from its defeat by Ohio State last week to smother Wisconsin's young Badgers, 40-12. . . . Sáenz scored three times for Great Lakes."

The *Chicago Tribune's* writer saw it this way: ". . . in the last few minutes of the opening period, the sailors from the Great Lakes, particularly Jim Mello and Eddie Sáenz, moved the ball from their own 20 yard line to the Badgers' one yard line. In the first play of the second quarter, Sáenz was stopped, but he tried again, and this time slipped through Wisconsin's right guard for the score."

As it turned out, Sáenz was just whetting his appetite. In the third quarter he scored with runs, one from the 40 yard line. The other was described by the *Tribune* this way: ". . . the sailors recovered a Badger fumble on their own 23 yard line. Four rushing plays and a penalty later, the ball was spotted on the Wisconsin 25 yard line. Sáenz took a lateral from quarterback Jim Youel and charged the remaining 21 yards for the touchdown."

Great Lakes scored its fifth touchdown of the game, with Sáenz sprinting for yardage on the next set of offensive plays and finally galloping around right end for 40 yards and his third score of the contest.

In spite of his late season start, his rushing in the Wisconsin game advanced Sáenz to the high end of the stats. He was second in team scoring and also in rushing. His 135 yards against Wisconsin increased his season rushing yardage to 288 yards in 36 carries, and his three touchdowns moved him to 30 points, second only to Jim Mello.

Sáenz started at halfback for the rest of the season in games against Third Air Force, Marquette, Fort Warren, and Notre Dame. He scored against Marquette with a 9-yard run. Great Lakes finished the season with an impressive 9-2-1 record, and Sáenz finished third on the team in scoring with 36 points and second in rushing with 465 yards. He accumulated 568 total yards and was named one of the most valuable players on the now legendary Great Lakes team.

A month after finishing the season, in December 1944, Sáenz received his orders and shipped out to the west coast. While on duty he got the news that he had been selected as the thirteenth-round draft choice of the Washington Redskins. But it would be some time before he would be able to play in the NFL.

In 1946 Seaman Sáenz joined the Redskins and played six hard seasons in Washington. In the days when few Latinos lived or worked in the nation's capitol, Sáenz was remembered well. The quick Sáenz had a knack for evading the defensive protection schemes of so many NFL teams. Frequently on the receiving end of Sammy Baugh's passes, in 1947,

Edwin "Eddie" Sáenz

Rushing

Year	Team	No.	Yds.	Avg.	TDs
1946	Washington Redskins	55	213	3.8	1
1947	Washington Redskins	51	143	2.8	0
1948	Washington Redskins	8	21	2.6	0
1949	Washington Redskins	53	170	3.2	0
1950	Washington Redskins	20	64	3.2	1[1]
1951	Washington Redskins	3	8	2.7	0[2]
		190	619	3.2	2

Pass Receptions

Year	Team	No.	Yds.	Avg.	TDs
1946	Washington Redskins	12	242	20.1	3
1947	Washington Redskins	34	598	17.5	4
1948	Washington Redskins	4	62	15.5	0
1949	Washington Redskins	23	251	10.9	0
1950	Washington Redskins	10	165	16.5	1
1951	Washington Redskins	1	9	9.0	0[3]
		84	1,327	15.79	8

Kickoff Returns

Year	Team	No.	Yds.	Avg.	Lg.	TDs
1946	Washington Redskins	11	264	24.0	55	0
1947	Washington Redskins	29	797	27.4	94	2
1948	Washington Redskins	8	173	22.0	-	0[4]
1949	Washington Redskins	24	465	19.4	-	0
1950	Washington Redskins	12	347	28.9	-	0
1951	Washington Redskins	9	145	16.0	-	0[5]
		93	2,191	23.5	94	2

Punt Returns

Year	Team	No.	Yds.	Avg.	TDs
1947	Washington Redskins	24	308	12.8	0
1948	Washington Redskins	2	26	13.0	0
1949	Washington Redskins	17	178	10.4	0
1950	Washington Redskins	14	125	8.9	0
1951	Washington Redskins	2	6	3.0	0[6]
		59	643	10.89	0

Notes

1 Telephone call to Washington Redskins Public Relations Office, for statistics on Eddie Sáenz, Monday, May 11, 1987.

2 David S. Neft, Richard M. Cohen, and Rick Korch, *The Football Encyclopedia: The Complete, Year-by-Year History of Professional Football from 1892 to the Present* (New York: St. Martin's Press, 1994), 233.

3 Ibid., 233.

4 Ibid., 208.

5 Ibid., 277.

6 Ibid., 233.

Edwin Sáenz, continued

Scoring

Year	Team	TDs	Total Pts.
1946	Washington Redskins	4	24
1947	Washington Redskins	6	36
1950	Washington Redskins	2	12
		12	72

NFL Kickoff Return Leader in 1947.

29 returns for 797 yards, 27.4 average and (2) Touchdowns.[7]

7 *The Official National Football League 1991 Record & Fact Book* (New York: Workman Publishing Company, 1991), 341.

Sáenz claimed the title as the NFL's most dangerous kickoff and punt return specialist. That year he returned 29 kickoffs for 797 yards and 2 touchdowns. His longest return was 94 yards, a feat he accomplished twice during the 1947 season. Against the Philadelphia Eagles, the *New York Times* recounts, "The Eagles and Redskins smashed all NFL scoring records today with the Eagles finishing on the long end of 45-42 count before a crowd of 35,400 at municipal stadium . . . Steve Van Buren personally conducted the Eagle back into the lead on a 95-yard kickoff return before the half ended . . . each team scored twice in the third period, the Redskins counting on the opening kickoff as Eddie Sáenz raced 94 yards with the ball for a touchdown."

In the Giants game, noted *New York Times* sportswriter Joseph Sheehan describes Sáenz's second kickoff return for a touchdown: "Paced by the incomparable Sammy Baugh and the mercurial Eddie Sáenz, the Washington Redskins sent the New York Giants down to their second straight NFL defeat 28-20. . . . After a New York threat fizzled, Baugh hit Sáenz with a long pass and the fleet Californian galloped the last 40 yards of a 74-yard pass play untouched, to make it 21-7 in the third period. In the final quarter, Sáenz took the next kickoff on his 6 yard line, burst into the clear on the 20 and went all the way, four blockers convoying him past Ken Strong and into the end zone."

But Sáenz's career in the pros was also a difficult one. Injuries cut Eddie Sáenz's career short at the end of the 1951 season. And although he never publicly complained about it, he was at the receiving end of a lot of anti-Mexicano discrimination.

In six productive seasons (1946-51) with the Washington Redskins, Sáenz caught 84 passes for 1,327 yards, rushed 190 times for 619 yards, returned punts for 643 yards, and returned 93 kickoffs for 2,191 yards.

Never one to seek the mundane or the ordinary, Sáenz returned to California to become a leading stuntman in the motion picture industry. Westerns were at their peak and Sáenz became a specialist in fights and falls, working as a double for Tyrone Power, Steve Cochran, Anthony Quinn, Charles Bronson, and many more.

Eddie Sáenz died April 28, 1971, survived by his wife Helen, eight sons, and one daughter. His football exploits against college opponents, against a host of NFL teams, and against innumerable celluloid bad guys are all remembered. Sáenz had an illustrious career for a talented yet unheralded athlete.

Big John Sánchez
Little All-American

"**B**ig John Sánchez, Little All-American" could be the title of an epic football story. In many ways the title fits, except for the little in front of All-American. This gentleman/athlete was not only big in stature but big in heart as well. From the very beginning he would be someone to be revered.

Born on October 12, 1920, in Los Angeles, California, John Sánchez's genealogy is a mixture of Old and New World roots. His father was from Asturias, Spain, and his mother from Mazatlán, Mexico.

In high school Sánchez established himself as a force to be reckoned with on the football field. He was a one-man show and at 6'2" and towered over his prep teammates.

After high school, Sánchez enrolled at Los Angeles City College and became an integral part of the football program. A *Compton Tartar Shield* article describes Sánchez in his premier collegiate season: "Rugged redheaded Johnny Sánchez is an outstanding tackle. The 6 foot 2 inch, 206-pound lineman has proven this, racing down the field with the agility of an ambitious hepcat and being as immobile as the rock of Gibraltar."

In the 1940 season the Los Angeles City College team posted a record of 6 wins, 3 losses, and 1 tie. They beat Bakersfield, Ventura Junior College, Long Beach City College, USC Freshman, Glendale Junior College, and Santa Monica City College to clinch a tie for the Metropolitan Conference title. Sánchez played in every game with his best efforts coming against Ventura and Glendale. In both these games the stalwart soul made spectacular tackles and turned in good all-around performances. The agile tackle also blocked eight punts that season. For his efforts, Sánchez earned spots on the All-Metropolitan Conference Team and the All-Southern California Junior College Teams for 1940.

The following year (1941) Sánchez transferred to the University of San Francisco (USF) on a football scholarship. A growing athlete, Sánchez now measured 6'4" and weighed 245 pounds. He played defensive tackle for the USF Dons. They expected big things from Big John and he delivered more than expected.

The singular highlight of the 1941 season came in the game against the Santa Clara University Broncos when Sánchez blocked a Santa Clara punt in the third quarter.

In the 1942 season, USF tackle John Sánchez reached stardom, contributing to the USF Dons wins over the University of Nevada, Arizona State, San Jose State, Fresno State, Alameda Coast Guard, and the team from Albuquerque Air Base. "Giant Johnny Sánchez's particular genius tends toward smacking down ballcarriers. The rugged Sánchez is fighting his way to prominence as the best tackle in recent Don history and certainly as one of the better on Coast gridirons," noted the *San Francisco Examiner* before the Fresno State game.

Competing against the St. Mary's Gaels, the Dons lost 6-0, but Sánchez and captain Carrol Vogelaar put on star performances. Bill Leiser, sportswriter for the *San Francisco Chronicle,* wrote, "El señor Johnny Sánchez, the booming, busting, battering bundle of dynamite from San Diego will do as the best tackle on the coast and as one of the best in the country. The red-haired star of USF football has inscribed for himself a niche in the Don Hall of Fame by playing the greatest game of his life against the Gaels of St. Mary's. He played exactly 59 minutes 44 seconds of the game and made 60% of the tackles."

In the game against the University of Santa Clara, Sánchez gave probably one of the greatest exhibitions of individual ability and doggedness ever witnessed on the West Coast. Santa Clara and USF were locked in a vicious struggle. At the close of the first half, Santa Clara, in possession, employed an end sweep over the left side of the USF forward defensive wall. Sánchez flung his body across the phalanx of interference and stripped all protection away from the ballcarrier by wiping out three Santa Clara players. Sánchez was cleated severely around the mouth and received a gash that required 13 stitches, which he received at half time. A tough competitor, Sánchez returned in the second half to give Santa Clara a defensive beating unequaled to anything the Broncos had encountered throughout the year. Sánchez personally accounted for 70 percent of the tackles in the second half. At the conclusion of the contest, Santa Clara's Lawrence "Buck" Shaw said, "[Sánchez is] the finest defensive tackler I've laid my eyes on in six years as head coach of Santa Clara."

At season's end, Sánchez received numerous honors for his football playing efforts. *San Francisco Examiner* named Sánchez to the 1942 All-Northern California Football Team. Sports writer L.D. "Spud" Lewis comments on Sánchez's football ability: "Sánchez was one of the most consistent players of the season, never turning in a bad game. Usually, he was the best lineman on the field. A giant in stature, Sánchez usually played a smashing, charging game."

The Associated Press placed Sánchez on the eighteenth Annual All-Pacific Coast Football Team. Sánchez was the first player from USF to gain a place on the number-one team. Also, the bulky star from USF was selected to the Little All-American Team at the tackle position.

The recognition continued long after the 1942 season had ended. Sánchez, a 20-year-old sophomore, was presented the Martin O'Brien Trophy, awarded to the player at the university who shows the greatest degree of development in all-around play and performance.

University of San Francisco head coach Jeff Cravath had nothing but admiration for Sánchez. He declared, "I've never seen or coached a better sophomore tackle than Sánchez."

Awaiting the next football season, and basking in his football glories, Sánchez also played rugby for USF in 1941-42. But the war abruptly interrupted his collegiate athletic career. John Sánchez enlisted in a Naval VT-12 training program and transferred from USF to the University of the Redlands (California) in 1943. As a Marine Corps officer candidate, Sánchez received initial training at Redlands and then was sent to Parris Island, South Carolina. He was commissioned a first lieutenant and served in the Pacific campaign with the Second Marine Division at Okinawa.

However, prior to his deployment to Okinawa, Sánchez did get a chance to display his football talents at the University of the Redlands. Although he played a short season with the Redlands Bulldogs in 1943, he played so well, the university announced it was permanently retiring football jersey 71, in honor of Big John Sánchez, tackle who had worn the number for the past seven years at San Diego High School, Los Angeles City College, USF, and Redlands. A university spokesperson estimated Sánchez had made about 50 percent of the Redlands' tackles in 1943 and that 60 percent of the Bulldogs' yardage was made over his side of the line. Sánchez captained the Redlands Bulldogs until his departure to the U.S. Marines.

In 1946 Marine combat veteran Sánchez returned from the war to the University of San Francisco. Immediately, he became the captain of the Don's 1946 football team. That season, USF posted victories over the University of Nebraska, Kansas State, and the University of Wyoming. Sánchez experienced a fine season, doing what he did best. His defensive efforts were reflections of the 1942 season.

In 1946 Sánchez signed to play football with the San Francisco Clippers of the Pacific Coast Football League, a local semi-pro league. The *San Francisco Examiner* reported that "Johnny Sánchez, senior tackle at USF, signed with the San Francisco Clippers and will perform against the Hollywood Bears in a Pacific Coast Football League game at Kezar Stadium."

Sánchez graduated from USF in 1947 with a bachelor of science degree in romance languages and pursued his dream of playing in the NFL. While in the Marines,

Sánchez had been drafted in 1944 by the New York Giants of the NFL. But their ninth-round choice could not join them until 1947.

At the beginning of the 1947 season, Sánchez experienced some difficulty with the New York club and subsequently signed with the Chicago Rockets of the rival All-American Football Conference (AAFC). Sánchez played for the Rockets; however, he quickly became disenchanted with them and signed on with the Detroit Lions. Once again Sánchez became uneasy about his team. Sánchez expressed his concern, and in a waiver agreement between the Lions and Washington Redskins, Sánchez went over to the Redskins. The *Washington Post* reported the deal between the two teams: "Still another new face was added to the Redskins' roster yesterday when John Sánchez, a tackle, was sent by the Detroit Lions in their half of the waiver deal that moved guard Bill Ward to Detroit. Sánchez, who starred for the University of San Francisco last year, will be in uniform this Sunday to play Detroit."

Once settled, Sánchez finished out the 1947 season on a positive note with the Redskins. Against the Boston Yankees, John Sánchez set up the team's final score when he intercepted Yankee quarterback Maley's pass on the Yankees' 20 yard line. Redskins quarterback Sammy Baugh stepped in and threw a touchdown pass to Joe Tereshinski. The final score: Redskins 40, Boston Yankees 13.

Sánchez played with the Redskins through the beginning of the 1949 season. During his time in Washington he was converted to an offensive tackle and many times opened holes for fellow Mexicano teammate and running back Eddie Sáenz.

After three games into the 1949 season, Sánchez returned to the New York Giants in what was termed "one of the best moves the Giants made." Sánchez was immediately placed into an offensive tackle position and played regularly for the remainder of the season.

In 1950 Sánchez played his final year of professional football. In his last season, Sánchez finished on a winning note, helping the New York Giants post 10

John C. Sánchez

Interceptions						
Year	Team	No.	Yds.	Avg.	Lg.	TDs
1947	Washington Redskins	1	1	1.0	1	0

Source: David S. Neft, Richard M. Cohen, and Rick Korch, *The Football Encyclopedia: The Complete, Year-by-Year History of Professional Football from 1892 to the Present* (New York: St. Martin's Press, 1944), 291.

victories, 2 losses, which placed them in a tie with the Cleveland Browns for the American Conference Championship and forced a playoff game between the two teams. The game was a defensive battle from the start. The Browns defeating the Giants by the score of 8-3, with the game decided on a late quarter field goal and a safety with 8 seconds remaining to play.

Sánchez recalls, "The game was closely contested on frozen ground, Connerly was quarterbacking and it was Kelly Note who dropped the pass in the end zone. Had he caught it, we would have won the game and championship."

After the 1950 season, Sánchez left professional football to accept a construction job on the West Coast. However, realizing that Sánchez would be difficult to replace on the offensive line, the Giants contacted him and offered him a two-year, "no release" $10,500 annual salary contract to come out of retirement and play for them once again. Sánchez considered the proposal but declined the offer and stayed in California and the construction business.

Since 1950 Sánchez has worked for licensed contractors Pierce Enterprises and Rollie French. A very successful businessman, John Sánchez can boast of over 40 years experience in the construction industry.

USF alumni relations director Tom Rice describes Sánchez as a redheaded, good-looking Mexican, a great leader well liked by all. Rice praised Sánchez for his athletic accomplishments and his sterling character. As a tribute to his fine collegiate football days at USF, Sánchez was inducted into the University of San Francisco's Athletic Hall of Fame in November 1975. Beyond any doubt, it was a well-deserved tribute to a great athlete and stellar individual. Now in retirement, John Claude Sánchez resides in Hayward, California.

Gonzalo Morales

The moment Gonzalo Morales took to playing football marked the beginning of a journey that would lead him to the NFL and the Pittsburgh Steelers. As a young athlete, Morales ran for glory on high school gridirons throughout San Francisco, establishing himself as one of the city's top athletes. In college he steadily improved and entered the pro ranks after his junior year at St. Mary's College. The Philadelphia Eagles chose him in the draft, but his stay with the team was short. Nonetheless, the Eagles looked forward to his arrival and described him in their *1947 Philadelphia Eagles Press Guide* as "a brilliant triple-threat player," and Gonzalo Morales lived up to this billing whenever he donned a football uniform.

Morales was born in San Francisco, California, on June 10, 1922, the son of parents who had migrated to the Unites States from a small town outside of Madrid, Spain. He grew up in San Francisco and achieved football fame at Mission High School.

At 6'1", "Ganzie," as he was called, was a natural athlete. Not only was he strong and fleet a foot, but he also was adept at throwing the football. In his senior prep year, Morales was named captain of the All-City Team, was its most valuable player, and was offered a scholarship at St. Mary's College of California in nearby Moraga. In those days St. Mary's played a top flight football schedule and was considered one of the best independent college teams in the country.

Morales accepted the scholarship and soon convinced his benefactors he could play their brand of collegiate football. As a freshman in 1941, Morales became the starting quarterback and could also play any position in the back field. In 1942, his sophomore year, he was considered one of the finest all-around collegiate prospects on the West Coast. Morales's long-time friend Al Corona had this to say about him: "He played both offense and defense, offensively at half-back and defensively in the secondary. His outstanding speed, strength, and coordination made him a valuable asset at both positions." The St. Mary's Gaels had a good season, but Morales had a great season.

In postseason play, Morales played in the East-West Shrine All-Star game and was a featured running back along with teammate Herman Wedemeyer. In the

Gonzalo Morales

Rushing

Year	Team	Games	No.	Yds.	Avg.	Long	TDs
1947	Pittsburgh Steelers	7	29	96	3.3	18	0
1948	Pittsburgh Steelers	10	13	29	2.4	8	0
		17	42	125	3.0	18	0

Passing

Year	Team	Games	No.	Comp.	Yds.	Avg.	TDs	Int.
1947	Pittsburgh Steelers	7	27	8	78	9.75	1	4
1948	Pittsburgh Steelers	10	4	3	30	10.0	0	0
		17	31	11	108	9.8	1	4

Punt Returns

Year	Team	Games	No.	Yds.	Avg.	Long	TDs
1947	Pittsburgh Steelers	6	88	14.6	20	0	
1948	Pittsburgh Steelers	8	83	10.4	20	0	
		14	171	12.2	20	0	

Kickoff Returns

Year	Team	Games	No.	Yds.	Avg.	Long	TDs
1947	Pittsburgh Steelers	5	113	22.6	27	0	
1948	Pittsburgh Steelers	3	62	20.7	26	0	
		8	175	21.8	27	0	

Interceptions/Recoveries

Year	Team	Games	No.	Yds.	Avg.	Long	TDs
1947	Pittsburgh Steelers	1	1	5	5	5	0
1948	Pittsburgh Steelers	2	2/1	–	–	–	1
		3	3/1	–	–	–	1

Source: Phone call to Pittsburgh Steelers Public Relations Office for statistics on Gonzales Morales, Tuesday, May 19, 1987.

contest Morales rushed once for 4 yards and played in the defensive secondary for the West team. Other postseason accolades for Morales included a selection to the 1942 All-Northern California Football Second Team (players selected from the five major college teams in the San Francisco area) and the *San Francisco Examiner* All-Coast Team.

With World War II in progress in 1943, Morales interrupted his collegiate career to enlist and serve with the U.S. Coast Guard. During his military tenure, Morales found time to play on their service football team. The Coast Guard team fully utilized his gridiron talents and he became a vital player on the team. For Morales's efforts and contributions, he was named to the All-Coast Guard Service Team.

Honorably discharged from the service in 1945, Morales returned to civilian life. Unfortunately for Morales, during his absence, underclassman Herman

Wedemeyer had gained prominence and had helped take the St. Mary's Gaels to the 1945 Sugar Bowl in New Orleans, Louisiana. In 1946, Morales returned to St. Mary's but was relegated to a secondary role behind Wedemeyer. St. Mary's new coach Jimmy Phelan had decided to concentrate on Wedemeyer and ignored Morales, generally recognized as the better all-around player.

That season the Gaels won five games, defeating University of Nevada, Washington, Fordham, Santa Clara, and University of San Francisco, with defeats only to Pacific Coast Conference teams California and UCLA. Their successful season earned them an invitation to play Georgia Tech in the Oil Bowl in Houston, Texas.

Morales, not Wedemeyer, provided the biggest thrill of the game. Midway in the fourth quarter, Morales returned a Georgia Tech kickoff 62 yards. All that Wedemeyer could muster offensively in the game was 41 rushing yards.

The Philadelphia Eagles drafted Morales in the fifth round of the 1945 NFL lottery. He never played a game with the Eagles, however, as they traded him across state to the Pittsburgh Steelers. With the Steelers, the galloping Morales played both single wing halfback and defensive secondary for two years (1947-48).

His rookie season with Pittsburgh, the team won 8 and lost 5 games, including an Eastern Division playoff loss to the team who had originally drafted Morales, the Philadelphia Eagles. Morales finished the year with 378 total offensive yards and one pass interception. In 1948 Morales's best game came against the New York Giants in Pittsburgh. Morales recovered a New York fumble and ran 36 yards for a touchdown, as the Steelers defeated the Giants 38-28.

Statistically, Morales accumulated 204 total offensive yards and, in addition to the fumble recovery, intercepted 2 passes.

After the 1948 season, Morales decided to retire from professional football to spend more time with his wife Helen, whom he had married after he joined the Steelers. Despite a personal letter from Steelers owner Art Rooney asking that he reconsider his decision to retire, Morales chose to return to San Francisco. When asked about his collegiate, Coast Guard, and professional football careers, Morales summed it up succinctly: "Football to me has always been a team game. Games are won usually on what a team does as a whole, rather than by individual effort. If I did excel in a single game, it was with the help of my teammates."

An ardent pro football fan, Morales concedes the pro game has become more refined since he played it. However, he does not think the players are that much better. "We played more for the love of it than the money. Of course, we didn't make the money the players are making now, but we weren't concerned with the money aspect. We were able to concentrate more on the game itself. I also think we were closer as a team."

Morales went on to join the San Francisco Police Department and recently retired after more than 27 years of service in law enforcement. At present, Morales and his wife Helen reside in San Francisco, California. Their children, Adrienne and Robert, and grandchildren live in southern California.

But the football story of Gonzalo Morales is one that remains unfulfilled. Coaching mistakes at the college level and an early retirement from pro football brought an end to a career that could have been outstanding; Morales had the stuff to be an All-Time great in the NFL.

Dan Garza
An Officer and a
Gentleman

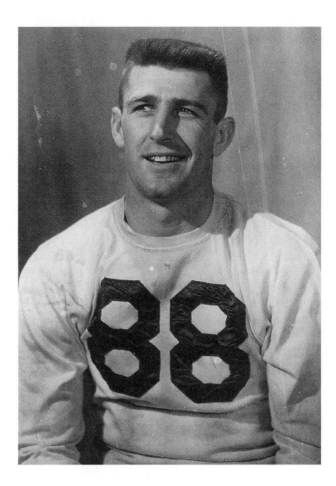

To this day, the memory of being cheated out of going to the Rose Bowl is still very vivid to football great Dan Garza. He played end on a University of Oregon team that was unjustly denied the trip to Pasadena. This football memory is one of many for the son of a career Navy man from San Antonio, Texas.

Dan Garza was born on February 21, 1924, in Anderson, South Carolina. His family moved around a lot due to his father's military duty. They lived in Anderson, South Carolina, and Weslaco and San Antonio, Texas, but the experience was an educational one for the young Garza.

The rites of passage for Garza centered on the old football field at Brackenridge High School in San Antonio. Arriving there as a junior, Garza realized he was a natural to play football and, by comparison, towered over most of his teammates. He was a two-way starter who achieved stardom in district play for the Brackenridge Eagles in 1940-1941. Observing his talent and potential, his coach George "Red" Forehand asked him about playing football at the college level. Garza recalls he initially did not give any thought to attending college, but the prospect was appealing and he eventually accepted a scholarship to play at North Texas State University in 1942.

However, the timing for college and football coincided with the Unites States' entry into World War II.

Although Garza had a college deferment from military service, this was only temporary. His father's patriotic example and his own personal convictions led him to enter the war effort. At North Texas he joined the VT-12 Naval program and transferred to Central Missouri State College in 1943. Unfortunately for North Texas State, Garza played only one season and did not return to their football program.

At Central Missouri Garza, whenever he was not in officer training, found time to play service football to keep his skills in tune. Upon completing the program at Northwestern University, he was commissioned as an ensign in the U.S. Navy.

Once in the regular Navy, Garza volunteered for the Underwater Demolition Team (UDT) and received orders to train at Fort Pierce, Florida. During the war the UDT were referred to as Navy frogmen, and they conducted special operations against the enemy. Today this group of Navy specialists are called SEALS. Ensign Garza also trained in Hawaii and in 1945 served as staff officer at Buckner Bay in Okinawa.

Upon conclusion of the war, Garza left the Navy in Seattle, Washington. On his way back to Texas, anxious to resume college and football, he took a few tours of colleges in Washington and Oregon. He visited the University of Washington and Oregon State before making one last stop at the University of

Oregon in Eugene. There two persuasive coaches, Tex Oliver and Vaughn Corley, both from Texas, convinced him to stay and play for the Ducks.

Even though he had been away from the sport a couple of years, his pass-receiving skills were not diminished. He signed to play three seasons (1946-48) for Oregon, but in 1946 Garza broke his leg in a scrimmage a week prior to the opening game and missed most of the year. At season's end, the pass-catching expert as he was called, had played only 62 minutes.

In those years the Oregon team was highly rated because of quarterback Norm Van Brocklin and Dan Garza. According to Oregon coach Jim Aiken, "Garza can do everything an end should do and does it well. He was one of the 'iron men' of the 1947-48 teams, playing the majority of the time on both offense and defense. Most Oregon opponents found it extremely difficult to make consistent yardage outside of Garza's end. He excels as a blocker as well as a pass receiver on offense."

During the 1947 season, Garza scored five touchdowns, two of which were on defense. He intercepted a University of San Francisco pass and ran it in for a score. Against Washington State, the quick Garza blocked a punt, recovered it, and ran for glory.

In 1948 the Associated press poll listed Oregon ninth in the country, a notch about Southern Methodist University (SMU). It was a great season for Garza and the Ducks. PAC-10 historian John D. McCallum describes the 1948 Oregon team: "The most important element was Van Brocklin's passing, but the Ducks were also strong on fundamentals and team discipline. The team was solid at every position. Van Brocklin was murder in the air. His co-assassin, rangy Dan Garza, one of the coast's best all-around ends, gives his a terrific target."

Oregon finished the regular season 9-1 and tied California for the Pacific Coast Conference title. Since Oregon had not played California during the season, they challenged the Bears to a playoff to determine the Rose Bowl representative. Conference officials approved the playoff but California refused to play. The matter was put to a vote and league coaches chose California to play Northwestern in the Rose Bowl. It was a shocking decision Garza won't forget. Recently, Garza talked to sportswriter David Flores about the decision: "We had a great team in 1948 and when we didn't play in the Rose Bowl, it demolished me. A lot of us were World War II veterans and had fought for equality, fairness, and justice. It was pretty hard to take."

Instead, Oregon opted to play SMU in the thirteenth annual Cotton Bowl. Disappointed but undaunted, Garza and his teammates turned their attention to Dallas, Texas, and a talented SMU team.

Pregame media rated Oregon stronger on the line and SMU better in the backfield. The contest boiled down to defending against the Van Brocklin passing game and an Oregon defense to stop a powerful SMU running game. As expected, the game was superbly played and All-American Doak Walker and Kyle Rote carried SMU to victory over Oregon by 21-13. Van Brocklin engineered two sensational last-quarter touchdowns to cap a brilliant contest. Garza on the other hand, was held scoreless but tied up an additional defensive player, freeing other targets for Van Brocklin. The end of the season for the Ducks was anticlimatic but successful nonetheless. Post-season honors for Garza included selection to the All-Coast, All-Pacific Conference and All-American teams in 1948.

The New York Giants of the NFL drafted him in 1948, but Garza was preparing for dental school and did not respond to the Giants offer. A year later, the Brooklyn-New York Yankees of the fledgling All-American Football Conference (AAFC) selected him in the seventh round of their 1949 draft, and this time Garza was motivated to play.

He joined the Yankees and played offensive end. During his rookie year he caught 9 passes for a total of 193 yards. The highlight of that season was his effort against the Buffalo Bills. Garza caught a 47-yard pass from quarterback Dan Paciera in a 17-14 win over the Bills. The Yankees finished third in the AAFC with a record of 8 wins and 5 losses. In the playoffs the Yankees lost to San Francisco to mark not only the end of the season but also the demise of the AAFC.

At year's end the AAFC disbanded, as three of the teams went over to the NFL. The remaining players of the other AAFC teams were then drafted by NFL teams. During the scuffle for players, Garza was reclaimed by the New York Giants, who had drafted him previously and then traded him to the New York Yanks. Garza's recollections of the 1949 season were mixed because of the uncertainty of the league and his desire to begin his dental career.

In 1950, as the NFL season got underway, Garza was attending classes at the University of Oregon Dental School. He was determined to be a dentist, but he would have one more year of pro football before finishing school. Garza mentioned he was very impressed with the Yanks coach Norman "Red" Strader, who encouraged him to play. "Strader was very fair and kept his word about playing me. With the Yankees this wasn't the case."

The next season, Garza was wearing a New York Yanks uniform and played splendidly throughout the year. In particular, he gave outstanding performances in games opposing the Chicago Bears and the Green Bay Packers. The following excerpts from the *New York Times* illustrate Garza's contributions to the Yanks and the four touchdowns he scored in 1951: "Yanks quarterback Bob Celeri came right back to account for another Yank tally against the Bears, hitting Dan Garza for 16 yards . . . and Dan Garza tallied for the Yanks on a double pass play good for 69 yards. The play went from George Taliaferro to Bob Celeri to Garza. . . ." Against the Packers, "Celeri pitched a 52-yard touchdown pass to Garza . . . and the amazing Bob Celeri had apparently saved the day for the Yanks by hitting Dan Garza in the end zone from 15 yards out, to give the Yanks a 27-26 lead over the Packers. Unfortunately for the Yanks, the Packers kicked a 16-yard field goal with 11 seconds left to beat them 29-17." The Yanks concluded their season by defeating the Packers the second time they played, 31-28, for their only victory.

Garza finishing the 1951 schedule with a noteworthy 31 receptions for 470 yards and 4 touchdowns. At the conclusion of the season, the sure-handed Garza left professional football to complete his dental education. He returned to the University of Oregon Dental School and, barring any more temptations, finished school and graduated with a doctorate in Dentistry in 1955.

At this point in his life, Garza planned for the future and decided to go back into the Navy. He re-enlisted and served as a dental officer for the next five years. However, the Navy had changed and Garza once again made a career change. He left the Naval Dental Corps and began his own dental practice in 1960 in Portland, Oregon. Dr. Garza remained there for the next 32 years serving the citizens of Portland until his retirement in 1992.

It was a remarkable journey for this athlete, officer, and gentleman. He did many things, saw a lot of places and influenced many people. In 1990 Oregon State University and the State of Oregon honored him by inducting him into their respective sports halls of fame. Five years later, in 1995, the University of Oregon Athletic Department conducted an extensive survey to name All-Time Most Outstanding Oregon Football Players by position. The results of the survey named Dan Garza to both the ends and tight ends. It was quite a tribute to Garza, who thought he might have been forgotten. Not a chance. Dan Garza cannot be forgotten because he has done so much for so many. Among his other accolades, he also has the distinction of being one of the early Mexicano pro football players in the history of the sport.

Dan Garza

Pass Receptions

Year	Team	No.	Yds.	Avg.	TDs
1949	New York Yankees (AAFC)	9	193	21.4	0[1]
1951	New York Yanks	31	470	15.1	4[2]

Kickoff Returns

Year	Team	No.	Yds.	Avg.	TDs
1949	New York Yankees (AAFC)	1	21	21.0	0[3]

Notes

1 *The New York Yankees Press-Radio-TV Guide 1951*, 29.

2 *The New York Times,* October 14, October 28, and December 9, 1951; and David S. Neft, Richard M. Cohen, and Rick Korch, *The Football Encyclopedia: Year-by-Year History of Professional Football from 1892 to the Present*, 221, 235.

3 Ibid., 221.

The Fifties

Chapter III

The Pride of Kansas
Ray Romero

In America's heartland, once traversed by Spanish explorers in their search of the fabled seven cities of gold, was born a proud and determined soul who, in the early years of his life, learned that being a Mexican American in Kansas was going to be difficult. But he overcame these difficulties with strong character and outstanding football skills.

Ray Romero, born December 31, 1927, in Wichita, Kansas, was the second of three sons and one daughter in the Romero family. His parents, JT and Delfina, were from Chihuahua and Guadalajara, Mexico, respectively. They migrated north in search of a home and settled in Kansas.

Romero grew up in Kansas and learned as a youth that he was looked at differently by others. He recalls, "I remember many incidents that happened to me as a boy in Wichita, Kansas. But the most outstanding was when I was forced to leave a movie theater because I had taken a seat on the first floor with an Anglo friend from school. The Mexicans were to sit only in the far balcony that was roped off. A Mexican in Wichita, Kansas, in the early years of my life was considered stupid, dirty, and immoral." Proudly, Romero added, "My parents were decent, hard-working people who raised four children. They taught us

to be proud of our heritage and to be the very best at what we did."

With this guidance, Romero solidified his character and overcame many of the obstacles placed before him. At North High School in Wichita, Romero became an exceptional athlete, excelling in football and wrestling. In the heavyweight division Romero captured the state wrestling championship with the heart and vigor symbolized by the Spanish conquistadors who found and explored Kansas.

After high school Romero won a scholarship to Kansas State University to play football and wrestle. He lettered in both sports all three years (1947-49) but is best remembered for his feats on the football field. Romero was an offensive lineman whose fierce blocking and competitive drive fortified the Wildcats' offense.

In 1947 the Wildcats were winless. The following season (1948), Romero and fellow Wildcats managed a win over Arkansas State. In 1949 they improved by a game by beating Fort Hays State and the University of Colorado.

In 1949 Romero played in only the first three games of the season. Against the Cornhuskers of Nebraska, he sustained a shoulder separation and was out for the remainder of the season. Not withstanding, Romero received Honorable Mention recognition on the All-Big 7 Conference Team at season's end.

With the shoulder healed and prospects of playing professional football a possibility, Romero waited but was not selected in the 1950 NFL draft of college players. Instead Philadelphia Eagles' line coach Jim Trimble recommended and encouraged Romero to attend the Eagles' training camp. Romero went to camp, made the team, and was signed on June 18, 1951, as a free agent for the 1951 NFL season. Ray remembers his opportunity to play professional football, "At 5 foot 11 inches, 200 pounds and average ability, I made up the difference in determination and hard work." True to his competitive drive, Romero beat out nine-year veteran Duke Moronic for the starting job.

Romero played offensive guard for the Eagles through November 1951. Unfortunately, the Korean War was on and Ray's selective service number came up. The Army ordered him to report to duty, so the Eagles had no choice but to place him on the military reserve list three games before the end of the season.

Until the draft notice appeared, Romero successfully held down the first-string guard position. He played alongside future hall-of-famers Steve Van Buren, lineman Chuck Bednarik, and receiver Pete Pihos.

In the Army Romero was stationed in Indiantown Gap, Pennsylvania. No sooner did he arrive there than he was recognized and acknowledged in the *Army Times*: "Fifth infantry division football officials are excited over the possibilities of being able to use Ray Romero at guard next fall. The 24-year-old Romero last season ranked as one of the most promising lineman in the tough National Football League." During that period, the Army as well as other service teams played regular schedules against neighboring colleges and other service teams. Romero had a tremendously successful year on the Indiantown Gap Army Team.

The Red Devils of Indiantown Gap opened the 1952 season with a 34-0 win over the Chambersburg Cardinals. The Red Devils went on to score impressive victories over the Shenandoah Maroons 45-0, Camp Brackenridge 34-27, and the Harrisburg Bears 53-0; but lost to the Parris Island Marines 21-13 and Quantico 48-7.

Romero was among the players nominated for a spot on two *Army Times* All-Star teams. He was a leading vote getter on the All-Army team, All-Service team, and most valuable player. The *Army Times* describes him: "Ray Romero, Indiantown Gap's hardworking lineman remained in first place among Army football's guards . . . as the *Army Times*' poll to pick

the season's 11 outstanding soldier gridders neared its finish. The selection board will announce the mythical line-up December 13 . . . Romero and Red Devils teammate John Callaghan are also in the running for the Most Valuable Player."

With all the votes in, Ray was unanimously selected to both the All-Army and All-Service teams and was a runner-up in the balloting for the most valuable player that year.

Upon discharge from the U.S. Army, Romero returned to civilian life and football with the Philadelphia Eagles. In the meantime, his younger brother Eli Romero had just concluded a successful collegiate football career at Wichita State University and was drafted by the Eagles in 1953. Romero looked forward to again playing in the NFL. He re-signed with Philadelphia on September 8, 1953. However, a week later, the Eagles placed him on waivers, so he did not play that season. His brother also was released before the start of the regular season. Undiscouraged, the determined Romero brothers stayed in shape and went to the Chicago Bears' training camp the following year. They both made the team and signed on as free agents.

Ray played on the Bears' offensive line until he pulled a hamstring muscle. Unable to fully recover from the injury, Romero again was placed on waivers, signaling the end of his professional football career. (His brother Eli was let go after the Bears' last preseason game.)

Romero returned to Kansas to continue graduate studies at Wichita State University. He earned a master of science degree and began a teaching career.

Romero's collegiate, military, and professional football career spanned seven years. Reflecting on his football career, Romero relates the following observation: "The recognition of an offensive lineman for an outstanding game is overlooked in many cases. Blocking for a back that scores gives one personal satisfaction."

After his successful football career, Romero continued to strive to be a positive influence on everyone he came in contact with. An educator for 37 years, Romero is an "All-Pro" with his students and colleagues because he cares and respects them. His dedication rewarded, Romero was among the eight national honorees at the 1993 annual awards dinner of the Hispanic Heritage Leadership Conference in Washington, D.C. He was honored for his success as an educator and given tribute for being one of the first Mexicans to play in the NFL.

On the occasion of Romero's being honored by the Hispanic Heritage Leadership Conference, sportswriter Greg Cote of the *Miami Herald* wrote, "Romero stands out because he is a common man, extraordinary in his context. Yes, he briefly played pro football 42 years ago, one season before the military draft intervened. It is the niche as one of the first Hispanics to play in the NFL that is ostensibly why Romero gets his glory. Truthfully though, Romero's fling with football is merely a good excuse to honor a good man, a man who earned this recognition by overcoming poverty and prejudice."

Remembering that time in the theater when he was forced to leave, Romero comments, "Later I realized that moment was a positive one. It motivated me to show I was just as good as anyone."

In the years since then, Romero did just that. With a little irony he says, "I can remember when I was put down for being Mexican, and now I am being honored for being Mexican . . . I guess you live long enough, things change."

"From the Halls of Montezuma . . ." Lupe Joe Arenas

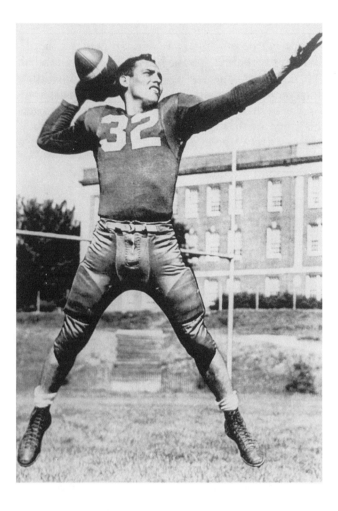

The states that comprise the Great Plains of this country have a rich and glorious history. From their fields of dreams emerge extraordinary individuals. One such person is Guadalupe Joe Arenas, who was born in Cedar Rapids, Iowa, December 12, 1925.

Arenas, the son of Mexican migrants, grew up during some difficult times. No sooner was he out of high school in Lincoln, Nebraska, than the Japanese bombed Pearl Harbor and Arenas's dreams of attending college were put on hold.

With World War II a reality, Arenas enlisted in the U.S. Marines and served in the Pacific Campaign. The young Mexicano Marine would see the horrors of war and survive its carnage. On February 19, 1945, Arenas and the 27th Marines landed on the Far Eastern island of Iwo Jima. During the 26 days of heavy fighting, Arenas was wounded and decorated for his bravery. He saw the American flag wave in victory atop Mt. Suribachi. When the war was over, Arenas returned stateside to his new home in Nebraska and the halls of the University of Omaha.

While pursing an education, Arenas decided to give collegiate football a try. He had not played in high school, but with his natural athletic ability and hard work, he developed into a triple-threat in the backfield.

In 1948, Arenas's sophomore season, the University of Omaha Indians won 5 and lost 4 in gridiron play. The versatile Arenas passed for 4 touchdowns and rushed for 2 scores. Against Morningside University of Iowa, Arenas rallied his team with a brilliant second-half attack to defeat Morningside. In the fourth quarter of the game Arenas completed 2 passes covering 50 yards to set up the winning score, Omaha 13, Morningside 6.

Against Washburn, Omaha scored first when Arenas tossed a 16-yard aerial to Don Gorman for six points. Arenas then kicked the extra point. Omaha's second touchdown also came from an Arenas pass to Bud Gorman. In the winning drive Arenas advanced the ball to the 3-yard line, where teammate Hooten catapulted over the middle of the line for the tying touchdown. In the point-after attempt Arenas faked a kick and completed a pass to Gibbons for the winning points, Omaha 20, Washburn 19.

Against Doane College, Arenas scored a 3-yard touchdown. Later in the game he rushed for gains of 7 and 9 yards, to set up the winning touchdown, Omaha 13, Doane 6.

Playing courageously in a losing effort against Wayne University, Arenas and Howard Bryan were the Omaha stars. The Wayne offense was overpowering; Arenas managed only a couple of scores to finish

Wayne 46, Omaha 20. At the conclusion of the season, the Indians named Arenas their most valuable player.

The following season (1949) was one of heartbreak for Arenas and the University of Omaha. They fell short of the success they experienced in 1948, winning 3 games and losing 5. Despite the team's difficulty, Arenas continued to lead the Omaha offense. Opposing Nebraska Wesleyan, Arenas took over in the second half to break a 6-6 deadlock. His passing and running resulted in scoring plays to Bud Gibson, Dusty Johnson, and Archie Arvin. In the Omaha homecoming, Lupe Joe was once again the leader and star. He scored from the 2-yard line in directing his team to a 47-7 victory over Colorado Mines.

Arenas had his best game of the 1949 season against Wayne University of Detroit. Arenas, who was favoring an injured knee, threw 4 touchdown passes for 219 yards, completing 13 of 39 passes. Although Omaha lost to Wayne 38-26, the score was not indicative of the otherwise splendid game played by Arenas and his teammates. Arenas finished the season as the team's number-two scorer with 27 points.

But the best of Arenas was yet to come. The following year was historic for Omaha University. Arenas's university yearbook had this to say: "Someday sports historians may look at the 1950 Omaha University football season and regard it with awe. Here is a university which gave no scholarship, no room and board, and no subsidizations, yet fielded a football team which won 6 games while losing 3, the best record in 16 years."

This campaign was to be Arenas's best. The season opened with a 33-7 Omaha victory over rival Nebraska Wesleyan. Regrouping after losses to Saint Ambrose and Northern Illinois, Omaha destroyed Washburn 26-6 on their home field. Still on their winning track, Omaha added Doane and Colorado Mines to their string of victories. But the sweetest win of the season came against Wayne University. For the first time in three years the Omaha Indians played giant-killers and swamped heavily favored Wayne 32-13. Arenas led the charge offensively and capped his defensive performance by intercepting a Wayne pass and returning it 32 yards for a touchdown.

Completing his best season, Arenas led the Indians in rushing yardage, 461 yards; scoring, 46 points; passing yardage, 813 yards; and 15 touchdowns. Also, he led the team in total offense with 1,264 rushing/passing yards. Nationally, Arenas ranked sixth in total offense in the National Collegiate Football Association. His fabulous collegiate career led to a selection to the Little All-American Team in 1950.

Arenas's next stop was professional football. The San Francisco 49ers chose him in the 8th round of the 1951 NFL collegiate draft. Known by his 49er team-mates as the "fighting Marine," Arenas played seven seasons with San Francisco, and in a change from his college quarterback days, Arenas specialized in kickoff and punt returns. When he first arrived at the 49ers' camp, Arenas remembers looking around to assess the competition. Although a little apprehensive initially, he recalls thinking to himself and saying, "If I survived a world war then I'm here to stay to play football." Attesting to Arenas's convictions is legendary 49er quarterback Y. A. Tittle. He writes in his autobiography,

> . . . Speaking of Arenas, he was the fighting spirit of the 1951 49ers. He typified the hustle and aggressiveness of the entire squad. Here was a young man who came out of Omaha as an unheralded draft choice and wasn't given much chance of winning the left halfback job . . . But Joe Arenas hadn't come all the way to San Francisco to be sent home again. We found this out the first day in training camp.
>
> Coach Frankie Albert called the squad together and said, "Let's line up out there and run some plays." Well, Norm Standlee steps in at fullback and Stryzkalski or Perry at halfback. Bill Johnson takes the center spot and Bruno Banducci and some of the other veterans fill in along the line.
>
> But before anyone else can make a move, Arenas hops in at left halfback. Rookies aren't supposed to take such liberties, but there he is, big as life. Everyone looks at everyone else in amazement. The same questions is going through our minds: "Who the hell does this little guy think he is, stepping in there when we are going to run some plays?"
>
> I must say that Joe wasn't too popular in the beginning. There were some 49ers who didn't like him. They had him figured as a brash, cocky kid. He may have been, too, but he was a hardnose with a tough attitude. They never did get him out of the left halfback spot after that first day in camp. He stayed there and his fighting spirit soon infected the rest of the squad.

From that day forward Arenas was a runner to be reckoned with. A *New York Times* game account illustrates Arenas's ability: "San Francisco's Forty-niners, scoring a touchdown after a sensational 51-yard punt return by rookie halfback Joe Arenas, defeated Detroit 21-17. Arenas, a swift 180-pounder from Omaha University, playing his first season of professional football, set the stage for the Forty-niners upset victory." Arenas dodged and weaved downfield to the Detroit 18-yard line, where quarterback Y. A. Tittle scored on a 1-yard line bootleg run. It was performances like this that made Arenas's initial pro season an exciting one. He led the 49ers in punt-return yardage that year and became a starter for the duration of his career at San Francisco.

Toward the end of the 1951 season, sportswriter Dink Templeton complimented Arenas's rookie performance:

If you like great football but missed seeing Joe Arenas last Sunday, I'm sorry, there isn't much I can do about it, but you just missed the sweetest running back of a whole season of great running backs.

There seems little sense in raving about Arenas' beautiful performance. I supposed no one would believe me. The game stories said he had a good day, and all of them patted him gently on the back. I had great difficulty in placing the plug I read about with the brilliantly blazing star who riddled the Green Bay defenses and sent me home from Kezar with the firm belief that the kid from Omaha University is the most valuable property in the National League, and if this costs Mr. T. Morabito a healthy raise from the gut so much the better. He sure deserves is.

It was the start of a great career for the speedy Arenas, who in a couple of years would take home the NFL kickoff return title.

The 1953 NFL gridiron war was the best showing for the 49ers in years. As a team they finished second to the Detroit Lions and, individually, several 49ers had outstanding seasons. Arenas gathered the momentum he needed to be numero uno in the NFL in kickoff return yardage. He returned 16 kickoffs for 551 yards—a 34.4 average. His teammate Joe Perry gained more than 1,000 yards rushing is a single season, and Gordy Soltau was the league's top scorer for the second straight year. Arenas's season highlights included an 82-yard kickoff return against the Philadelphia Eagles and a touchdown reception from Y. A. Tittle. In subduing Chicago, Arenas sped 60 yards for a touchdown to insure a 35-28 win over the Bears from the Windy City. Against the Green Bay Packers, Arenas rushed for 2 touchdowns en route to a lopsided victory over the Packers.

For the next two seasons the 49ers finished third and fifth in NFL play. During those two campaigns, Arenas successfully ran back punts and kickoffs to lead the team in both categories. In 1956 Arenas experienced another exceptionally good year. At Kezar Stadium on November 4, 1956, Arenas kept the Detroit Lions at bay with a spectacular 90-yard kickoff return for a touchdown.

On December 16, 1956, an Arenas kickoff return and interception for a touchdown helped the 49ers beat the Baltimore Colts 30-17. Bob Brachman, sportswriter for the *San Francisco Examiner* writes: "Chunky Joe Arenas, the San Francisco 49ers' go-ahead kid with the heart of a lion, had two spectacular run backs, a kickoff return of 96 yards and a punt return of 67 yards for a touchdown. The swarthy dynamiter from Omaha University took all the fight out of the aroused Colts and carried the Forty-niners to a tremendous 30-17 win in their 1956 NFL windup."

Brachman describes Arenas's effort in the third quarter: "It was on the ensuing kickoff that Arenas cut loose for the first time. Starting from his own 2-yard line, little Joe flew through the pack as he started upfield. Only Raymond Berry stood in his way from the Baltimore 35 to the 15. They played cat and mouse with Joe dodging his way to avoid the back-tracking Colt. At the 15, Arenas sensed the big opening and took off. Berry, a quick one, made a last desperate lunge from behind and almost miraculously managed to grab a piece of Joe's jersey. Arenas broke loose, but there was enough contact to cause the 49ers runner to stumble and, ultimately, tumble at the 2-yard line after the second longest run back in San Francisco history." When the dust had cleared the 49ers kicked a field goal.

In the fourth quarter, Arenas delivered the death blow. The Colts punted to the 49ers and the punt bounced in front of Arenas and Hugh McElhenny. Arenas hesitated momentarily in the face of several on-rushing Colt tacklers. It didn't look as if he was going to field the ball. Arenas moved up on it nonchalantly as some of the Colts eased up in their pursuit, which was all he needed. In a flash, with a fancy side-step, he was gone. As the crowd went mad, McElhenny leveled one Colt, Bob St. Clair obliterated another, and Arenas galloped away.

The following year (1957) was one of the most emotional and dramatic seasons in 49er history. It was a season of the unexpected, aptly described in the *1983 San Francisco 49ers Media Guide:* "Every game was a cliffhanger and the 'Alley-Oop' pass from Y. A. Tittle to rookie R. C. Owens became a household word. Emotions reached a peak when the founder of the 49ers, Tony Morabito, died of a heart attack during the Chicago Bears game played on October 27. The 49ers trailing 17-7 fought back to beat the Bears 21-17."

In the 1957 playoffs, the 49ers lost to the Detroit Lions 31-27 after giving up a third-quarter lead. This was Arenas's final year in professional football. At seasons end, Arenas lamented his decision to retire: "I loved football and at the time figured I still had another three years to play before hanging up the old proverbial cleats, but within me it was time to leave the game and I did so reluctantly." Gone but not forgotten, Arenas left a set of numbers that keep his memory alive and well in 49er history.

Arenas ranks second and fifth in kickoff and punt returns, respectively, in San Francisco 49er all-time

Joe Arenas

Rushing

Year	Team	No.	Yds.	Avg.	TDs
1951	San Francisco 49ers	34	183	5.4	0
1952	San Francisco 49ers	44	183	4.2	1
1953	San Francisco 49ers	72	380	5.3	6
1954	San Francisco 49ers	11	77	7.0	0
1955	San Francisco 49ers	37	150	4.1	0
1956	San Francisco 49ers	(No rushing stats)			
1957	San Francisco 49ers	5	14	2.8	1
		203	987	4.8	8[1]

Pass Receptions

Year	Team	No.	Yds.	Avg.	TDs
1951	San Francisco 49ers	1	12	12.0	1
1952	San Francisco 49ers	5	47	9.4	1
1953	San Francisco 49ers	10	113	11.3	1
1954	San Francisco 49ers	2	12	6.0	0
1955	San Francisco 49ers	13	255	19.6	2
1956	San Francisco 49ers	14	226	16.1	1
1957	San Francisco 49ers	1	10	10.0	0
		46	675	14.7	6[2]

Kickoff Returns

Year	Team	No.	Yds.	Avg.	Long	TDs
1951	San Francisco 49ers	21	542	25.8	49	0
1952	San Francisco 49ers	12	291	24.2	—	0
1953	San Francisco 49ers	15	551	34.4[3]	82	0
1954	San Francisco 49ers	16	362	22.6	41	0
1955	San Francisco 49ers	24	594	24.8	42	0
1956	San Francisco 49ers	27	801	29.7	96	1
1957	San Francisco 49ers	24	657	27.4	64	0
		139	3,798	27.3	96	1[4]

Punt Returns

Year	Team	No.	Yds.	Avg.	TDs	
1951	San Francisco 49ers	21	272	13.0	51	0
1952-53	San Francisco 49ers	15	133	8.8	-	0
1954	San Francisco 49ers	23	117	5.1	23	0
1955	San Francisco 49ers	21	55	2.6	7	0
1956	San Francisco 49ers	19	117	6.2	67	1
1957	San Francisco 49ers	25	80	3.2	26	0[5]
		124	774	6.2	67	1

Notes

1 David S. Neft, Richard M. Cohen, and Rick Korch, *The Football Encyclopedia: The Complete, Year-by-Year History of Professional Football from 1892 to the Present* (New York: St. Martin's Press, 1994), 235, 241, 247, 253, 259, 265, 271.

2 Ibid.

3 NFL Kickoff Return Leader in 1953. 15 returns for 551 yards and a 34.4 average (*Official 1991 National Football League Record & Fact Book*, 341).

Joe Arenas, continued

San Francisco 49ers Career Statistics

Joe Arenas ranked #2	Kickoff return yardage, 3,798 yards for the years 1951-1957.[6]
#5	Punt return yardage, 774 yards for the years 1951-57.
#2	Number of punt returns, 124 returns for the years 1951-57.[7]
	Highest average for kickoff returns in 1953 (minimum 15) for 34.4 average, 16 for 551 yards.[8]

NFL All-Time Records—Top 20 Kickoff Returners

Ranking	Player	Years	No.	Yds.	Avg.	Long	TDs
#5	Joe Arenas	7	139	3,798	27.3	96	1[9]

Notes

4 *1983 San Francisco 49ers Media Guide,* 186.

5 Ibid., 188.

6 Ibid., 181.

7 Ibid., 180.

8 Ibid., 182.

9 *Official 1991 National Football League Record & Fact Book,* 336.

statistics. In NFL all-time career statistics, Arenas ranks fifth among all kickoff returners. The speedy Mexicano, who went from player to coach shortly after his pro playing days, had a superlative seven-year career with the 49ers.

After retiring from professional football, Arenas worked as an assistant football coach for the University of Houston Cougars. In his 23 years at Houston, the ex-Marine and former pro football star helped coach Cougar receivers and kick returners. He developed some of the best receivers and kick returners in Houston Cougar football history, many of whom became successful professional football players. Ken Herbert, Riley Odons, Elmo Wright, Don Bass, and Lonell Phea are just a few of Arenas's proteges.

During Arenas's coaching tenure at the University of Houston, the Cougars played in various postseason bowl games, including the Astro Blue Bonnet, Cotton, and Garden State Bowls. Thinking back a few years, Coach Arenas recalls:

As an assistant coach at the University of Houston, we had several great Bowl games. I guess a memorable one had to be the Nortre Dame game played in freezing weather at the Cotton Bowl. We had them beat in the third quarter 34 to 12, and Joe Montana came out of the dressing room after being sick most of the second half. He put together one of his come-from-behind performances and beat us 35-34. But the most memorable one was the following year when we beat the University of Nebraska at the Cotton Bowl. Beating Nebraska, which always has one of the best teams in the nation, had to be a great win. The score was 17-14, and it was my receiver who caught the final touchdown of the game.

Today the former member of the San Francisco 49ers back field that included quarterback Y. A. Tittle, and running backs Hugh McElhenny and Joe Perry, enjoys his retirement in Galveston, Texas.

Genaro "Mean Gene" Brito All-Pro

Of all the Latinos to play professional football, one individual stands above the rest. He was a five-time All-Pro player, four times in the NFL and once in the Canadian Football League (CFL). He was an outstanding defensive end whose specialty was bone-jarring tackles and fumble recoveries. A great athlete who helped turn a tragic Redskins team around and whose popularity attracted the attention of a U.S. President. That individual was Genaro Herman Brito.

Brito was born on October 23, 1925, in Huntington Park, California, a suburb of Los Angeles. The son of Genaro Brito and Trecia Chávez, Brito grew up in East Los Angeles and attended Lincoln High School during the early years of World War II. At Lincoln High he began his football career and also excelled in basketball, baseball, and track. For most young men during wartime, graduation from high school meant military service and for Brito it was no different. He joined the U.S. Army and served with the paratroopers, attaining the rank of staff sergeant.

Honorably discharged from the Army at war's end, Brito returned to Los Angeles and enrolled at Loyola University. While at Loyola, Brito embarked upon a great football career. Of his four seasons of football at Loyola University, his last two years were the most outstanding. The 1951 *Loyola University Yearbook* had this to say about the 1950 season: "An unprecedented winning streak, national recognition, and captivation of the public fancy were all achieved by last year's Loyola Lions varsity . . . The 1950 Lions rolled off seven straight victories over Pepperdine, St. Mary's, San Jose State, College of the Pacific, Nevada, Hardin-Simmons, and Fresno State before falling to giant-killer Santa Clara, then rebounding to over-whelm the University of San Francisco Dons."

Brito starred both on offense and defense and was rated as Loyola's finest end. He never missed a game during his four years at Loyola, and his offensive sta-tistics for the 1950 season included 15 receptions for 199 yards and 1 touchdown. At the end of his senior season, "Mean" Gene Brito, as he was called by both teammates and opponents, was named to the UPI All-Coast Independent College Team.

In the spring of 1951 the Washington Redskins picked the highly regarded Gene Brito as their 17th-round draft choice. Brito was drafted as an offensive end but shifted to defense in 1953. The shift to defen-sive end would be a beneficial one for Brito and the Redskins.

Now a professional, Brito began to carve his niche as a Redskins star. The 1951 season for Washington was dismal. Veteran Sammy Baugh was in the twilight of his career and back-up quarterback Gilmer was still a journeyman. Nevertheless, "Mean" Gene hauled in 24 passes for 313 yards. The following year (1952) the Redskins made a coaching change as Earl "Curley" Lambeau took over as head coach, but the Redskins offense still struggled. After a 2-2 start, the Redskins lost 6 in a row until "Slinging" Sammy Baugh, who had broken his hand earlier in the season, returned to the starting line-up to lead them to 2 victories. During all the quarterback problems, Brito had 21 pass recep-tions for 270 yards and 2 touchdowns. At this point in his career, Brito switched over to defensive end and it proved to be the right move.

In 1953 the Redskins won 4 of their last 6 games to finish third in their conference with a record of 6 wins, 5 losses, 1 tie. The key to the Redskins' suc-cess, according to Beau Riffenburgh's *The Official NFL Encyclopedia*, was a strong defense built around end Gene Brito, tackle Dick Modzelewski, linebacker Chuck Drazenovich, and defensive back Don Doll.

The next season (1954) Brito and quarterback Eddie LeBaron left Washington to play in the Canadian

Football League (CFL). Brito left the Redskins after a feud with Coach Curley Lambeau. In Canada Brito played with the Calgary Stampeders. Utilized on both offense and defense, Brito caught 5 passes for 60 yards, returned a kickoff for 16 yards, and was a superlative defensive standout for the Stampeders. His defensive play was rewarded with a selection to the CFL Western Conference All-Star Team at the defensive end position, the first of 5 All-Pro selections in his pro football career.

Brito and LeBaron rejoined the Redskins in 1955. All-American halfback Vic Janowicz had also signed with Washington. The three stars rejuvenated the team. Grateful he had returned to Washington and reflecting on the 1955 season, Brito reversed the old saying by showing that a good defense sometimes is the best offense. The Redskins finished second in the Eastern Conference with 8 wins, 4 losses. Brito was named to the NFL All-Pro Team and selected to play in the Pro Bowl, where he garnered the game's Most Valuable Player award. Adding to his accolades, the Touchdown Club of Washington selected him as the Pro Football Player of the Year, to cap a sensational year for Brito.

The following season was darkened with tragedy when, while at training camp, running back Vic Janowicz was killed after he was thrown from a car and struck a tree. This demoralized the team, and Washing-ton could only muster 6 wins and 6 losses. However, Brito continued to shine on defense and was once again named to the All-Pro Team at defensive end.

The 1957 season was not any better for the tragic Redskins. They lost another player during training camp, when defensive back Roy Barni was shot to death in a bar-room brawl. The Redskins struggled through most of the year, but toward the end of the season the defense, led by the reliable Brito, jelled once again and held Chicago, Pittsburgh, and Philadelphia to a combined total of 13 points. For the third consec-utive year, his teammates selected Brito as the most valuable Redskins player. In 1958 Brito continued to smack opposing ballcarriers and quarterbacks to the ground, in hopes of turning around the team's misfor-tune. At season's end, and for the fourth consecutive time, Brito was selected to the All-Pro Team. He played in the annual Pro Bowl game and was voted the Outstanding Lineman in the contest.

But Brito was now considering a life away from football. Prior to the Pro Bowl game, Brito announced his retirement from professional football. Modestly he said, "My greatest thrill as a pro came when I made the Redskins squad in 1951."

He never missed a game with the Redskins and played 84 straight regular season games. Brito had never been penalized until the 1958 season, when he received a penalty for jumping offsides. When Brito announced his retirement in the nation's capital, then–Vice President Richard Nixon commented about his decision to retire: "Brito symbolized the kind of spirit which, win or lose, has made the Redskins a great team to watch."

Brito formally retired from pro football in January 1959. He returned to his home in Los Angeles and planned to devote his time to teaching and coaching at his alma mater, Lincoln High School. However, no sooner was Brito back in town than the Los Angeles Rams announced they had obtained the four-time NFL All-Pro defensive end from Washington in exchange for Larry Morris.

When notified of the trade, Brito said, "A trade of this type never occurred to me at the time I announced my retirement last December. But a chance to play with the Rams and at the same time to begin to establish myself in the Los Angeles area is a tremendous opportunity for me and my family, particularly in light of the fact that I'm still in love with football."

Now a Ram, Brito prepared himself for another NFL campaign. However, in the second game of the 1959 season, he suffered a fractured ankle in the contest against the San Francisco 49ers and missed the rest of the season.

In 1960 Brito returned to play with the Rams in what turned out to be his final season in pro football. At preseason training camp, Brito was in top form and eager to play. "He's quick as a cat," praised Ram coach Bob Waterfield. "He's not favoring that ankle at all . . . To watch Brito work is a football education in itself. He spins, fakes, dips, and relies on 8 years of NFL experience to slip past an offensive lineman and smother the ballcarriers on passes."

Brito started every game that 1960 season as the Rams finished sixth in the standings with wins over Detroit, Dallas, Green Bay, and Baltimore and a tie with the Chicago Bears. Defensively, it was a good season for Brito but not an All-Pro year.

The next football season would be Brito's 10th year in the NFL. As in years past, he looked forward to playing football again, but at the Rams summer training camp in Redlands, California, he was stricken with a paralyzing disease described as peripheral neuritis, an inflammation of the nerves of the lower body. Peripheral neuritis is the same disease that claimed the life of another great athlete, Yankee baseball player Lou Gehrig. As fate would have it, the handsome and fearsome All-Pro defensive end was forced to leave the game that he loved so much.

In a *Los Angeles Times* article, Brito said, "I wish I could play this year, but I've had 10 years in this league and that's more than most. It's all been great!" Rams General Manager Elroy "Crazylegs" Hirsch hailed Brito as "a wonderful person and player who will be missed by the game of football."

Since training camp, Brito had been in and out of hospitals but always maintained a cheerful, courteous attitude. Confined to a wheelchair, he played the toughest game of his life, tackling his paralysis head-on for four years until his death on June 8, 1965.

Mal Florence, sportswriter for the *Los Angeles Times* writes, "The former All-Pro football player who waged a gallant, uphill fight against an undefined, paralyzing disorder died Tuesday afternoon at the City of Hope Medical Center in Duarte, California." His death brought expressions of sorrow from his many friends in the sports world. "The example of courage he set for us will live long after his football feats are forgotten," said Daniel F. Reeves, president of the Los Angeles Rams.

"He was an inspiration to me as a man and a player," said Ram coach Harlan Svare. "It's a very sad thing; the sports world has lost a true champion," lamented former teammate and Ram star Les Richter, a close friend of the Brito family.

The then former Vice President Richard Nixon had this to say about Brito: "His example of courage, determination, and spirit in the face of overwhelming odds, both on the football field and in his great battle for life, will be a lasting memorial to one of America's truly great athletes."

Years later, President Nixon nominated Brito for induction into the Pro Football Hall of Fame in Canton, Ohio. The president's comments were recorded by *New York Times* reporter Arthur Daly: "During his stay with the Redskins, he played 84 consecutive games receiving the title of Iron Man." The president recalled one of his many performances sixteen years past:

A measure of his effectiveness against opposing passers took place in 1955 against the Cleveland Browns. Going into the Redskins-Browns clash, the Washington team had never won a game. Cleveland's peerless passer Otto Graham faded back to pass and was surprised to find he didn't have the ball. The charging Brito was upon Graham so fast the great quarterback had the ball snatched from his hands and Washington's ace defensive end was racing downfield to set up the winning touchdown.

Although not inducted into the Hall of Fame, Brito will be long remembered for his football feats. The late great Gene Brito continued to be a source of inspiration to all who knew and heard of him even after his death. Not only was he one of pro football's best, but he was also a caring and extraordinary man. In between gridiron campaigns, Brito gave back to the community he came from. In the off-season he taught at his alma mater, Lincoln High School. According to friend and author Bob Addie, Brito specialized in teaching incorrigible and disadvantaged children.

Gene Brito

Pass Receptions

Year	Team	No.	Yds.	Avg.	TDs
1951	Washington Redskins	24	313	13.0	1
1952	Washington Redskins	21	270	12.8	2
1953	Washington Redskins	2	35	17.5	0[1]
1954	Calgary Stampeders (CFL)	5	60	12.0	0[2]
		52	678	13.0	2

Kickoff Returns

Year	Team	No.	Yds.	Avg.	Long	TDs
1951-53	Washington Redskins	4	39	9.7	—	0[3]
1954	Calgary Stampeders	1	16	16.0	16	0[3]
		5	55	11.0	16	0[2]

Notes

1 Telephone call to Washington Redskins Public Relations Office for statistics on Gene Brito, Monday, May 11, 1987.

2 Canadian Football League individual statistical record for Gene Brito.

3 Telephone call to Washington Redskins Public Relations Office for statistics on Gene Brito, Monday, May 11, 1987.

"The fact that I'm a football player makes it also easier," Brito once told Addie, "but the problem with these kids is that they need love, kindness, and attention. I've sacked many a quarterback and have made many a tackle, but to me the greatest thing I've ever done in life is to see some of these kids come back after a few years as good citizens of the community." He had a magic with children and continued to work with the youth of Los Angeles until the very end.

His dedication to kids, passion for football, and heroic battle against the disease that claimed his life, along with being one of the all-time great Washington Redskins players, prompted the Touchdown Club of Washington, D.C., to establish an award in his honor. "The Gene Brito Achievement Award," established in 1976, is presented annually to persons who, in the estimation of the Touchdown Club demonstrate "Faith, Perseverance, and Fortitude."

Recipients of the prestigious award included physically-challenged individuals who overcame their disabilities to succeed in sports. Past award winners include Edward M. Kennedy, Jr.—amputee; Darryl Stingley—paraplegic; Jimmy Huega—multiple sclerosis; and Rocky Bleier—wounded Vietnam Veteran.

The award was presented to eleven individuals prior to 1987. A permanent plaque for the award, along with Brito's jersey and helmet are on display in the trophy room of the Touchdown Club of Washington, D.C.

In September 1982, seventeen years after his death, Brito was elected to the Washington Hall of Stars for his playing performance, fan popularity, and contribution to the sports history of the District of Columbia. As part of the induction ceremony, Brito was given posthumously a gold and ruby ring. His portrait hangs in the StarPlex Clubhouse in RFK Stadium, and his name-plaque of red letters on white background is displayed on the mezzanine railing around RFK stadium.

For Genaro "Mean Gene" Brito, the remembrances and honors were many, and in 1988 he received an additional recognition by being selected into the Italian-American Sports Hall of Fame located in Arling-ton Heights, Illinois. This honor was based on his football greatness and the part-Italian ancestry of one of his grandparents. It was a special tribute to the handsome Latino, who joined other sports legends such as Doug Buffone, Nick Buoniconti, Gino Cappelletti, and Vince Lombardi in this prestigious Sports Gallery.

By any standard, Brito was indeed an unforgettable paragon. He played a great game both on and off the field and is a lasting monument not only to the sport he loved so much, but also to the people he touched and inspired.

El Presidente
George Maderos

The fabulous '50s in pro football continued to see Latino athletes in the skilled positions. One was a defensive back named George Maderos who played two seasons with the San Francisco 49ers. He was a multitalented athlete whose surname resembled that of former Mexican President Francisco Madero. They were not related, for the California-born Maderos entered this world on November 3, 1933, in Chico, to parents of Portuguese and German ancestry.

The prodigal Maderos quickly developed into an athlete of promise to compliment an already developed interest in academics. Upon graduation from high school, he received an academic scholarship to attend hometown Chico State University. During his time at Chico State (1951-55), Maderos turned out to be one of the finest all-around athletes in the history of the university.

Primarily a basketball player, Maderos also excelled in football and boxing. In basketball, he rewrote the record books at Chico State. In round ball action his career 2,377 points scored and 21.2 scoring average are just two of the nine game-season-career individual records he still holds at the school.

According to a Chico State public relations spokesperson, it appears these records will stand for a long time to come. Maderos played four years to accumulate those statistics.

In addition to basketball, Maderos excelled at football and was the team captain for three consecutive years. In 1953 the Chico State Wildcats won the Far West Conference Championship, a highlight in Madero's collegiate gridiron career.

His accolades included being selected to the UPI Little All-Coast Team and the Little All-American Team in 1954, and he played in the East-West Shrine All-Star game.

Whenever Maderos was not on the court or the football field, he entered the ring and boxed in collegiate tournaments. His claim to fame as a pugilist was a runner-up finish in the light heavyweight division of the Pacific Coast Conference Intercollegiate Boxing Tournament.

In 1955 Maderos became the twenty-first draft choice of the San Francisco 49ers and was their starting defensive back. He had a good rookie year with San Francisco and was expected to be nominated for

George Maderos

Kickoff Returns

Year	Team	No.	Yds.	Avg.	Long	TDs
1956	San Francisco 49ers	2	21	10.5	—	0

Source: David S. Neft, Richard M. Cohen, and Rick Korch, *The Football Encyclopedia: The Complete, Year-by-Year History of Professional Football from 1892 to the Present* (New York: St. Martin's Press, 1994), 265.

the Rookie of the Year Award, until he was injured in the seventh game of the season.

His best defensive performance of 1955 came in the game against the Chicago Bears, where he intercepted a pass and recovered a fumble to help preserve a 20-19 victory over the Bears.

Maderos also blocked for fellow Latino teammate Joe Arenas, who returned kickoffs and punts for the 49ers. Maderos played with San Francisco in 1956 and then left professional football.

Maderos returned to Chico State, where he received a master's degree. In 1958 he began his career at Chico State as the track coach. However, unexpected coaching vacancies prompted his being named head football coach, and remained in that capacity through 1967. At age 25, Maderos was the youngest head football coach in the nation, and he looked upon it as quite an accomplishment. His record as a coach was 36 wins, 59 losses, and 1 tie.

In 1968, still an instructor at Chico State, Maderos took on the challenge to coach semi-pro football in nearby Sacramento, California. He coached the Sacramento Capitals of the Continental Football League for two years (1968-69).

He left football for nearly a decade but returned in 1979 to coach the Twin City (Yuba City and Maryville, California) Cougars of the California Football League. He coached three years and then retired from football altogether.

A sportsman to no end, the talented Maderos can look back on a very successful athletic career. Both as an athlete and a coach, he could do it all. Had it not been for an injury, his tenure in pro football could have been a long and successful one.

Possessing a wealth of experience and not one to be far from sports, Maderos has added another sport to his repertoire—golf—and he is currently the golf instructor at Chico State University. Sports are in his blood, as anyone who knows him can attest. To him they give meaning to life, and a day without a visit to the gym, field, or golf course would be incomplete for "El Presidente."

The Rick Casares Express

According to various NFL football historians, the decade of the 1950s was a fabulous one. It was an era when the iron men of football played and extreme toughness was required to survive the gridiron wars. In this backdrop, a young Latino entered the tough NFL neighborhoods and held his own against the toughest of the league. His name is Ricardo (Rick) Jose Casares, who for the years 1955-66, played a fierce game of football and became one of the Chicago Bears' all-time power runners.

Born in Tampa, Florida, on July 4, 1931, Casares grew up strong and tough in the Florida sunshine. The son of Spanish and Italian parents, he became a legendary prep star and distinguished himself as a high school All-American in 1948. Recognized as a triple-threat athlete, the Casares reputation stretched statewide and collegiate coaches watched this future star closely. Casares chose the University of Florida in Gainesville and played collegiate football for the Gators during the years 1951-53. He was a fast and powerful runner, considered by many experts of the time as the best fullback in the South.

In 1952, Casares quickly established his prominence by averaging 28 carries per game, rushing for 635 yards, scoring 7 touchdowns, converting 21 of 28 extra points, and averaging 41.2 yards in 24 punts. He led the Gator offense to a successful season in Southeast Conference play and the team earned an invitation to play the University of Tulsa in the eighth annual Gator Bowl.

The contest was closely matched—a penalty determined the winner. In the clash, Casares rushed for 86 yards, scored a touchdown, and kicked 2 extra points. As it happened, the second extra point by Casares was no good and a Tulsa penalty allowed him a second try. With the game in the balance, he made good on the extra point which gave Florida a 14-13 victory.

After only two games into his senior season, Gator co-captain Casares received a draft notice from the US Army. Although a soldier for the time being, he was not far from the football field. Casares displayed his talents on the Fort Jackson Army team in 1954, and during his brief stay with his Army team, he picked up All-Army, All-Service accolades; played in the Chicago Collegiate All-Star game; and was selected by the Chicago Bears in the second round of the 1954 NFL draft. He reflects on his military service and says he got bigger, stronger, and faster while he was in the Army, and received training that actually prepared him for pro football.

Upon separation from the Army in 1955, Casares donned a Bears uniform and quickly established himself as a formidable running back in the tough NFL trenches.

His rookie season was an explosive one, as the Latino fullback slashed his way through the staunch lines of NFL defenses. A highlight of Casares's premier season was an 81-yard touchdown run which became the Bears' longest run from scrimmage that season. In the game against Baltimore, Bears halfback Bobby Watkins had just run two plays to set up a third down and 5 yards to go. Casares recalls quarterback Ed Brown calling a halfback toss and Watkins telling Brown his head was spinning from the two previous plays. Casares suggested that he move to the halfback position. Watkins traded places with the rookie to the astonishment of quarterback Brown. Casares took the pitch-out and on his first pro football carry not only slammed through the Baltimore line but also into fame on his way to an 81-yard touchdown run. What better way to start a pro football career! Casares's recollection of that run was exuberant. "I'll never forget that as long as I live," he says. "I can see it as if it were yesterday—all my cuts, one guy hitting me across the

head. Practically everybody got a shot at me. Five yards from the end zone, somebody took a dive at me, so I went diving in and wound up lying on my back. I was so filled with exultation that I raised my legs up on my neck. I was so happy, well, I stood on my head." The end zone celebration symbolically announced that Casares had arrived in the NFL.

In his second NFL season (1956), the rambling Casares rushed for 1,126 yards on 234 carries to lead all the NFL ground gainers. He set his rushing mark in the game against the Detroit Lions, a game marred by fisticuffs and mayhem. From the opening kickoff, fights broke out on the field for reasons unknown and they continued all through the game. Casares himself tangled with his foes and left the game with an injured wrist, six and a half minutes left to play in the contest.

But despite leaving the game early, Casares played a tremendous game, rushing for 190 yards, including a 68-yard touchdown run. His rushing yardage not only gave him the NFL rushing title but also bettered the old Bears' rushing mark of 1,004 set in 1944 by Hall of Famer Beattie Feathers.

The Bears won the Western Title, so they readied themselves for the next obstacle—the championship game against the powerful New York Giants. Although the Bears were 3-point favorites, the 20-degree icy weather hampered Chicago's offense. The Giants scored quickly and furiously to lead 34-7 at halftime. The stunned Bears could not recover, and managed to score only after New York's Emlen Tunnel fumbled away a punt on the Giants' 25-yard line. A few plays later, Casares tallied from 9 yards out to account for the only Bears score in the championship game. The Giants' formula for success was its defense, which limited Casares, the NFL's leading rusher, to only 43 yards.

Although lacking the NFL championship to cap a great season, the Latino star was named to the NFL All-Pro Team in 1956 and he played in the first of 5 consecutive Pro Bowls in his NFL career.

The Bears had winning seasons in 1958, 1959, 1961, and 1962. Time and time again, Casares pounded the NFL defenses for yardage, until 1962, when injuries sidelined him temporarily. At this point in his career, he had been the Bears' rushing leader for the years 1955-60.

The 1961 NFL collegiate lottery was significant for Chicago and Casares. The Bears selected as their number one choice, tight end Mike Ditka from the University of Pittsburgh. Within a couple of campaigns, Ditka, quarterback Bill Wade, Casares (in a limited role), and the other Chicago veterans formed the core of the championship team of 1963. Ditka recalls first meeting Casares. "He was one of the most inspirational guys I ever played with. . . . It was exciting to get into

Rick Casares

Rushing

Year	Team	No.	Yds.	Avg.	TDs
1955	Chicago Bears	125	672	5.3	4
1956	Chicago Bears	234	1,126	4.8*	12
1957	Chicago Bears	204	700	3.4	6
1958	Chicago Bears	176	651	3.6	2
1959	Chicago Bears	177	699	3.9	10
1960	Chicago Bears	160	566	3.5	5[1]
1961-64	Chicago Bears	319	1,261	4.0	10
1965	Washington Redskins	(Injured Reserved)			
1966	Miami Dolphins	43	135	3.1	0
		1,429	5,810	4.06	49

Pass Receptions

Year	Team	No.	Yds.	Avg.	TDs
1955-64	Chicago Bears	182	1,538	8.5	10
1966	Miami Dolphins	8	45	5.6	1[2]
		190	1,583	8.33	11

Chicago Bears Scoring Leader

Year	Team	TDs	Pats	FG	Total Pts.
1956	Chicago Bears	14	—	—	84
1959	Chicago Bears	12	—	—	72[3]

Notes

1 *Chicago Bears 1986 Media Guide,* 131.

2 Telephone call to Miami Dolphins Public Relations Office for Statistics on Rick Casares, Wednesday, May 20, 1987.

3 *Chicago Bears 1986 Media Guide,* 134.

the huddle with him and look into his eyes because you knew he was all business. He did everything by example, nothing by word; he was a tough guy that didn't wear it on the outside." This was quite a tribute from a former teammate whose toughness and hard-nose style of football is well known in the NFL.

The 1963 season for the Bears was one of change and success. The Bears' defense made some adjustments and became the strongest in the NFL. The team lost only 1 game all season. Offensively, Casares, Joe Marconi, and Willie Galimore ran exceptionally well while Ditka caught 59 passes. Casares, in particular, was having a good year until he broke his ankle in the November 17 game against the Green Bay Packers and was out for the remainder of the season. The Bears tied their next two games and then beat San Francisco and Detroit to advance to the NFL Championship.

This time it would be a different outcome from last year's championship game. Playing in 8-degree weather at Wrigley Field, the Bears' defense rose to the occasion and intercepted five Y. A. Tittle passes to shut down the Giants' offense. It was sweet revenge as the Bears defeated New York 14-10, to capture their first NFL Championship since 1946.

In 1964, Casares played his 10th and last season with the Chicago Bears. Nagging injuries kept him from performing 100 percent, and the quiet warrior reluctantly gave way to other Bear runners like Joe Marconi, Jon Arnett, and Ron Bull. He left Chicago as their all-time career rushing leader (Walter Payton surpassed his record in 1979). At season's end, the Bears traded Casares to the Washington Redskins. In the first Redskins game of the season against the defending NFL Champion Cleveland Browns, Casares

Rick Casares, continued

Chicago Bears Career Statistics

Rick Casares ranked #1	Touchdowns consecutive games, 8 touchdowns (11-1-59 thru 9-25-60).[4]
#2	Career leading rushers, 5,675 yards on 1,386 attempts, average 4.08 per attempt, 49 touchdowns, 1955-64.[5]
#2	Rushing attempts lifetime, 1,386 attempts, 1955-64.[6]
#2	Rushing touchdowns lifetime, 49 touchdowns, 1955-64.[7]
#2	Touchdowns lifetime, 59 touchdowns, (49 rush, 10 receptions).[8]
#3	Touchdowns season, 14 touchdowns (12 rush, 2 receptions), 1956.[9]
#7	Career leading scorers, 354 points, (49 rush, 10 receptions), 1955-64.[10]
#10	Career leading receivers, 182 catches for 1,538 yards, average 8.5 per catch, 10 touchdowns, 1955-64.[11]
#19	Career leading receivers, yardage, 1,538 yards on 182 catches, average 8.5 per catch, 10 touchdowns, 1955-64.[12]
	* NFL rushing leader in 1956.

Notes

4 Ibid., 106.
5 Ibid., 128.
6 Ibid., 107.
7 Ibid., 110.
8 Ibid., 106.
9 Ibid., 106.
10 Ibid., 129.
11 Ibid., 131.
12 Ibid., 130.

sustained a season-ending rib injury. Casares was put on waivers and returned to Florida.

At this time, the American Football League (AFL) was expanding and Miami was granted a franchise in 1965, to begin playing in 1966. On June 19, 1966, the new Miami Dolphins announced the free-agent signing of Rick Casares. Dolphins coach George Wilson said this about the signing: "When I was at Detroit, I twice tried to trade for him. When I was the head coach of the West one year in the Pro Bowl, he played for me and turned in an outstanding performance. Last year (1965), I was an assistant at Washington and we were counting on him to be the number one full-back before he was injured and I feel that with his experience and all-around ability, he can be of tremendous help to our offense."

In Miami's AFL debut against the Oakland Raiders, the aging Latino fullback caught a touchdown pass, but the Dolphins were unable to mount a serious offensive threat and lost to the Raiders 23-14. For Miami, it was going to be a year of organizational and player problems associated with any expansion team. For Casares, it was his last glory and he retired prior to the end of the 1966 season, bringing to a close a twelve-year career in professional football.

From the beginning, Casares seized the opportunity to play football and had all the right instincts to be great. Nothing about the game escaped him and only injuries curtailed his football immortality. In retirement, the reclusive Casares wondered in 1977 about playing again. "If anything," he said, "I've just about realized that I'm not going to make a comeback, but I'd make a deal with the devil tomorrow if I could trade 10 years of my life for one season with my full capabilities. Some players say football is just another game, but it was everything to me."

Throughout his career, Casares was respected by friends and foes alike. To him actions always speak louder than words and he is not only remembered for the football records he set but also by the vigorous way he set them. Beyond a doubt, this gentleman and athlete is the "Gran Corredor Latino" of all time.

LSU's Pressure Man Vincent González

Louisiana State University football coach Paul Dietzel called Vincent Joseph González one of the best pressure athletes he had ever seen. González was as dependable as they come, and delivered the clutch performances when called upon to get first-down yardage, set up a crucial play, or convert an extra point.

This Latino star was born on May 20, 1933, in New Orleans, Louisiana, a town known for its Mardi Gras and rich cultural diversity. He was the son of Mexican and Italian parents, who for personal reasons went to Brooklyn, New York and left their son to be cared for by his grandmother. Under her care and guidance, young "Vicente" grew into a superb individual. Growing up in New Orleans and nicknamed "Chico," he prepped at Holy Cross High School, where the football team made a habit of winning the city championship three years in a row. In 1951, the three-time city champion González was named the Outstanding High School Athlete in New Orleans. Having achieved acclaim in high school, González was offered, and accepted, a football scholarship to LSU.

In the 1950s, LSU was renowned for producing outstanding running backs—players like Steve and Ebert Van Buren, Jim Taylor, Billy Cannon, and others. When González began his LSU career, he too became part of that tradition. Not wasting any part of the scholarship, González was a four-year letterman for the Tigers during the years 1952-55. In his sophomore year, he reached for the stars, compiling 175 offensive yards, most of them in kickoff returns. His junior season, he tripled his offensive output and was the Tigers' second leading rusher. His junior season success began immediately in the 1954 opener against the University of Texas. The Tigers called upon González to rekindle their offense. He responded and dazzled players and spectators alike with a brilliant 44-yard touchdown run to account for the only LSU score. Appearing on the cover of the sports section of the *San Antonio Express-News*, González is shown taking off on his touchdown gallop. *Express-News* sportswriter Dick Peebles writes, "The Longhorns had controlled the ball for the first half of the game, but the LSU Tigers came out for the second part determined to make a game of it. With Texas kicking off to LSU to open the second half, González stepped in and within a few offensive plays ran for glory." Dick Peebles describes, "Vincent González poured new hope into the Tigers when he sliced through right tackle, cut to the outside and sprinted down the west sideline 44 yards for a touchdown . . . it was a great run for González who was LSU's number one ballcarrier with 60 yards in six attempts."

For the rest of the season, González delivered the goods, including a spectacular catch of a Win Turner pass in the third quarter against Tulane, which produced a 14-13 come-from-behind victory. His senior year, the quick and evasive Latino hammered the Southeast Conference turf for yardage and big plays. He caught 2 touchdown passes in the season opener over Kentucky for a 19-7 win. Throughout the season, González terrorized the enemy defenses, accumulating 639 offensive yards and 5 touchdowns. His extra point conversion preserved a tie with Tulane, 13-13 in the season finale.

Postseason accolades for González included a selection to the All-Southeast Conference Second Team and the opportunity to play in the Annual Blue-Gray College All-Star game, held in Montgomery, Alabama. On the All-Star roster, González was listed as the number two fullback and saw action in the closely contested ballgame. He produced the key play in the game by converting the extra point, with little time remaining, to give the Gray team a thrilling 20-19 victory.

With college behind him, González contemplated a number of pro football offers. In 1956, he was the twentieth pick of the Washington Redskins of the NFL and an offer to play for the Hamilton Tiger-Cats of the Canadian Football League (CFL). They made an offer he liked and González received a $1,000 signing bonus to play north of the border. Leaving the Bayou State, González ventured into a short but interesting Canadian adventure.

The previous year, the Hamilton team had been a semifinalist en route to the Grey Cup and hoped to advance to the CFL championship in 1956. At the Hamilton training center, the eager Latino practiced hard and earned a starting position playing all the pre-season games. However, the rigors of preseason exacted a toll on González when he dislocated his shoulder just prior to the start of the regular season. Disappointed and on the injured list, he watched from the sidelines, hoping the shoulder would heal quickly. Playing without the services of González, the Tiger-Cats posted a 7-7 season record to finish second in the CFL Eastern Conference, just one game away from the Grey Cup finals. Unfortunately for González, the shoulder injury forced him into early retirement. It was a sad day for pro football to lose so great a talent, but such is the glory and agony of the sport.

González moved back to Baton Rouge, which had been his home during his collegiate days at LSU. With his playing days concluded, González looked forward to coaching at the high school level and embarked on an illustrious coaching career. For twenty-eight years, Coach González mentored football and baseball in the greater Baton Rouge area. His teams were highly successful. In particular, his baseball teams of 1965 and 1966 were the Louisiana State Champions and Runners-up, respectively.

Recognized for his success and achievement in coaching high school sports, González was inducted into the Redemptoris Sports Hall of Fame in 1988. His induction into the Baton Rouge–based Hall of Fame was a fine tribute to a dedicated and committed sportsman.

Today, the former LSU football star, CFL player, Hall of Fame coach and father of four daughters and two sons is still very involved in sports. His many responsibilities include assigning officials for the Capitol City Umpires Association in Baton Rouge. He is a respected community leader who continues to inspire others and is remembered as one of the All-Time Latino football greats.

Fast Hombre Alex Bravo

Probably the fastest Mexicano alive during his time was speed merchant Alex Bravo. Like Mercury in Greek mythology, Bravo was swift of motion and used his gift to streak through a stellar collegiate and pro football career.

Bravo was born on July 27, 1930, in Tucson, Arizona, one of three children in the Bravo family.

During his early childhood, the family left the sweltering heat of Tucson and moved to scenic Santa Barbara, California. In Santa Barbara, the young Bravo grew up and attended Santa Barbara High School. As a prep athlete, he excelled in football and track, and earned All-California Interscholastic Federation (CIF) honors.

So vast was Bravo's talent that nearby California State Polytechnic University at San Luis Obispo (Cal-Poly) took a keen interest in the fleet Bravo and offered him a scholarship. He accepted and embarked on a fabulous collegiate career.

Described in the Cal-Poly yearbook as "one of the fastest and greatest offensive backs in the history of Cal-Poly football," Bravo ran the 100 yards in 9.7 and the 220 yards in 21.2 seconds. Without a doubt, he was a key player in the two consecutive conference championships won by the Cal-Poly Mustangs in 1952-1953.

As a sophomore in 1951, Bravo established his leadership by setting two school records, one for the longest run from scrimmage; 77 yards and a touchdown against the Fresno State Bulldogs. The other came in the same game for a single game total of 159 yards rushing to break the old Cal-Poly record set by Bud McDougal in 1949 at 140 yards.

In other gridiron campaigns, the Cal-Poly Mustangs posted victories against Southern Oregon, Chico State, Santa Barbara, and Los Angeles State. Bravo's most sensational performance during the 1951 season came against the University of Santa Barbara Gauchos. He was brilliant in bringing the Mustangs from behind in the fourth quarter with two long touchdown runs, defeating Santa Barbara 14-7. *The San Luis Obispo Telegram-Tribune* recorded his efforts: ". . . Bravo broke up the ballgame with two brilliant runs, one a 37-yard gallop and the other for 57 yards, both good for touchdowns. But more than that the fans had seen the 180-pound back spark the Mustangs throughout the game. He carried the ball 18 times during the game for a total gain of 159 yards."

His first score came after Santa Barbara bulled their way to a touchdown early in the fourth period. After a fumble and a punt, Cal-Poly took possession and netted 27 yards on two plays and a first down. A pass to Bravo was good for 24 yards and then, "on the next play, Bravo followed his interference around the left side of the line, ran along the sideline for about 15 yards, dodged several would be tacklers and then streaked the rest of the way to the goal line. Clive Remund kicked the extra point to tie the score 7-7 and put the Mustangs back in the ballgame." The second Bravo touchdown came after Santa Barbara once again punted to the Mustangs. "On the first play, Bravo sliced through left tackle, slipping his way untouched through the middle of the Gaucho team to again score for Cal-Poly. Remund's second kick was good and the Mustangs held a 14-7 lead." A lead they would not relinquish. It was a great game for Bravo, who finished the season as the California Collegiate Athletic Association (CCAA) leader in rushing yardage, total offense, and scoring.

The following 1952 collegiate season Bravo continued making the big plays. In the season opener against the Lobos of Sul Ross College, Bravo's brilliant broken-field run for 48 yards was Cal-Poly's lone touchdown. Two weeks later, well on their way to the CCAA football championship, Cal-Poly dumped the San Diego State Aztecs 20-18. Bravo rang the bell for Cal-Poly four minutes after the game began. He took a 30-yard pass from quarterback Neal and scampered his way into the end zone.

In his hometown of Santa Barbara, Santa Barbara State College was smothered by Cal-Poly by the score of 19-0. In this contest, Bravo added to his touchdown collection by scoring on a short yardage play. However, the best was yet to come. In the city by the bay, against the San Francisco State University Gators, Bravo tallied two touchdowns—one on a 49-yard pass reception, the other on a record-breaking 85-yard sprint.

The *San Luis Obispo Telegram-Tribune* describes the Bravo run for glory. "Midway in the third period, the Mustangs were back on their own fifteen . . . on a pitchout, Bravo sped around the left end, slowed down long enough to draw several Gator tacklers and then turned on the steam for an 85-yard touchdown run." He finished the game, a 34-26 victory, with a total of 169 yards to break the record he earlier established for rushing yards in a single game.

Against the Los Angeles State Diablos, Bravo scored on a 28-yard run, leading the Cal-Poly Mustangs to a 32-7 victory and its first conference title since joining the CCAA in 1947. Cal-Poly ended its championship season by defeating the Missouri Valley Vikings 27-14. In the sweetness of the victory, the speedy Bravo scored on a 25-yard touchdown run at the end of a 12-play, 82-yard drive.

The following season, the Cal-Poly Mustangs posted an unbeaten, untied record to win their second straight CCAA championship. Again, Bravo played flawlessly and the Mustangs played near perfection in capturing their second consecutive title. The season's highlight was the Mustangs' win over once previously beaten Redlands Bulldogs 51-6. Bravo, who played one of his best defensive games, intercepted a Bulldog pass and returned it 54 yards for a touchdown.

While at Cal-Poly, Bravo established three school career records; most yards rushing for the years 1951-53, 2,238 yards; most total yards/pass receiving, 2,848; and most points scored, 151. Additionally, he was named to the All-CCAA and UPI All-Little Coast teams three consecutive years. Also, he was selected to the UP All Southern California Small Colleges Team, and in his senior year received Honorable Mention on the prestigious Little All-American Team.

Alex Bravo

Rushing

Year	Team	No.	Yds.	Avg.	Long	TDs
1956	Saskatchewan Roughriders (CFL)	72	399	5.54	96*	2

* Alex Bravo had season record in 1956 for longest run from scrimmage, 96 yards.

Pass Receptions

Year	Team	No.	Yds.	Avg.	Long	TDs
1956	Saskatchewan Roughriders	8	209	26.1	43	1

Scoring

Year	Team	TDs	PATS	Total Points
1956	Saskatchewan Roughriders	3	—	18[1]

Interceptions

Years	Team	Int.	Yds.	Avg.	TDs	Long
1960-61	Oakland Raiders (AFL)	6	64	10.7	0	37[2]

Notes

1 Canadian Football League, Individual Statistical Record for Alex Bravo.

2 *Decades of Destiny, 1960-1984 The Historic First 20 Years* (Los Angeles: CWC Sport Publications, 1985), 80.

After a very successful collegiate career, Bravo became a ninth round draft selection of the Los Angeles Rams in 1954. However, the military draft called, and he served two years in the US Marine Corps. Upon discharge from the Marines in 1956, Bravo returned to football and after some consideration accepted an offer to play professional football in the Canadian Football League with the Saskatchewan Roughriders rather than play for the Rams.

When Bravo signed with the CFL, Los Angeles Rams general manager Tex Schramm filed a protest with Sidney Halter, registrar of the CFL, alleging breech of agreement between the two leagues over the recruitment of players. According to Jack Geyer of the *Los Angeles Times,* "Bravo was highly regarded by the Rams, particularly for his speed . . ." The Rams and the Roughriders reached an agreement to allow Bravo to play in Canada for one year and then return to the Rams.

As a Saskatchewan Roughrider, Bravo set a record for the longest run from scrimmage, 96 yards, in a game against the Winnipeg Blue Bombers. For the rest of the season, Bravo cranked out 399 rushing yards, hauled in 8 passes for 209 yards, and scored 3 touch-downs. Bravo and the Roughriders went to the conference playoffs, losing to the Edmonton Eskimos for the championship, and concluding his one and only season in the CFL.

In 1957, Bravo returned to the NFL and the Rams. The Rams converted him to a defensive back to utilize his speed and quickness. This proved to be a wise move as evident midway through Bravo's premier NFL season. In the game against Cleveland, which took place on November 24, 1957, Bravo played a sensational defensive game. Twice, Bravo ran down and tackled the legendary Jim Brown from behind. Brown was about to break away for touchdowns when Bravo, from the safety position, made the plays to prevent the scores. Years later when asked about his defensive performance, Bravo smiled and commented, "Brown was fast but I was faster."

In 1958, at the Rams training camp, Bravo sustained knee and ankle injuries which sidelined him for several weeks. Upon resuming practice, he pulled the hamstring muscle which caused him to miss most of the 1958 season. During his rehabilitation, Bravo taught and coached at Hawthorn High School in Hawthorn, California.

After a year and a half and still unable to play, the Rams released Bravo to free agency. In 1960, the fully recovered speedster signed with the newly formed Oakland Raiders of the American Football League (AFL). He was one of the original Raiders, like teammate Tom Flores, and for the next two seasons started every game for Oakland at safety. In the Raider's publication, *Decades of Destiny 1960-1984, The Historic First 25 Years,* Bravo is acknowledged for his play and contributions: "Among those who contributed on the field as the Raiders played their initial 1960 campaign were defenders like safety Alex Bravo."

The 1961 season was one of continued development as the new team managed only 2 wins against the Denver Broncos 33-19 and the Buffalo Bills 31-22. A constant threat to the passing game of opposing quarterbacks, Bravo solidified his safety position and had 6 interceptions during those two seasons.

After the 1961 AFL gridiron campaign, the veteran Bravo decided to conclude his pro football career and returned to teaching/coaching at the high school level. Also, Bravo returned to the collegiate turf in another capacity, to officiate junior college football games in the highly competitive Los Angeles Metropolitan Football Conference.

Remembered for his speed and football accomplishments, the extremely likable Alex Bravo was indeed a star and remarkable individual. Now that he is no longer wearing the black and white striped shirt, Bravo and family homestead in sunny southern California in a place called Manhattan Beach.

Collegiate Champion Primo Villanueva

Very few collegiate football players can boast about playing on a National Championship Team. Even fewer players have the distinction of leading their teams to the much sought-after championship. However, UCLA tailback Primo Villanueva has the bragging rights on both counts. This Latino athlete did everything he could to pace the 1954 UCLA Bruins to the national title. Despite these achievements, he entered pro football an unsung hero and played just four seasons in the Canadian Football League (CFL).

Primo Villanueva was born in the badlands of Tucumari, New Mexico, on December 2, 1931. The oldest of twelve Villanueva children, Primo and his younger brother Danny were successful athletes and played professional football for different teams in different eras and different countries.

Although originally from Tucumari, New Mexico, the Villanueva family, for economic and religious reasons, moved to Calexico, California to work in the rich agribusiness of Southern California. In Calexico, Villanueva grew up and developed into a superb athlete. He attended Calexico High School, where he played football under the direction of Coach Earl "Ace" Parker. An overnight success, Villanueva was a triple-threat player and earned a spot on the All-Imperial Valley

Team for three consecutive years. Later, he was named to the All-Imperial Valley First-Half Century Team.

Upon graduation from high school, Villanueva enrolled in the University of California as Los Angeles (UCLA) and gave collegiate football a try.

"You've never seen a 19-year-old boy quite as lost as freshman Primo Villanueva was in September of 1951, when he left his hometown of Calexico, population 6,433, to enroll at UCLA, population 13,398," says a UCLA news bureau press release.

A shy boy of Mexican American ancestry, Villanueva went to UCLA and became one of the all-time great tailbacks in UCLA football history. In his sophomore year, Villanueva got his first real taste of college football. Dick Hyland, sportswriter for the *Los Angeles Times* writes,

> Primo Villanueva was as green as any pea could be when he entered the Rice game in his sophomore year. Paul Cameron was injured, Teddy Narleski was tired and needed a rest . . . in went Primo, the kid from Calexico, with orders to merely control the football. In doing so Villanueva marched the Bruins 62 yards to a touchdown that broke the Rice Owl's back. Also, in the same year, he came close, very close to taking the USC Trojans out of the Rose Bowl at the end of the season. Forced to the sideline when the Trojans were leading 14-12, Primo made a leaping off-balance pass that was caught by Don Stalwick 26 yards downfield. A little more lead on that one and that would have been the ball game. Primo was great to even complete the throw the way the Trojans swarmed in on him.

In his senior year, Primo continued to develop and excel in the Bruins backfield, as both a quarterback and a running back. UCLA won 8 and lost only to Stanford 21-20, on their way to winning the Pacific Coast Conference championship. The conference championship meant the Bruins would face Michigan State in the Rose Bowl. In the official Rose Bowl game program, Villanueva was listed at left halfback starting behind All-American halfback Paul Cameron. Villanueva played sparingly against Michigan State in the Rose Bowl. All season long Cameron had been sidelined with injuries while Villanueva carried the Bruins' offense. Then came the Rose Bowl, and Cameron came to life, turning in a stellar performance in a losing effort. Michigan State outlasted the Bruins, beating them 28-20. In preparation for the 1954 senior season Villanueva had some obstacles to overcome. As *Los Angeles Times* writer Jack Tobin describes, "Primo Villanueva, UCLA's soft-spoken, reticent Mexican tailback was preparing for the Bruins' Pacific Coast Conference debut and during their first spring practice, was carried from the field with a severely sprained

ankle." Villanueva comments, "I was ready to go back to Calexico and the vegetable fields right then, but I had to stay because I couldn't walk. I was on crutches for a week and everything seemed to go wrong. I was having a terrible time with my classes: we had a little boy and it was hard to make ends meet. In fact, I was mowing lawns and doing anything I could on Sundays to make some money. Finally, Mother convinced me that I had to take full advantage of the opportunity for a college education that none of the other eleven kids had; that 's why I am still here."

Against USC last year it was Primo who came in after Cameron couldn't muster a scoring drive and marched the Bruins to the USC 2-yard line, where Bob Davenport bulled over and the Bruins' date at Pasadena's Rose Bowl was assured. Often Primo has been asked how it feels to run in Cameron's spot and he always has the answer, "I've been there before. I'm no Cameron and I never will be; I'm not as good as Paul and there's nothing I can do about it. All I can do is just the best I know how."

Fully recovered from his ankle injury, Villanueva set the tone for the 1954 season in the game against the University of Maryland. "It was Villanueva's work on this dazzling 10-yard clutch run to the 1 yard line that sealed Maryland's doom. That run vaulted Villanueva to the head of UCLA's tailback pack," wrote Jack Tobin for the *LA Times*. According to Tobin, this is how the season went:

> After a slow start against San Diego Naval and an extremely disappointing performance against Kansas, the test was applied in the Los Angeles Coliseum before 73,000 as UCLA and Maryland battled for top honors . . . With third down and 6 yards to go on the Maryland 9 yard line, it was a do or die play as the freshly inserted Villanueva took the ball from center on a fake pass and ran to the left. Primo faked the throw, made another deep fake to run off-tackle, then came up still waving the ball as he skirted his own left end for 8 yards and a first down on the one yard line. From there, Bob Davenport drilled into the line for the winning score.

Villanueva went on to truly superb performances, completely outshining Paul Larson, George Shaw, and other All-Americans. In the University of Washington contest, Villanueva went 2 yards to score the winning touchdown, UCLA 21-Washington 20. Against Stanford, the *New York Times* reported that "UCLA's football team, led by Primo Villanueva, handed Stanford University its worst defeat in history, as the Bruins ran up a 72-0 score before 70,555 fans in Memorial Coliseum. The worst loss by a Stanford team since the 49-0 defeat in 1901 by Michigan . . . it was the largest score ever compiled by UCLA.

Villanueva, the little senior left halfback had a hand in the first five scores, making two of the touchdowns."

Against Oregon State, Villanueva scored 1 touchdown in a 61-0 rout of their northern neighbors. In the game against California, Villanueva led the powerful Bruins to their seventh straight victory as he scored 2 touchdowns and passed for a third in a 27-6 triumph. Villanueva ran 40 yards to set up the score in the first quarter and later went around end for 8 yards and the tally. In the second quarter, on a pass-run option, Villanueva slipped down the sidelines for 26 yards and a score. In the same game, the versatile Villanueva completed a pass to end Bob Long for 24 yards and one to halfback Jim Decker for 30. Villanueva then engineered a 50-yard march in the fourth period, with the pay-off, his pass into the end zone to halfback John Hermann from 8 yards out. In the contest, Villanueva carried the ball 13 times for 108 yards and completed 7 of 10 passes for 120 yards.

After the California game, the fans waited for Villanueva outside the locker room. Harry Culver, writer for the *Los Angeles Herald Express* described the scene: "We want Primo . . . the surging chant of victory made Bruin students create a din that echoed in Strawberry Canyon (Pasadena). . . they were gathered outside the UCLA dressing room and they wanted to see Villanueva, hero of the triumph over California, who had scored two touchdowns, pitched another, and set up a fourth. Finally Primo, last to leave the quarters, faced the rooters, looked down at his shoes . . . 'Say something, Primo,' the Bruin students implored. 'Adios,' said Primo and fled to the waiting bus."

Villanueva, known affectionately to his teammates as "Da Preem," may have been shy, but he found himself at left halfback for the undefeated, untied UCLA gridders shooting for the mythical National Football Championship.

In the University of Oregon game, the first time UCLA got the ball they marched 70 yards in 8 plays, scoring on a 16-yard pass from Villanueva to Ronnie Loudd, as UCLA blanked Oregon 41-0.

In the season finale, the nation's top-ranked UCLA Bruins faced cross-town rivals the USC Trojans before 102,548 fans in Memorial Stadium. The second time the Bruins had the ball after the opening kickoff, they scored on a 48-yard pass from Villanueva to end Bob Heydenfelt. On the following kickoff, Trojan tailback Jon Arnett fumbled on the 15 and UCLA guard Hardiman Cureton recovered the ball. Villanueva passed 13 yards to Harry Debay for the third score. Villanueva was involved in three of the five touchdowns, as he passed for 2 and made a key run that helped set up another. The season ended perfectly for the Bruins as they captured their second straight Pacific Coast Conference Championship. Villanueva

was, beyond a doubt, instrumental in its success. He was no longer the shy, lost kid from Calexico, but a confident, alert, sharp young man who made the UCLA team go. He was a significant member of the UCLA team that won the first Grantland Rice Award, which goes annually to America's number 1 collegiate football power.

Sports author John D. McCallum in 1982 writes, "One of the greatest elevens ever assembled in the United States was the 1954 UCLA Bruins. Ironically, a no-repeat clause in the Big Ten/Pacific Coast Conference pact kept the Bruins out of the Rose Bowl. Instead, Red Sanders and his Bruins had to satisfy themselves with the number 1 ranking in the United Press Poll.

The Bruins were the National Collegiate Champions due in part to the outstanding play of Primo Villanueva. He carried the ball 101 times to gain 380 net yards; completed 23 of 50 passes for 371 yards and a 46 percent completion ratio; scored 6 touchdowns and contributed to 8 others during the 1954 championship season.

For his stellar performances in 1954, Villanueva was selected to the All-Pacific Coast Conference First Team. In talking to Villanueva about his collegiate career, he said, "Beating USC and being the National Champions were the highlights of my career at UCLA; it is something I will never forget."

In postseason play, Villanueva was selected as a college All-Star to play in the ninth annual Hula Bowl in Hawaii. The *New York Times* describes the event: "The contest was between the college cream of the mainland and the local military and Hawaiian players, fortified by the presence of 5 pro football stars . . . Otto Graham, Gordon Soltau, Elroy Hirsch, and Jim Clark. The Collegians were in control of the game, as linemen ripped big holes for backs like Hardy, Dick Moegle, and Primo Villanueva of UCLA. The final score of the game was a 29-yard touchdown toss to Villanueva, as the College All-Stars won 33-13."

Professionally, Villanueva was not drafted by any NFL Teams in 1955. A *Los Angeles Herald Express* article questioned the motives of the NFL teams: "How come that in 360 draft choices by 12 clubs of the National Football League, not one picked up either Marvin Goux of USC or Primo Villanueva of UCLA in last week's big lottery in New York?"

"The $64 question was put to a Los Angeles Rams spokesman just home from the big ivory hunt . . . 'well, it's this way, neither man according to all the best information gleaned by every club in the league, is either big enough to make the grade in pro football. What the Rams' file shows on Villanueva, 5 feet 10 inches, 172 lbs., good deception, good competition, too small, no speed, and is no specialist.' " Although

Primo Villanueva

Rushing

Year	Team	No.	Yds.	Avg.	Long	TDs
1955	British Columbia Lions (CFL)	63	317	5.0	26	2
1956	British Columbia Lions	25	97	3.8	20	0
1957	British Columbia Lions	40	247	6.1	58	1
1958	British Columbia Lions	11	72	6.5	16	1
		139	733	5.27	58	4

Passing

Year	Team	No.	Comp.	Yds.	Pct.	Long	TDs	Int.
1955	British Columbia Lions	4	4	62	.100	23	1	1
1956	British Columbia Lions	29	16	297	.551	46	2	0
1957	British Columbia Lions	46	21	406	.456	64	4	3
1958	British Columbia Lions	1	—	—	—	—	—	—
		80	41	765	.512	64	7	4

Pass Receptions

Year	Team	No.	Yds.	Avg.	Long	TDs
1955	British Columbia Lions	16	234	14.6	37	2
1956	British Columbia Lions	1	12	12.0	12	0
1957	British Columbia Lions	9	175	19.4	44	2
1958	British Columbia Lions	3	34	11.3	17	0
		29	455	15.6	44	4

Punts

Year	Team	No.	Yds.	Avg.	Long	Blk.
1955	British Columbia Lions	4	124	31.0	40	0

Punt Returns

Year	Team	No.	Yds.	Avg.	Long
1955	British Columbia Lions	14	105	7.5	20
1956	British Columbia Lions	2	0	0.0	0
1957	British Columbia Lions	1	0	0.0	0
1958	British Columbia Lions	1	7	7.0	7
		18	112	6.22	20

Primo Villanueva, continued

Kickoff Returns

Year	Team	No.	Yds.	Avg.	Long	TDs
1955	British Columbia Lions	3	42	14.0	15	0
1956	British Columbia Lions	3	72	24.0	40	0
1957	British Columbia Lions	5	94	18.8	28	0
1958	British Columbia Lions	4	71	17.7	20	0
		15	279	18.6	40	0

Scoring

Year/s	Team	TDs	Converts	Total Pts.
1955-58	British Columbia Lions	8	1	49

Fumbles

Year	Team	No.
1955	British Columbia Lions	4
1956	British Columbia Lions	2
1957	British Columbia Lions	2

Interceptions

1956	Team	No.	Return Yds.	Avg.
1955	British Columbia Lions	5	87	17.4
1956	British Columbia Lions	1	13	13.0

Source: Telephone call to Larry Robertson, Information Officer and Statistician, Canadian Football League Office, for statistics on Primo Villanueva, Thursday, July 30, 1987.

not substantive enough to exclude Primo from the NFL draft, one wonders what the real reasons were. Although not drafted, Villanueva received an offer to attend the Washington Redskins camp, and received a call from the British Columbia Lions of the Canadian Football League (CFL). Villanueva made the CFL team and signed a contract to play for the 1955 season. His pay was $7,500.

On the Canadian gridiron, Villanueva played on offense, defense, and special teams for the British Columbia Lions. He finished the 1955 season with a total of 5 interceptions, including 3 interceptions in the game against the Calgary Stampeders. In that game he also punted once for 32 yards, returned 2 punts for 21 yards, had 1 pass reception, completed 3 of 5 passes thrown, the longest for 23 yards and 1 touchdown. Last, he rushed 7 times for 29 yards. Statistically, this game was typical of Villanueva's versatility in each of the games he played for the Lions.

Villanueva played four brilliant seasons with the British Columbia Lions. Although the team did not

fare will in Canadian Football League play, Villanueva, the competitor, was a key factor in the success of the 18 games they won during the 1955-58 seasons.

In 1959, the Lions traded Villanueva to the Montreal Alouettes. However, Villanueva decided to retire from professional football. Instead he ventured into the restaurant business and gave Canadians a taste of Mexican cuisine. Today his restaurant business is very successful and has expanded to a chain of Mexican restaurants throughout Canada. Recently, he turned over the ownership of the restaurants to his son and now owns and operates the manufacturing company that supplies the restaurants. Today one can find this superb individual and his family in Surrey, British Columbia.

Primo Villanueva had a great football career including a national collegiate football championship, a distinction only a few athletes can claim. From very humble beginnings he rose to national stardom at the college level, and had a notable and exciting pro football career in Canada.

Danny Villanueva

One would never have guessed that Danny Villanueva had been a quarterback at one time in his football career. As a matter of historical fact, he had been a quarterback at Reedley Junior College in California, then at New Mexico State University when a shoulder injury intervened and forced the young Villanueva to learn other football skills. Actually, Villanueva could not bring himself to tell his mother he was going to be cut from the team, so the former quarterback hurriedly learned to placekick the football.

This move by the short and portly Villanueva was a wise one indeed for two reasons. First, Villanueva did not have to have his mother's scorn as an ex-football player, and second, he would surely become a pro-caliber punter and kicker.

Born on November 5, 1937, in Tucumari, New Mexico, Danny Villanueva was the ninth of twelve children born to Reverend Primitivo and Pilar Villanueva. Without a doubt, the Villanuevas were blessed in many ways. Their eldest son Primo was a star tailback for the 1954 UCLA National Collegiate Football Championship team and Danny would become an NFL pro football kicker.

Villanueva began his football career at Reedley Junior College in 1957. It was a short-lived experience due to injuries, and Villanueva returned to New Mexico to pursue an education and play football at New Mexico State University. It was there that Villanueva learned to kick a football. For two seasons, he doubled as the punter and placekicker for the New

Mexico State Aggies. In his senior year, Villanueva kicked 7 of 8 field goals, the longest one from 47 yards.

His name absent from the NFL draft in 1959, Danny Villanueva became a teacher. It appeared as though Villanueva's gridiron would be the classroom. However, in Los Angeles, California, the Rams coaches expressed a need for a kicker and Chuck Benedict, a radio broadcaster, remembered Villanueva as a great high school player and suggested to the coaches that Villanueva should be given a tryout.

Villanueva flew to Los Angeles and reported to the Rams training camp in Van Nuys. Once there, he kicked for the Rams coach Bob Waterfield, a Pro Football Hall of Fame member. In a *Los Angeles Times* article, Villanueva recalls, "I thought he was the greatest thing I'd ever heard of and so I kicked and I kicked. I don't recall the exact number anymore, but it was 30-something in a row and I never missed, and he said, 'I've seen enough,' so they offered me a contract."

The $5,500 a year contract was a bargain for the Rams because Villanueva was utilized as both a kicker and a punter. The Rams' rookie free-agent enjoyed a good season. He converted 28 of 28 extra points and 12 of 19 field goals to lead Los Angeles in scoring. His biggest thrill of the rookie campaign was a game-winning field goal with 22 seconds left to play to best the Green Bay Packers, 33-31.

The following season (1962), Villanueva set a Rams club record by averaging 45.5 yards per punt and scoring 56 points. The next year was another robust and productive year for the developing Villanueva. He finished third among NFL punters with a 45.4 average and once again led the Rams in scoring with 52 points. His best punting day came in the game against the Chicago Bears on October 12, 1963. In that game, Villanueva averaged 51 yards on 5 punts, the fifth highest game average in Rams history. His placekicking skill, the only highlight of the Rams' less than successful season, upset the Minnesota Vikings 27-24, ending an 8-game losing streak. His kicking also led to a defeat of the favored Baltimore Colts 17-16.

In his last year with the Rams, before being traded to the Dallas Cowboys, Villanueva was used solely as a punter. It was not that his placekicking ability had lessened, but the emphasis was being placed on his punting. His 82 punts averaged 44.1 yards as the Rams continued to struggle through the 1964 season. In 1965, Villanueva was traded to the Dallas Cowboys for end Tommy McDonald. Although there was some bitterness over the unexpected trade, Villanueva kept a positive outlook. Al Wolf, Los Angeles sportswriter writes, "Villanueva may have nothing but kind words for his five years with the Rams, but he also has this to say about the Times Charity game between the clubs. . . . 'I'd like nothing better than to start my Dallas career by kicking a winning field goal against the Rams.' "

For the next two seasons, Villanueva led the Cowboys in scoring in 1965 and 1966 with 85 and 107 points, respectively. The 1966 season was a stellar one for the Mexicano kicker. His 107 points were second best in the NFL and his 56 consecutive extra points in one season set a NFL record. (Ray Wersching of the San Francisco 49ers tied the record in 1984.) An added glory for Villanueva that season was his successful kick against the Washington Redskins, where he kicked a 20-yard field goal with 15 seconds left in the game to defeat the Redskins 31-30. Dallas Cowboys historian Carlton Stowers described the Cowboys' memorable drive to set up Villanueva's historic placement:

It was a game which had all the earmarks of defeat for the Cowboys, then still smoldering the stigma of not being able to win the big one. The fading minutes of the clock were fast escaping when Washington punter Pat Richter, protecting a 30-28 lead, punted the ball inside the Cowboys' five-yard line.

On the sidelines, Danny Villanueva had no reason to be nervous. This one he knew would not come down to him. There was simply not enough time. However, Cowboys quarterback Don Meredith had not given up. [He threw] a long pass to Pete Gent and then one to Pettis Norman. Dan Reeves caught one coming out of the backfield and the miracle was beginning to take form.

It became a real possibility when Meredith, rolling out to his right was knocked out of bounds and tackled by an over-zealous Redskins defender after he was clearly off the field of play. As the official stepped off the 15 yard penalty, 11 seconds showed on the clock. It had come down to Villanueva. Villanueva remembers, "It was just over 30 yards. But it looked a lot further. The holder Reeves bobbled the snap and I had to wait. There was no timing on the kick. I just tried to nurse it over the goal posts. I've never in my life been so relieved to see an official raise his arms."[1]

As a souvenir of the winning field goal, the fan who caught the football was Pete Richert, former Los Angeles Dodgers and Washington Senators pitcher, who was seated in the end zone with his son. In a thoughtful gesture, Richert returned the game ball to Villanueva after the game. Surprised to retrieve the ball, the elated kicker noticed Richert's son had hopes of keeping the ball, so he got another ball from the equipment manager and traded him. The exchange was a happy one.

Danny Villanueva

Punting

Year	Team	No.	Yds.	Avg.	Long	Blk.
1961	Los Angeles Rams	46	1,845	40.1	53	0
1962	Los Angeles Rams	87	3,960	45.5	65	1
1963	Los Angeles Rams	81	3,678	45.4	68	0
1964	Los Angeles Rams	82	3,616	44.1	58	0[2]
1965	Dallas Cowboys	60	2,508	41.8	58	0
1966	Dallas Cowboys	65	2,548	39.2	58	1
1967	Dallas Cowboys	67	2,707	40.4	57	0[3]
		488	20,862	42.8	68	2

Scoring

Year	Team	Pats	FG	Total Pts.
1960	Los Angeles Rams	28	12	64
1961	Los Angeles Rams	32	13	71
1962	Los Angeles Rams	26	10	56
1963	Los Angeles Rams	25	9	52[4]
1965	Dallas Cowboys	37	16	85
1966	Dallas Cowboys	56	17	107
1967	Dallas Cowboys	41	9	68[5]
		245	86	503

Field Goals

Year	Team	Atts.	Made	Pct.	Long
1960	Los Angeles Rams	19	12	.631	—
1961	Los Angeles Rams	27	13	.481	—
1962	Los Angeles Rams	20	10	.500	51
1963	Los Angeles Rams	17	9	.529	—[6]
1965	Dallas Cowboys	27	16	.593	41
1966	Dallas Cowboys	31	17	.548	37
1967	Dallas Cowboys	23	9	.391	34[7]
		164	86	.524	51

Notes

1 Carlton Stowers, *Journey to Triumph: 110 Dallas Cowboys Tell Their Stories* (Dallas: Taylor Publishing Company, 1982), 122.

2 Telephone call to Los Angeles Rams Public Relations Office for statistics on Danny Villanueva, Monday, May 11, 1987.

3 *1986 Dallas Cowboys Media Guide,* 125.

4 Telephone call to Los Angeles Rams Public Relations Office for statistics on Danny Villanueva, Monday, May 11, 1987.

5 *1986 Dallas Cowboys Media Guide,* 126.

6 Telephone call to Los Angeles Rams Public Relations Office for statistics on Danny Villanueva, Monday, May 11, 1987.

7 *1986 Dallas Cowboys Media Guide,* 126.

8 *Los Angeles Rams 1982 Media Guide,* 122.

9 Ibid, 121.

10 *1986 Dallas Cowboys Media Guide,* 122.

11 Ibid, 147.

12 Ibid, 148.

13 *Official 1981 National Football League Record Manual,* 224.

14 Ibid, 224.

15 Ibid, 282.

Danny Villanueva, continued

Dallas Cowboys Career Playoff Records

Scoring

	Yrs.	Games	TDs	PATs	FG	Total Pts.
Listed #13	1965-67	3	0	12	4	24[11]

Los Angeles Rams Individual Records

Danny Villanueva Tied for #1	Longest field goal, 51 yards vs. Dallas Cowboys in 1962.
Listed #2	Highest average distance, game, 52.5 average (6 punts for 206 yards vs. San Francisco 49ers in 1962).[8]
#3	Most punts, season, 87 punts, 45.5 average in 1962.
#3	Most punts, game, 11 punts, 50.0 average vs. Dallas Cowboys in 1962.[9]

Dallas Cowboys All-Time Leaders

Danny Villanueva Listed #5	Punting, 192 punts for 7,763 yards, 40.3 average for the years 1965-67.
#5	Field Goals, 42 field goals out of 81 attempts, .519 percentage, for the years 1965-67.[10]

Dallas Cowboys Single Game Playoff Record

Danny Villanueva— Extra Points Attempted	Made 7 of 7 vs. Cleveland Browns on December 24, 1967.[12]

NFL All-Time Records

Danny Villanueva Listed #1	Most points after touchdown, no misses, season, 56 points with Dallas Cowboys, 1966.[13]
#3	Highest points after touchdown percentage, career (200 points after touchdown), 97.93 percentage, with Los Angeles Rams, 1960-64; Dallas Cowboys, 1965-67, 236 PATs of 241 attempts.[14]
#10	Top ten punters, 488 punts for 20,862 yards, 42.8 average, longest 68 yards, 2 blocked, for the years 1960-67.[15]

But Villanueva's jubilation that followed the Cowboys' victorious return to Dallas was tempered when he found out that his two-year-old son Jimmy had been saved from drowning by his conscientious neighbor, Robert Somerall. The near tragedy occurred about the same time that Villanueva had just split the uprights for the win.

The victory propelled the Cowboys into the playoffs for the very first time in the history of the franchise. It was also the beginning of the Dallas Cowboys' winning dynasty.

After Villanueva's dramatic kick in the Washington game, the Cowboys won the next 3 of their 4 remaining games. The Cowboys played the defending NFL Champion Green Bay Packers in the first round of the playoffs. Villanueva contributed 2 field goals and 3 extra points although it was not enough to seal a Cowboys victory.

His final season (1967) was business as usual. The Villanueva kicking game was effective and Dallas returned to the playoffs. They battled the Cleveland Browns for the Eastern Conference Championship, but unlike the year before, the Cowboys savored victory, beating the Browns 52-14. Villanueva was perfect in his placements, converting 7 for 7 extra points and was 1 for 1 in field goals.

The weather was a formidable foe as Dallas prepared to play the world champion Packers in the championship game. The teams played a closely contested game which came to be known as the "Ice Bowl." Leading 17-14 late in the fourth quarter after a Villanueva field goal, the Cowboys braved the elements up until the final 14 seconds. As fate determined, Green Bay quarterback Bart Starr sneaked over for the score and Green Bay won their third consecutive championship.

After eight successful seasons in the NFL, on July 20, 1968, Villanueva announced his retirement from professional football to embark on a new career as a Spanish language sports broadcaster with KMEX (Los Angeles). Beginning with five-minute sport shows, Villanueva progressed to news director, TV station manager, general manager, and then president of the Spanish International Communications (SIN) Corporation in Los Angeles, California. Realizing the importance of the primarily Mexicano community in the Los Angeles area, Villanueva expanded the station's community involvement. What his Father Primitivo had always professed "to serve others," his son Danny is now doing on a grand scale. A tireless and dedicated man, this extraordinary Mexicano is a true success, whose work has always been well done.

The Sixties

Joe Kapp
Roses, Grey Cup, & Super Bowl

During the course of pro football history, many colorful and memorable players have come and gone, but nonetheless, are remembered for the courage they displayed, the excitement they caused, and the success they achieved. One such player was Joseph R. Kapp, who arrived in the NFL as a 29-year-old rookie, and led the Minnesota Vikings to Super Bowl IV. Kapp accomplished this feat with a unique and fierce style of leadership never before seen in professional football.

He was as tough as they come and overcame adversity under which any normal man would have buckled. The era in which he played was a turbulent one with the Vietnam War, civil rights, and social upheaval. Not to be spared, the status quo of the NFL would also be challenged and what tougher man to do it than Joe Kapp.

Kapp was born on March 19, 1938, in Santa Fe, New Mexico, and grew up in the California valleys of San Fernando and Salinas. As a youngster, he devel-

oped a physical toughness that became his most notable characteristic during his football playing days. In high school, the teenage Kapp discovered his ability to play sports and became a great competitor in football and basketball and earned All-California Interscholastic Federation (CIF) honors in both sports.

The University of California Golden Bears offered Kapp a basketball scholarship, but it was football that distinguished his athletic career.

During the first three years at California, his performances in both basketball and football in Pacific Coast Conference play were outstanding. He played on the California Golden Bears basketball team that defeated West Virginia and Jerry West to win in the 1959 NCAA championships.

The Golden Bears football team, however, was undergoing some hard times. They had not won a conference title in years and in the previous two seasons had won a total of three games. Bothered by his team's lethargy, Kapp worked diligently to motivate his teammates at every practice. His diligence paid off as he led his team to one of the most dramatic one-season turnarounds in college history. The Golden Bears finished with a 7-3 season, and won the Pacific Coast Conference title and a date to play Iowa in the 1958 Rose Bowl.

The powerful Iowa team wreaked havoc on Kapp and the Golden Bears. Ron Fimrite wrote about Kapp in *Sports Illustrated,* "I remember it was a beautiful day," says Kapp, "because I spent most of it lying on my back looking up at the blue sky." Ron Fimrite, in a *Sports Illustrated* article, quoted Willie Fleming, Iowa's star halfback, later Kapp's teammate on the British Columbia Lions in the CFL, remembering the game for something else. "In the game, I'm in the end zone after scoring and I see this mad man running straight at me and it's Kapp alright. He grabs me by the jersey and says, 'We're gonna kick your ass,' and I tell him, 'Hey, there's five minutes left and we're way ahead', but he said that with such conviction, he had me believing we were in trouble."

For his leadership, Kapp was selected to the All-American Team by the Football Writers and *Time* magazine. He was the team's Most Valuable Player, received the Andy Smith Trophy (awarded yearly to the varsity player with the most playing time), and was named to the All-Pacific Coast Conference Second Team.

Eager to play football at another level, Kapp anticipated NFL offers to roll in, but the 1959 NFL collegiate draft proved to be disappointing. The Washington Redskins chose him in the 17th round, but never contacted him. With no NFL offers, Kapp opted to play in the Canadian Football League (CFL). He signed a three-year contract with the struggling Calgary Stampeders. No sooner did Kapp arrive in Calgary than things began to happen. Kapp recalls, "The ink was hardly dry on the contract before I got into a battle that produced these scars on my face. It was a hot, humid night during the training season, and most of the Stampeders were sitting around drinking beer. We'd had the annual rookie show earlier and nobody felt like going to bed, and around one a.m., I walked into a room where the guys were talking. Without warning, a big linebacker broke a quart bottle across my jaw and raked it across my throat. We started to tangle, but there was so much blood spurting out around the room that the other guys jumped in and broke it up. At the hospital, they gave me 100 stitches and the doctors said the broken glass had missed the jugular by about half and inch. The reason for the attack was never fully explained, but order was restored and differences set aside."[1] The season opened auspiciously as the Stampeders beat Saskatchewan 28-8

and Kapp passed for two touchdowns. They beat Winnipeg and posted a 29-17 win over British Columbia to take over first place. After Labor Day, however, the Stampeders faltered and finished one game short of the playoffs.

The rookie Mexicano played brilliantly in his first pro season, rushing for 606 yards and completing 196 passes for 2,990 yards with a stellar 59.7 percent completion rate. He played even better the next season.

Calgary's 1960 season opener ended in a tie, but Kapp had an impressive game. For the rest of the season he continued to out-pass his opponents and the Stampeders played beyond expectations. A head coaching change early into the season did not hamper Kapp's plans to lead Calgary into the playoffs. Against British Columbia, and needing only a tie to qualify for a playoff berth, Kapp engineered a 22-10 Stampeders win. Calgary returned to the playoffs after three years only to have their momentum stopped by the Edmonton Eskimos, who went on to play in the Grey Cup championship.

At the start of the 1961 season, in what appeared to be a salary dispute, Kapp informed Calgary management he wanted to play out his option and go to another team, preferably the BC Lions. Through the exhibition season and the early part of the schedule, Kapp played unsigned while the situation worsened. The Calgary press and fans criticized Kapp's reluctance to reconsider staying in Calgary, but football is a business and Kapp knew he was a hot commodity. After successful negotiations between Calgary and British Columbia, Kapp got his wish. Canadian sportswriter Denny Boyd called it "the greatest trade in Canadian football history. . . . The BC Lions gave up three players and the Canadian rights to a fourth for Calgary quarterback Joe Kapp."

Although he did not want to see Kapp leave, Calgary general manager Jim Finks commented on the trade, "I think we got all the best of the deal. Otherwise, we wouldn't have made it." Finks also would later figure in Kapp's move from British Columbia to the Minnesota Vikings of the NFL.

For the BC Lions, the trade appeared to be a gamble because of Kapp's previous knee injury. Word around the league was that he was washed up. However, off-season surgery restored mobility to his knee, and in the 1962 campaign Kapp set a CFL season record of 3,279 passing yards. Highlighting the record-breaking season for Super Mex was his performance against the Edmonton Eskimos. Kapp threw for 433 yards and 6 touchdown passes to set a BC Lions career record for most touchdowns in a single game. It was a tremendous performance, which Kapp would supersede in the NFL.

Kapp led his team to the league title game, where the BC Lions beat the Hamilton Tiger-Cats 34-24 to capture the coveted Grey Cup.

To the victor belong the spoils, and Kapp was selected to CFL All-Pro teams in both 1963 and 1964. He garnered the Jeff Nicklin Memorial Trophy for being the Western Conference most valuable player and was runner-up for the Schenley Award as the most outstanding player in the CFL.

In 1966, Kapp played out his option with the BC Lions and requested waivers that would let him play in the NFL. Lions management refused to waive him and continued to negotiate a deal to keep him with the Lions. Behind the scenes, however, Kapp had initiated his own talks with representatives from the Houston Oilers. This sent shock waves through both leagues.

Kapp struck a deal with the Oilers, signing a two-year contract at $100,000 a season. The contract with the Oilers also stipulated that if Kapp could escape from the CFL a year early, in time for the 1967 campaign, he would be given a $10,000 bonus. To NFL commissioner Pete Rozelle, this looked like tampering which violated the NFL and CFL's long-standing agreement to respect each others' players' contracts. In one fell swoop, Rozelle voided the Houston-Kapp agreement to temporarily end the matter.

North of the border, the BC Lions realized they didn't want a reluctant player on their hands, so they sold their rights to Kapp to the Minnesota Vikings for $50,000. Once again it was Jim Finks, now with the Vikings, who handled the complicated negotiations. Finks apparently had to make a deal with Washington, who had drafted Kapp back in 1959, to release Kapp from the Redskins' reserve list. Finks signed Kapp for two years plus an option season at $100,000 per year. Kapp's desire to play in the NFL was now realized.

In his second season with Minnesota, as he had done previously at California, Calgary, and British Columbia, Kapp provided the inspiration that turned the Vikings from a last-place team into a winning one and to one that claimed the Central Division title in 1968. Once again, Kapp's leadership and intense drive infused the Vikings to new heights of NFL play.

In the 1969 season, Kapp led Minnesota to a 12-2 record, the NFL Championship, and the Vikings' first shot at the Super Bowl. Along the way to that glory, Kapp recorded one of the truly remarkable performances in pro football history. On September 28, 1969, in a game against the defending NFL champion Baltimore Colts, Kapp passed for 449 yards and 7 touchdowns to become just the fifth man in NFL history to throw 7 scoring passes in a single game, matching the accomplishments of pro football greats Sid Luckman, Adrian Burk, Y. A. Tittle, and George Blanda. The *New York Times* describes the game: "Joe Kapp shredded the Baltimore defense for a league tying seven passes and smashed the NFL champion Colts, 54-14. . . . Kapp's scoring strikes of 18, 83, 21, 13, 41, 1, and 15 yards went to six different receivers, with Gene Washington taking in the 83 and 41 yard bombs."

In Super Bowl IV, the Vikings met the Kansas City Chiefs and their Cinderella season ended less than successfully. Kapp recalls, "In my opinion, somebody should have seen our trouble developing early, right after the NFL championship game when we didn't party enough, didn't have enough fun. In the middle of our practice week in New Orleans, Gary Cuozzo and I had a little talk. 'Something's not right,' Gary said, 'we're flat and I don't know why.' "

Without knowing they were the prophets of doom, the Vikings turned in a poor performance in Super Bowl IV. Turnovers and mistakes rendered Minnesota's game plan ineffective. Toward the end of the contest, Kapp ran a bootleg into Chiefs Buck Buchanan and Aaron Brown; Brown clinched the tackle and pounded Kapp onto the turf shoulder to shoulder. This was the end of the game and a dream for Kapp. He not only left the game disappointed, but with a separated shoulder and torn ligaments as well. Lamenting the loss to Kansas City, Kapp praised the overall team effort by the Chiefs, and was positive about his team's performance. "Now my attitude is simply that we Vikings will have to go out there and do it all over again—the hard way; I don't mind."

As the 1970 season approached, further contract negotiations forced Kapp eastward to Boston. The Vikings offered Kapp $100,000 a year, but Kapp was asking for more money and Minnesota was not willing to offer more than 100 grand. The Vikings' front office gave Kapp an ultimatum to take the offer or leave it. Stunned and hurt by the Vikings' refusal to negotiate, Kapp responded, "I don't answer to ultimatums; I'm not some kind of slave."

In the meantime, Boston Patriots head coach Clive Rush called Kapp about the possibility of playing in Boston. Two days later, Kapp flew to Boston, signed a three-year, no cut, $200,000 contract, and became the Patriots' second-string quarterback. At the time the three-year deal represented the biggest contract in football. Rather than a standard contract, however, Kapp signed a "Memo of Agreement" covering the general terms that would eventually be included in the standard players' contract. This was an exception to the usual procedure but NFL commissioner Pete Rozelle allowed it to expedite the signing, although he expected Kapp to sign a formal player's contract as soon as possible.

It appears Kapp did not want to sign a standard player's contract because it was too rigid and binding. He was looking for some flexibility in negotiating, and the contract did not allow for that. Once the contract was signed by a player, he gave up his rights and became the property of the team and the NFL. If a player angered his coach/owner, they could throw him out of the NFL and pro football, but they would not release him from their contract without compensation, and they could prevent him from playing with another team. This was the business of football that Kapp was trying to change. Unfortunately, it cost him his career.

Kapp got a great deal when he didn't sign a standard contract. However, it angered the NFL, Pete Rozelle in particular, and he had to be made an example.

"Super Mex," as he was called, went to Boston and played in the fourth game of the 1970 season. The Patriot fans expected miracles from Kapp for two reasons: first, he was being handsomely paid to turn the pathetic Patriots into winners; and second, his reputation had preceded him, and they were curious to see if this acclaimed Mexicano was what they had heard him to be. Kapp did not falter, and began the task of uniting his new team. Unlike the previous challenges that Kapp undertook, this one would be the most difficult. In responding to a Boston critic, Kapp said, "Some wise guy predicted I'd be overwhelmed by all the culture in Boston, but what the hell! Anyway, the Mexicans had a culture in California 300 years before there was even a Boston."

The 1970 season was a dismal one for Kapp and the Patriots. The Patriots won a single game and had an unsettling coaching situation. Kapp completed less than 45 percent of his passes for only 3 touchdowns, recorded 17 interceptions, and was sacked 27 times. It was a season of disorganized football that everyone wanted to forget. The next season would be an improvement, but the business of the NFL would once again cloud over his career. Back to haunt him was the not-so-standard player's contract Kapp had signed, and he would not be allowed to play the 1971 season unless he signed a traditional player's agreement.

In a twist of irony, while the storm clouds rumbled, the Patriots selected as their first player in the 1971 collegiate draft, another Mexicano quarterback, Jim Plunkett from Stanford University.

Kapp refused to yield to the Rozelle mandate and was ordered out of training camp indefinitely. He already had a *pro tempore* agreement with the Patriots, which was a legal contract, and all Kapp wanted to do was negotiate the best deal possible.

Nowadays, this is known as free agency but in the 1960s the NFL front office dictated the rules of the business. Unsettled by the whole affair, Kapp complained that the NFL establishment had been after him for years. In the book *New England Patriots:*

Triumph and Tragedy, author Larry Fox writes, "Remember this was a Chicano from Santa Fe talking. He and his people have been dumped on for years. They were used to it, expected it. There was a meager Redskins offer in 1959, the fact that he never got a call to return to the states until 1967, the voiding of his deal with the Oilers. It all spelled conspiracy to Kapp. He was hurt and in his opinion, the Vikings never really tried to keep him."

Out of football and out of a job, Kapp and his attorneys filed an antitrust suit against the NFL and all 26 teams, contending that he was being deprived of his right to earn a living. The suit asked for 12 million dollars in damages but because it was antitrust litigation, Kapp stood to collect three times that amount. When the case finally went to trial in December 1974, Kapp appeared to win a major victory when U.S. District Court Judge William T. Sweigert in San Francisco issued a summary judgment which found the NFL standard player's contract and their reserve system "patently unreasonable and illegal." The court held that the player's draft and the so-called Rozelle rule requiring compensation from a club signing a free agent to a team losing him were "unreasonable restraints under the antitrust laws."

However, the question of whether or not Kapp had been damaged by all of this was left to the jury to decide. Two years later in the same San Francisco courtroom, a jury of two men and four women deliberated for almost six hours and ruled that $200,000 a year, which Kapp was being paid, was not exactly slave wages (although he thought he was being treated like one). He could very well have signed and played and still sued, as the judge had pointed out. In other words, Kapp was not entitled to any damages. With subsequent appeals all the way to the Supreme Court, it took eight years to resolve the case. During this time, Kapp kept busy supporting his family with his real estate ventures, and acting in and producing TV and feature films. Most notably, he costarred in the Burt Reynolds film *The Longest Yard.*

Kapp had pioneered free agency in the NFL long before its time, but it cost him his career. Years later in a television interview, this tough Chicano recalled those difficult times, "I learned a lot about business and the power of the NFL, but as you look back you see the growth of it too; we fought some issues—the draft, the Rozelle rule—in the court of law and won." Kapp had won his legal battles except the one for damages, but more costly, pro football lost one of its most charismatic and colorful players.

While Kapp's courtroom drama unfolded, his replacement at New England,[2] Jim Plunkett, experienced a great rookie year and went on to have several great seasons with the Oakland Raiders. But by the time the U.S. District Court dealt Kapp the proverbial kiss of death for damages, Plunkett was a struggling and almost forgotten quarterback with the San Francisco 49ers. How symbolic that two Mexicano NFL quarterbacks, both in San Francisco at the same time but for different reasons, were victims of the so-called business of pro football.

According to a saying, "old quarterbacks never die, they just drop back and pass away." In a slight departure from the saying, the resilient Kapp would step back onto the football field, this time as head football coach of his alma mater, the University of California at Berkeley.

However, the opportunity to coach collegiate football would stir controversy for the toughest Chicano around. At California, the football program was struggling to produce winning seasons. The team, then coached by Roger Theder, posted a 2-9 record for the 1981 season, the worst in nineteen years for the school. The last time the California Golden Bears had won a Pacific Coast Conference championship and played for the "Roses" was in 1958—Kapp's senior year at Berkeley. On December 5, 1981, University of California Athletic Director Dave Maggard hired Kapp for the head coach position. Sportswriter Ralph Wiley from the *Oakland Tribune* gave Kapp a vote of confidence when he wrote, "Joe Kapp can make a great fist. His chin is square. He could stare down an eclipse. He makes even old men want to charge. He'll look good on the sidelines and if there is a way to light emotion under the California Bears, whom he will serve as head coach, Joe Kapp will find it." Nonetheless, the prodigal son returned amidst some criticism from the coaching community about the selection. They clamored that coaching experience was at issue and Kapp had none, but Kapp overcame the criticism.

Challenged by it all, Kapp donned his old letterman's jacket from years past, walked onto the field, and began the task of motivating his players into believers and winners. Short of a miracle, the 1982 season was historic not only for the California Golden Bears, as they won 7 and lost 4, but also for Joe Kapp. He was honored by his peers and named the Pac-10 Coach of the Year. This silenced the critics temporarily.

Under Kapp's leadership, winning football games returned to the California program. His players displayed the competitive drive that had been missing from previous football campaigns.

In their annual Pac-10 contest against rival Stanford University, California led the game until early in the fourth quarter when future NFL great John Elway rallied Stanford to a 20-19 lead. With four seconds remaining to play, the Stanford fans and band members began to celebrate their victory by coming on to the playing field. On the sidelines Kapp recalled,

"We tried to talk about the fact the game wasn't over and that they [the fans] were partying a little too early." In the kickoff return that has now become legendary, the California Golden Bears utilized 5 laterals and a key block by a Stanford band member to score the winning touchdown and snatch the victory from Stanford. It was one of the most bizarre plays in the history of collegiate football and Kapp credited his players for their desire to win. The climax of the 1982 season was a thriller and only a Kapp-coached team could have accomplished such an unusual feat to win a football game. Final score: Cal 25, Stanford 20.

The following year (1983), Kapp and the Bears posted a 5-5-1 record, but the record did not reflect the quality of football they played throughout the year. They tied Arizona when the Wildcats were one of the best teams in the country and nearly defeated UCLA, which went on to win both the Pac-10 and Rose Bowl championships.

In 1984 the California defense played well while the offense sputtered when it came to scoring points. Turnovers and missed field goals were costly mistakes for the Bears, who ended the season with a 2-9 record. The next two seasons were less than successful as California managed to win only another six games. Kapp and the Bears had reached a plateau and at the end of the 1986 season he stepped aside for another coach, leaving behind a renewed Cal football program with future hopes of gridiron success.

Just prior to the start of the 1984 season, Kapp was selected for induction into the Canadian Football League Hall of Fame. At last Kapp was being honored, and not scrutinized, for the skills and leadership he had displayed in the CFL for eight difficult but successful years.

With his induction into the CFL Hall of Fame he became the first ever Mexicano athlete to receive such an honor in professional football.

Kapp's football story would have one more stop before he returned to family and friends on a full-time basis. On June 1990, his former team, the British Columbia Lions, whom he led to the Grey Cup Championship in 1964, hired him as their general manager. It had been some time since Kapp was in Canada and the warrior returned for a brief sojourn in the business of pro football. The highlight of his short tenure was the successful contract negotiation and signing of NFL veterans Doug Flutie and Mark Gastineau. Flamboyant as ever, Kapp's marketing of these two players into the CFL and the BC Lions was a tremendous financial success to the team.

In September of the same year, the toughest Chicano around cleaned out the old locker and took his last walk from the dressing room, the stadium, and the office. He looked back nostalgically remembering

Joe Kapp

Rushing

Year	Team	No.	Yds.	Avg.	Long	TDs
1959	Calgary Stampeders (CFL)	113	606	5.3	21	5
1960	Calgary Stampeders	61	374	6.1	27	1
1961	British Columbia Lions	37	127	3.4	20	0
1962	British Columbia Lions	51	183	3.5	19	3
1963	British Columbia Lions	75	438	5.8	39	5
1964	British Columbia Lions	95	370	3.9	18	6
1965	British Columbia Lions	64	345	5.3	21	4
1966	British Columbia Lions	83	341	4.1	16	2[3]
1967	Minnesota Vikings (NFL)	27	167	6.2	24	2
1968	Minnesota Vikings	50	269	5.7	27	3
1969	Minnesota Vikings	22	104	4.7	18	0[4]
		620	3,324	5.3	39	31

Passing

Year	Team	No.	Comp.	Yds.	Pct.	TDs	Int.
1959	Calgary Stampeders (CFL)	328	196	2,990	59.7	21	14
1960	Calgary Stampeders	337	182	3,060	54.0	18	17
1961	Calgary Stampeders	22	9	139	40.9	0	1
1961	British Columbia Lions	209	85	1,580	40.6	9	15
1962	British Columbia Lions	359	197	3,279	54.8	28	18
1963	British Columbia Lions	339	183	3,011	53.9	20	15
1964	British Columbia Lions	329	194	2,816	58.9	14	13
1965	British Columbia Lions	423	219	2,961	51.7	15	19
1966	British Columbia Lions	363	211	2,889	58.1	11	18[5]
1967	Minnesota Vikings (NFL)	214	102	1,386	47.7	8	17
1968	Minnesota Vikings	248	129	1,699	52.1	10	17
1969	Minnesota Vikings	237	120	1,726	50.6	19	13[6]
1970	Boston Patriots	219	98	1,104	44.7	3	17[7]
		3,627	1,925	28,640	53.0	272	194

Joe Kapp, continued

Scoring

Year	Team	TDs	FG	PATs	Total Points
1959	Calgary Stampeders (CFL)	5	—	1	31
1960	Calgary Stampeders	1	—	1	7
1962	British Columbia Lions	3	—	—	18
1963	British Columbia Lions	5	—	—	30
1964	British Columbia Lions	6	—	—	36
1965	British Columbia Lions	4	—	—	24
1966	British Columbia Lions	2	—	—	12[8]
1967	Minnesota Vikings (NFL)	2	—	—	12
1968	Minnesota Vikings	3	—	—	18[9]
		31	—	2	188

Punting

Year	Team	No.	Yds.	Long	Avg.
1959	Calgary Stampeders (CFL)	69	2,735	80	39.6[10]

Minnesota Vikings Individual Records

Joe Kapp listed #1	Touchdowns passing, game, 7 touchdowns vs. Baltimore Colts, September 28, 1969. Ties NFL Record.
#2	Passing yards, game, 449 yards vs. Baltimore Colts, September 28, 1969.
#2	Longest Pass, 85 yards to Gene Washington vs. St. Louis Cardinals, October 8, 1967.[11]

NFL All-Time Records

Joe Kapp tied for #1 with 4 others	Most touchdown passes, Game 7, Minnesota Vikings vs. Baltimore Colts, September 28, 1969.[12]

NFL Outstanding Performers—400 Yards Passing in a Game

Joe Kapp	September 28, 1969 vs. Baltimore Colts, Passed for 449 yards and 7 touchdowns.[13]

Notes
1 Joe Kapp with Jack Olsen, "A Man of Machismo," *Sports Illustrated,* July 20, 1970.
2 The name change from Boston to New England Patriots can be attributed to a move from Boston to a new stadium in Foxboro, Massachusetts. The team previously played their games at Boston University, Harvard Stadium, or Fenway Park. On March 22, 1971, the team was renamed the New England Patriots and began that season in their own Schaefer Stadium.
3 Canadian Football League, Individual Statistical Record for Joe Kapp.
4 *Minnesota Vikings 1970 Fact Book,* 21.
5 Canadian Football League, Individual Statistical Record for Joe Kapp.
6 *Minnesota Vikings 1970 Fact Book,* 21.
7 *New England Patriots 1983 Fact Book,* 129.
8 Canadian Football League, Individual Statistical Record for Joe Kapp.
9 *Minnesota Vikings 1970 Fact Book,* 21.
10 Canadian Football League, Individual Statistical Record for Joe Kapp.
11 *Minnesota Vikings 1983 Fact Book,* 80.
12 *Official 1981 National Football League Record Manual,* 231.
13 Ibid, 276.

his glory days, the challenges, the disappointments, the battles he had fought and survived.

Above all, he loved football and he would miss it. But Joe Kapp was always an optimist and continued to move forward. Today he is remarried with a brand new family and life has taken on new meaning. He says, "The best team I'm in right now is my family; it's amazing what you learn from a 6-year-old, a 4-year-old and a 1-year-old. There is too much good life and I am an optimist who looks for those good things . . . of course you look back with some regret, but you learn from the past and try to make new and better decisions from the battles you fought."

A true champion and crusader, Joe Kapp will long be remembered after others have been forgotten.

Committed to Excellence: Original Oakland Raiders QB Tom Flores

Photo by: Robert L. Smith—Buffalo Bills Team

Before there were football fields for Tom Flores there were lettuce fields, fruit orchards, and berry patches. His family migrated from crop to crop in California, but life was good for the skinny Mexicano from a little town outside Fresno called Sanger, California. Back then no one would have guessed Flores would someday be a player and coach of a team that has won professional football's most prestigious award—the world championship. Even so, the firmly planted Flores never forgot who he was and where he came from. I was fortunate enough to meet and speak with him in the most unlikely of places.

The place was a high school cafeteria and the function was a local sports banquet. The guest speaker was the former Los Angeles Raiders coach Tom Flores, who incredibly enough, took time from his busy schedule to attend the banquet and honor a group of local athletes in a small south Texas town. Not surprisingly, the majority of the citizens and parents, mostly Mexicano, showed up to see and listen to the NFL's only Mexicano head coach.

He addressed a packed house and talked about commitment to a sport and the work necessary to succeed. Needless to say, his message was both motivational and inspiring. Without a doubt, the banquet would be a memorable event for the people of Alice, Texas.

Thomas Raymond Flores was born in Fresno, California, March 21, 1937, son of farmworker Tom Cervantes Flores and Nellie Flores. He rose from the fields of the San Joaquin Valley to the fields of dreams in pro football. On his way, Flores attended nearby Sanger High School where he starred in football, basketball, and baseball. He attended Fresno City College where he quarterbacked the 1954 and 1955 teams. The team captain in 1955, Flores received Junior College All-American Honorable Mention.

After two years at Fresno City College, Flores planned to transfer to San Jose State University, but a scholarship offer from College of the Pacific changed his mind and Flores headed to Stockton instead of San Jose, California. He played two seasons (1956-57) for the Pacific Tigers and received national acclaim for his outstanding play in 1956.

Flores split the quarterback duties with another Mexicano, Jim Reynosa, yet his numbers ranked him as the sixth rated college passer in the nation and fourth in total offense. His best college game was against the school he chose not to attend—San Jose State University. Flores connected on 12 of 14 passes for 195 yards and 3 touchdowns in the game against SJSU. The Mexicano from Sanger had a great performance and he would remember it well. End of season kudos included All-American Honorable Mention and All-Pacific Coast Teams.

The next season for Flores was not as productive but just as important. In 1957 he reinjured his shoulder, resulting in painful and disappointing game performances. Wracked with injury, Flores and the Tigers survived on guts and determination. Once recovered from his injury, Flores was selected to play in the East-West Shrine All-Star game as he waited to hear news from the NFL draft. The only notification he received was a telegram from the Cleveland Browns saying they were going to draft him, but they never did. Angered by his exclusion from the 1958 draft, Flores looked elsewhere to play pro football. Upon a recommendation, he went to Canada to try out for the Calgary Stampeders, but the recurring shoulder injury sent him packing.

He returned to College of the Pacific to work on his Master's degree and, with a little luck, finally made it into pro football with a semipro team named the Bakersfield Spoilers.

In 1959 Flores auditioned for the Washington Redskins, but once again was hampered by the shoulder problem. After a new surgical procedure permanently corrected the problem in 1960, Flores signed with the Oakland Raiders of the newly formed American Football League (AFL) and began a program to rehabilitate his shoulder. In his initial season of play in the AFL, Flores beat out a dozen quarterbacks for the starting job with the Raiders. As the original Raiders quarterback, he led the entire league with a 54 percent pass completion ratio and fewest interceptions (12). The following season, Flores finished second in the AFL in passing behind George Blanda of the AFL Champion Houston Oilers.

Missing the entire 1962 season after a severe case of tuberculosis, Flores miraculously returned as Oakland's quarterback in 1963. The Raiders finished strong with a 10-4 record, only one win short of the championship. In the last game of the 1963 season, Flores had his greatest moment in the AFL against the Houston Oilers. It would be a shootout in which Flores would outgun Oilers quarterback George Blanda.

On a rainy December 22, 1963, at the old Frank Youell Field in Oakland, California, one of the most memorable games in AFL history took place. Flores established his field leadership and played a magnificent game, completing 17 of 29 passes for 407 yards and 6 touchdowns, 4 of which went to teammate Art Powell. His opponent, the legendary George Blanda, completed 20 of 32 passes and 5 touchdowns.

In their first possession of the game, the Raiders' Hoot Gibson took the Houston punt, sidestepped a few tacklers and broke into the clear, returning it 68 yards for a touchdown. However, the Oakland fans had hardly begun to celebrate when Houston's Blanda evened the score with a 4-yard touchdown pass to Charlie Hennigan. Later in the first period, Blanda and the Oilers set up a 2-yard scoring run by Dave Smith. As the second quarter began, Houston led 14-7. Houston added another score when Blanda completed a 12-yard touchdown pass to Willard Dewveall.

Flores responded to Blanda's last touchdown pass, completing three passes in a row, hitting Powell for 23 yards, Bo Roberson for 4, and then another to Powell for 13 yards. He finished the drive with a 7-yard touchdown pass to Ken Herock. The score read Houston 21, Oakland 14.

Flores was hot. The next time Oakland went on offense, he put the ball in the air again. First, he connected with Powell for 15. Then calling an audible at the line of scrimmage, Flores passed to halfback Clem Daniels in the middle of the field. Daniels caught the ball and sped the 56 yards toward the end zone to tie the game at 21.

The Raiders fans were ecstatic, but the elation did not last. Houston came swinging back. Blanda tossed a scoring strike to Smith for the 35 yards and a touchdown. Undaunted, the cool Flores noticed the one-on-one coverage that Houston was using on Powell. In the huddle, Flores called for the deep pass pattern. On the snap of the ball, Powell raced downfield. Flores pitched the ball 62 yards to his favorite receiver of the day, and at the Oilers' 31, Powell picked the ball from the sky and waltzed into the end zone for an 81-yard touchdown. With Flores's quick thinking and Powell's swift feet the Raiders tied the game at 28.

Incredibly, Houston struck back just as quickly. Blanda moved the Oiler offense to the Raider one where with 1:09 left before halftime, Oiler fullback Charlie Tolar hammered his way into the Oakland end zone for yet another score. With the Houston offense in high gear, Flores and head coach Al Davis decided to pull out all the stops and go for the points needed to pull even in this amazing aerial classic. Flores hustled the Raider offense onto the field and three passes later, the Raiders were at the Houston 20-yard line. With six seconds remaining, Flores found Powell in the left end zone. Oiler defender Freddy Glick was faked out of his shoes as Powell caught the pass for the score. The Oakland crowd of 17,400 fans went wild as the Raiders tied Houston 35-35 at halftime.

Early in the third period, the Raiders regained the lead for the second time after Flores completed a 44-yard pass to Powell, who caught his third straight touchdown pass.

Blanda was equal to the task. It took him four plays to get the Oiler offense to Oakland's 26. Blanda fired straight and connected with Dewveall for a 31-yard score to even up the see-saw battle at 42, with 7:04 left in the third period.

The aerial attacks continued throughout the third quarter until with 4:37 left in the game, and with the game tied 49-49, the Raiders' Mercer kicked a 39-yard field goal to seal the victory. The magic of Flores, Powell, and the Raider offense had given Oakland a three-point advantage in a game that is considered one of the legendary contests in the history of the AFL.

Tom Flores

Passing

Year	Team	No.	Comp.	Yds.	Pct.	TDs	Int.
1960	Oakland Raiders	252	136	1,738	.539	12	12
1961	Oakland Raiders	366	190	2,176	.519	15	19
1962	Oakland Raiders	(missed season due to illness)					
1963	Oakland Raiders	247	113	2,101	.457	20	13
1964	Oakland Raiders	200	98	1,389	.490	7	14
1965	Oakland Raiders	269	122	1,593	.453	14	11
1966	Oakland Raiders	306	151	2,638	.493	24	14[1]
1967	Buffalo Bills	64	22	260	.343	0	8
1968	Buffalo Bills	5	3	15	.600	0	1[2]
1969	Kansas City Chiefs	6	3	49	.500	0	0[3]
1970	Kansas City Chiefs	(No statistics for season)[4]					
		1,715	838	11,956	.488	92	92
1971	(Quarterback coach with Buffalo Bills)						
1972-78	(Receivers coach with the Oakland Raiders)						
1979-88	(Head coach of the Oakland/Los Angeles Raiders)[5]						

Rushing

Years	Team	No.	Yds.	Avg.	TDs	Long
1960-61,						
1963-66	Oakland Raiders	81	307	3.8	5	31[6]

Coaching Record

Year	Team	Won	Lost	Pct.
1979	Oakland Raiders	9	7	.563
1980	Oakland Raiders	11	5	.688
1981	Oakland Raiders	7	9	.438
1982	Los Angeles Raiders	8	1	.889
1983	Los Angeles Raiders	12	4	.750
1984	Los Angeles Raiders	11	5	.688
1985	Los Angeles Raiders	12	4	.750[7]
1986	Los Angeles Raiders	8	8	.500[8]
1987	Los Angeles Raiders	5	10	.333
1988	Los Angeles Raiders	8	3	.727
1992	Seattle Seahawks	2	14	.125
1993	Seattle Seahawks	6	10	.266
		99	80	.888

Tom Flores, continued

Postseason Record

Year	Team	Won	Lost	Tie	Pct.
1980	Oakland Raiders	4	0	0	1.000
1982	Los Angeles Raiders	1	1	0	.500
1983	Los Angeles Raiders	3	0	0	1.000
1984	Los Angeles Raiders	0	1	0	.000
1985	Los Angeles Raiders	0	1	0	.000[9]
		8	3	0	.727

Los Angeles Raiders Individual Records

Tom Flores Listed #3	Career, most passes attempted, 1,640 for the years 1960-66.
#3	Career, most touchdown passes, 92, for the years 1960-66.
#3	Career, most passes completed, 810, for the years 1960-66.
#3	Career, most yards gained passing, 11,635, for the years 1960-66.
#3	Career, most interceptions, 83, for the years 1960-66.[10]

NFL Outstanding Performers—400 yards Passing in a Game

Tom Flores	On December 22, 1963 vs. Houston Oilers, passed for 407 yards and 6 touchdowns.[11]

Notes

1 *The Los Angeles Raiders 1986 Media Guide,* 100.

2 Telephone call to the Buffalo Bills Public Relations Office for statistics on Tom Flores, Friday, May 22, 1987.

3 *Kansas City Chiefs 1970 Yearbook,* 21-22.

4 Telephone call to the Kansas City Chiefs Public Relations Office for statistics on Tom Flores, Friday, May 22, 1987.

5 *The Los Angeles Raiders 1986 Media Guide,* 8.

6 *Decades of Destiny, 1960-1984, The Historic First 25 Years,* (Los Angeles: CWC Sport Publications), 1985, 77.

7 *The Los Angeles Raiders 1986 Media Guide,* 8.

8 Telephone call to the Los Angeles Raiders Public Relations Office for statistics on Tom Flores, Thursday, July 9, 1987.

9 *The Los Angeles Raiders 1986 Media Guide,* 8.

10 Ibid, 96.

11 *Official 1981 National Football League Record Manual,* 277.

12 Dave Newhouse, "Flores takes Charge of Raiders His Way," *The Oakland Tribune,* Friday, February 9, 1979, 45.

The 1963 season marked a turning point for both Flores and the Oakland Raiders. As Flores fondly reminisced about that memorable afternoon in Oakland, he laughed heartily, and then said, "We had come from a 1-13 season the year before, and that was the year I hadn't played. I had the lung ailment, actually I had tuberculosis. So I missed the '62 season, and that was my first year back, and Al Davis's first year as head coach. And we were on a roll, we really were. It was the last game of the year. We were 9-4 going into the game, and actually had a chance to win the division if San Diego lost that day, but they didn't lose. We ended up with the second best record in the league. I remember that we were hot, and it was a nice feeling to come back like that."

In his autobiography, *Fire in the Iceman,* Flores also remembers what transpired after the close of the 1963 season that angered him somewhat:

I finished the season with 11 touchdowns in the last two weeks and I was third in the AFL in passing. I thought that was a pretty good comeback for me and the Raiders. I felt I should have gone to the AFL All-Star game that year. Cotton Davidson was the other quarterback, and he won some games for us and played quite a bit, but I finished the season as the clear-cut starter and was third in the league in passing. His stats were half of my numbers and he was eighth in the league in passing.

However, when the season was over our public relations manager Scotty Stirling called me in and said that San Diego Chargers' Sid Gillman, who was coaching the West All-Stars, wanted one of our quarterbacks and he got Cotton Davidson. I immediately thought that was wrong because there was no question I deserved to go.

The two were close friends and after being notified, Davidson called Flores. He told him that Flores deserved to go instead, but that he did not want to turn down a big opportunity like this. According to Flores, they even flipped a coin and he lost. This further infuriated Flores.

The Raiders finished second in the Western Division of the AFL and Flores continued on as the Raiders quarterback through the 1966 season, after which he was traded to the Buffalo Bills. In 1969, Flores played with the Kansas City Chiefs and earned his first of four Super Bowl rings. After one year with the Chiefs, Flores packed his bags and became an assistant coach with the Buffalo Bills, and later returned to the Raiders in that capacity.

On February 9, 1979, Tom Flores made sports history when he was named as the head coach of the Oakland Raiders, replacing John Madden. Flores was the first Mexican American ever to be named to such a position. In 1980 only his second year as head coach, Flores guided the Raiders to a World Championship with a 27-10 triumph over the Philadelphia Eagles in Super Bowl XV. This championship was particularly significant in Hispanic Sports history because another Mexicano, Jim Plunkett, also played in the championship. Plunkett, who had been released by the San Francisco 49ers and written off by other NFL teams was signed by the Raiders. Plunkett wanted to be traded but Coach Flores kept him on and an injury to the regular quarterback Dan Pastorini gave Plunkett the opportunity to step in and lead the Oakland offense. When the gridiron dust had settled, the Raiders were the World Champions and a revitalized Plunkett was the game's most valuable player.

Following the 1982 NFL campaign in which the Raiders boasted a season record of 8-1, Flores reached another milestone in his career. He was given the honor of the league's Coach of the Year.

The next season (1983), Coach Flores led the Raiders to another World Championship in Super Bowl XVIII and added another Super Bowl ring to his collection.

On September 16, 1984, the date which commemorates Mexico's independence, Flores won his fiftieth game as the Raiders' coach, defeating the Kansas City Chiefs 22-20. Flores coached a few more seasons and then called it quits.

After twenty-nine years of pro football experience and weary from the game, Flores announced his retirement on January 20, 1988. However, his retirement was short-lived: Flores returned to the game on February 22, 1989, as the president and general manager of the Seattle Seahawks, and also took over as head coach for the 1992 and 1993 seasons. The situation seemed hopeless but what better man to take on the job. There is a saying that fits the situation: "There are no great men, only ordinary men forced by circumstance to greatness. . . ." Tom Flores is such a man.

Willie Crafts
All-American

To former Texas A&I All-American Willie Crafts, football is a way of life. But in the beginning the young Mexicano from Brownsville, Texas faced problems and uncertainty. Growing up in the citrus-producing valley of Texas, the young Crafts quickly realized that life was going to be a constant struggle and like other Mexicanos of his era, that struggle would help shape his character.

In high school, Crafts discovered there was more to school than just academics and the impressionable young man began directing his energies to football. Crafts worked hard to be the best he could. His coaches applauded his success, while his high school team struggled through their schedule. Crafts played on, not realizing his football talent would take him beyond the high school gridiron.

When Crafts graduated from high school, opportunity presented itself when Texas A&I offered him a football scholarship. Crafts recalls that he never thought nor expected he would be recruited to play collegiate football. For the South Texas native son, his arrival at Texas A&I was less than smooth. In the first practices he injured his ankle and then bruised his thigh. Additionally, Crafts did not escape the ravages of the flu that had reached epidemic proportions in Kingsville, Texas. He remembers going to the university infirmary for treatment and being startled by all the other students there for the same reason. To Crafts, this was not a good and healthy beginning for a football career.

Discouraged and homesick, Crafts returned to Brownsville, only to realize he had made a mistake in leaving his football career and college education behind. Texas A&I head football coach Gil Steinke called him with a second opportunity, and in less time than it took him to leave, Crafts returned to the A&I campus. Once back on campus, Crafts's positive outlook gave him a renewed vigor, and led to his development as a skilled defensive lineman.

During Crafts's junior and senior years (1959-1960), the Texas A&I Javelinas won two consecutive Lone Star Conference Championships, compiling 20 wins, 2 losses, and 1 tie. In 1959 the Javelinas also won the NAIA National Title. They shut out Hillsdale University of Michigan 20-0 in the semifinals and moved on to the championship game where they faced, and defeated, Lenoir Rhyne of North Carolina 20-6. The Mexicano from Brownsville who had left and then returned to A&I was now a champion.

Throughout the two campaigns with the Javelinas, Crafts played great defense and was one of the key reasons for the 7 shutouts the Javelinas posted during those two years. For his accomplishments, he was twice named to the All-Lone Star Conference First Team and, in 1960, became an Associate Press (AP) Little All-American selection on defense. It had been a successful collegiate career in many respects. Crafts matured as an individual and became a superior athlete. He shared his success with those he knew and respected, including running back Sid Blanks of Del Rio, Texas. From their very first meeting the two became very good friends. Crafts remembers that "Sid Blanks was probably the first Black player at Texas A&I and this sometimes presented problems to some of the other players. Sid was a very talented athlete and the fact that he also spoke Spanish enabled us to communicate all the better. We practiced together, shared some good times, and to this day are still very good friends."

In 1961, the two amigos parted ways. Crafts became the fifteenth-round draft selection of the Denver Broncos of the American Football League (AFL), while his friend Blanks remained at Texas A&I to fulfill his destiny of greatness and await his turn to play pro football. Also in 1961, the Minnesota Vikings of the NFL contacted Crafts. However, as was the practice back then, no one personally notified him about going to Denver or Minnesota.

The Canadian Football League also beckoned and a representative from the Edmonton Eskimos convinced him to play in Canada. The $3,000 signing bonus and a $12,000-a-year salary contract was by far more than AFL/NFL teams had offered, so Crafts signed and journeyed to Edmonton, Canada. He arrived in June 1961 and remembers being in awe by the beauty of the Edmonton countryside. For the next two years it would be his home and where he started his professional football career.

At the Eskimos camp, Crafts the rookie practiced at the guard position on both offense and defense. He enjoyed the level of play and impressed the Edmonton coaches with his performances in preseason games. When the regular season began, Crafts primarily played on defense. The Eskimos experienced an outstanding season. They won 10, lost 5, and marched all the way to the playoffs where they lost to the Calgary Stampeders. During the two-game playoff series, Crafts sustained a groin injury and could not play. The following year, the Eskimos finished in 5th place in the Western Conference, but for Crafts the season was marred by tragedy. His father passed away and it proved to be a difficult time for the young Mexicano lineman. At season's end, he returned to south Texas, concluding a two-year career with Edmonton.

With football still a big part of his life, Crafts traveled to Denver for the tryout he had missed a couple of years earlier. Crafts made the team and played through the 1963 exhibition season at offensive guard. On the final cut prior to the start of the regular campaign, Crafts remembers, "They had one too many guards in camp. I was listed fourth on the chart and

they were going to keep three. The guard they kept was from Colorado and he was a little larger and quicker than I."

Somewhat disappointed but not discouraged at not making the team, Crafts did the next best thing, and began to coach the game he loved so much. For the next six years, he coached high school football in south Texas and eventually returned to his college alma mater in Kingsville as an assistant coach in 1970. When Coach Crafts returned to the Texas A&I Javelinas, they were having a banner year. They once again won the NAIA National Football Championship and Crafts garnered his second national title, this time as a coach.

While coaching at A&I, the highly motivated Crafts also played minor league pro football in nearby San Antonio, Texas. Juggling his summer schedule, he found time to practice and play for the San Antonio Toros of the TransAmerica and the Southwestern Football leagues. However, after two all-star years with the Toros, Crafts curtailed his participation in favor of coaching.

He remained at A&I for a total of four years and for personal reasons, returned to coach at the high school level. He coached the Port Isabel High School team to the district championships.

Since then, the Crafts coaching train has made many stops throughout Texas, where he saw football take on special meaning to many young athletes. Nowadays, Coach Crafts is usually found on the football field at South San Antonio High School in San Antonio, Texas. The glint of gold you see when he raises his hand to point or give instructions comes from the NAIA championship ring he wears. This ring is a reminder of his accomplishments in his younger days and is also the reason that he coaches football. What drives him to coach is his character and the desire to help others to excel. According to Crafts, nothing is ever easy. Reflecting on his career, he said, "It was a struggle to survive in football because I did not have the size, but I did it for pride, fun, and recognition."

In Crafts's case, football did not build his character; instead it revealed it to all those who were ever associated with him. He overcame uncertainty through hard work and succeeded in the biggest game of all—life.

Tough Henry Rivera

When you first look at Latino Henry Rivera, you see a man of average build and height, who goes about his own affairs. He doesn't bother anyone and if you did not know him personally, you would never guess he was once a bone-crushing defensive back in college and pro football. But the toughness he developed, which at first is deceiving, he learned at a young age in the barrios of Los Angeles.

Rivera was born in the City of Angels (birthdate unknown) and like other kids before and after him, lived the experience of big-city life, poverty, and minorities seeking to better their lot.

In the barrios around Belmont High School, Rivera came into his own and earned his stripes in athletics. There the little big man showed early promise in sports and won varsity letters in football and track.

Upon graduation from high school after a very successful prep football career, Rivera took his talents to junior college powerhouse Los Angeles City College. While at LACC, Rivera honed his football skills and became an excellent tackler. His aggressive defensive plays became his trademark and he wreaked havoc throughout the Metropolitan Conference. For his hard-hitting style of play, Señor Rivera was twice

named to the All-Metropolitan Conference teams (1958 and 1959).

Recruited by various local and out-of-state universities, Rivera chose to transfer to Oregon State University to play in the Pacific Coast Conference. When he arrived there he was already "known as extremely tough and a good enough athlete to play anywhere," according to the university's media guide. Rivera specialized in defense, although he did play offense occasionally as a fullback, flankerback, and end.

Rivera's senior year at Oregon State (1961) was said to be one of the best teams in the school's history. In anticipation of a great year, the *1961 Oregon State University Media Guide* described it this way: "This could be one of Oregon State's best teams . . . Quarterback Terry Baker won't be alone; he'll have Don Kosso at left half and hustling Hank Rivera at wingback. They can both scoot and are senior veterans."

As the media guide predicted, the Oregon State Beavers did experience a successful season and earned Rivera a few accolades for his fine play. He was given an Honorable Mention on the All-Coast Football Team by UPI sportswriters. He concluded his OSU career with 516 yards total offense and intercepted 6 passes on defense. His versatility as a blocker, runner, receiver,

Henry Rivera

Kickoff Returns

Year	Team	No.	Yds.	Avg.	Lg.	TDs
1963	Buffalo Bills	1	20	20.0	20	0

Source: David S. Neft, Richard M. Cohen, and Rick Korch, *The Football Encyclopedia: The Complete, Year-by-Year History of Professional Football from 1892 to the Present* (New York: St. Martin's Press, 1994), 373.

and defensive ace were invaluable to Oregon State's gridiron efforts.

In postseason play, Rivera played in the East-West Shrine All-Star game in San Francisco, the Senior Bowl game in Mobile, the Chicago College All-Star game, and the All-American Bowl game in Buffalo, New York.

Of his all-star appearances, his best postseason performance was in the East-West Shrine game. Rivera played defensive safety for the West team and put on a defensive performance unequaled in the history of the Shriner's game. His two pass interceptions and bone-crushing tackles were chronicled in the newspaper accounts of the game.

Curley Grieve of the *San Francisco Examiner* writes, "60,000 shivering Kezar Stadium fans saw an inspired West squad thunder to a 21-8 upset triumph over the East in the thirty-seventh edition of the Shrine classic. Rivera played superb defense, intercepting two passes; one off Roman Gabriel, the other off Ron Miller." He goes on to describe Rivera as "the tough as nails safety man from Oregon State. . . . Rivera was the best man on the field in the defensive secondary. He did a wonderful job on passes and tackling. It was Rivera who jarred the teeth loose for Bob Ferguson in the fourth period and forced the great Ohio Stater to go to the bench for repairs." Other

notable players in that game included Roman Gabriel, Ernie Davis, Bob Ferguson, Joe Kuharich, Ron Bull, John Hadl, and Merlin Olsen.

In pro football's annual college lottery, two teams selected Rivera in 1962. He was picked in the fifth round by the Cleveland Browns of the NFL and was a tenth-round choice of the Oakland Raiders of the AFL.

Rivera chose the AFL and signed to play pro football with the Oakland Raiders. In preseason play, Rivera played defensive back in games against the Dallas Texans, Boston Patriots, and San Diego Chargers. Unfortunately, in the final preseason game against the Denver Broncos, Rivera injured his shoulder and had to undergo surgery. He missed the first ten games of the regular season, but recovered and played against the last four opponents. Unable to break into the win column, the Raiders, with Rivera back in uniform, achieved their lone victory in the final game, downing the Boston Patriots 20-0.

Other Mexicanos on the Raiders team were quarterback Chon Gallegos, who had a good passing game versus San Diego, defensive back Vernon Valdez, who intercepted 4 passes that season, and regular quarterback Tom Flores, who was on the roster but was out for the year with a lung ailment.

In 1963 Rivera departed the Raiders and signed as a free agent with the Buffalo Bills. He went from sun to snow and it proved to be a good move. After a slow start, the Bills came on strong and finished in a tie with the Boston Patriots for the Eastern Division Championship. At the end of the 1963 season, the tough Hank Rivera concluded a short but notable career in professional football.

Chon Gallegos

When the young AFL Oakland Raiders came unglued in a 1962 game against the San Diego Chargers, coach Marty Feldman sent in 5'9" quarterback Chon Gallegos to put a stop to the slaughter and keep the score respectable. In his very first pro football appearance, Gallegos put a halt to the Chargers' rampage and in six minutes' playing time threw two touchdown passes and a two-point conversion, and controlled the football.

It was indeed a remarkable performance by rookie Gallegos, who until that game was back-up quarterback to the errant Cotton Davidson. The regular Raiders quarterback was Tom Flores, who was out for the season with tuberculosis.

In reserve, Gallegos proved he could perform under pressure and in actuality saved the Raiders from being routed by the Chargers. Where did this young Mexicano athlete come from?

Chon Gallegos was born on September 28, 1939, in Gallup, New Mexico. In 1941, just before the outbreak of World War II, the Gallegos family moved west to the rich agricultural community of San Jose, California. In San Jose, Gallegos attended James Lick High School, where he participated in football and baseball. Upon graduation from high school, Gallegos attended San Jose City College, where he developed into an outstanding collegiate football player.

In 1959 he transferred to nearby San Jose State University on a football scholarship and embarked on an illustrious career. As a member of the 1959-61

San Jose State Spartans football team, Gallegos was an outstanding quarterback and put himself in the university's all-time career statistics record book. He completed 160 passes of 280 attempts for 1,939 yards, 17 touchdowns, and a remarkable 57.1 percent completion average. This accomplishment placed him ninth on the Spartans' all-time career pass completions.

The 1961 season was Gallegos's best year at San Jose State. He and the Spartans won 7 games, including victories over Washington State, Arizona State, and Stanford. That year, Gallegos led the nation in passing, was named to the UPI All-Coast Team, and received the Glenn "Pop" Warner Award for the most valuable senior football player on the West Coast. He won the award in a closed balloting poll of 400 sportswriters, sportcasters, and coaches. He nosed out Bobby Smith of UCLA by a few votes. (Past winners of the award include Eddie LeBaron, Ollie Matson, Bob Garrett, George Shaw, Bob Davenport, Jon Arnett, Joe Kapp, Chris Burford, and Bill Kilmer.)

According to Gallegos's collegiate coach Bob Titchenal, Chon was overlooked in the pro drafts because the pros felt he was too small (5'9", 170 lbs.). It seems the pros were wrong because Eddie LeBaron (5'7", 170 lbs.), who graduated from the University of the Pacific, had a great career in the pro ranks. "Additionally, Chon wants to go into professional football and I think he'll stick once some team gets a good look at him," said Coach Titchenal.

Chon Gallegos

Passing

Year	Team	No.	Comp.	Yds.	Pct.	TDs	Int.
1962	Oakland Raiders	35	18	298	.514	2	3[1]

Rushing

Year	Team	No.	Yds.	Avg.	TDs
1962	Oakland Raiders	3	25	8.3	0[2]

Notes

1 Oakland Raiders Press Information on Chon Gallegos, 1962.

2 David S. Neft, Richard M. Cohen, and Rick Korch, *The Football Encyclopedia: The Complete, Year-by-Year History of Professional Football from 1892 to the Present* (New York: St. Martin's Press, 1994), 361.

Although not drafting him, the Oakland Raiders asked Gallegos to come to their training camp for a tryout. He made the team and signed as a free agent with the Raiders. Initially, he played on the reserve squad and was then activated as a back-up quarterback to Cotton Davidson.

On September 30, 1962, Gallegos played his first professional football game against the San Diego Chargers at Frank Youell Field. Scotty Stirling, sportswriter for the *Oakland Tribune* describes his effort: "He entered the game late in the fourth quarter and the San Jose State kid passed beautifully to Dobie Craig for a 35-yard touchdown and hit Bo Roberson with a safety valve pass, who then made an incredible touchdown run, scampering and dancing past bewildered Charger defenders for 30 yards." Additionally, Gallegos completed a pass to John White for a two-point conversion.

Although the Raiders lost a 42-33 decision, Gallegos kept it close. His fourth quarter statistics show 4 pass completions of 7 attempts for 89 yards and 2 touchdowns. He also ran with the pigskin twice for 29 yards. Stirling goes to say, "The individual brilliance of Bo Roberson, Fred Williamson, and rookie quarterback Chon Gallegos, kept the score respectable." For his efforts in the Chargers game, Gallegos received a team award. Later in the season, Gallegos played in the game against the Denver Broncos and finished out the 1962 season.

The following year (1963), the Raiders placed Gallegos on waivers to conclude his professional football career. Decisively, Gallegos returned to San Jose State University to finish his education. In the spring of 1964 he graduated with a degree in physical education and pursued a teaching career.

Interestingly, Gallegos kept his connection with the NFL by coaching the young Jim Plunkett at James Lick High School in San Jose, California. In his book, *The Jim Plunkett Story*, Heisman Trophy Winner Plunkett mentions "having learned to throw a soft catchable ball from Chon." Presently, Chon is a teacher/coach at Santa Teresa High School in San Jose, California.

Jack Rabbit Joe Hernández

Pro football great Vince Lombardi is known for saying, "Winning is not a sometime thing. You don't win or do things right once in awhile, you do them right all the time." Although Lombardi might not have heard or known José M. Hernández, the essence of the quotation is very true of this California-born athlete. Born on February 2, 1940, in Bakersfield, California, Hernández began his football career and winning ways at an early age. At age ten he played football on the St. Francis Catholic School team that won the championship in 1950 and since then church-sponsored football has never been the same.

During high school, particularly in his senior year, Hernández was tagged with the nickname "Jack Rabbit Joe," and went on to rewrite football history at Garces Parochial High School. He compiled a phenomenal 3,366 yards total offense, averaging 259 yards a game and scoring 32 touchdowns in 13 games. As the 1957 school yearbook, *The Garcian,* stated, "Never in its ten-year history has Garces High School been gifted with such a talented athlete, and never has any football player given this school such great recognition through his gridiron exploits as Joe Hernández."

After high school, Hernández left California to attend New Mexico Military Institute in Roswell, New Mexico. As a freshman and in his only year at the Military Institute, Hernández made the transition from a prep football star to a stellar collegiate football player.

In 1958 the New Mexico Military Institute Broncos won the National Junior College Football Championship. They had an undefeated season in capturing the national title. The Broncos had four junior college All-Americans, including fullback Hernández. He led the nation in rushing yardage—1,848 yards on 191 carries, establishing an NCAA record. He also scored 23 touchdowns for a season total of 138 points, a feat unmatched in junior collegiate football. At the conclusion of that glorious season and his freshman year, Hernández returned to Bakersfield to play before the hometown crowds at Bakersfield College.

Not at all diminished by his trip to Bakersfield from Roswell, New Mexico, Hernández entered the Bakersfield College campus, donned a Renegades football uniform, and once again displayed his magic. In 1959 Hernández and the Bakersfield Renegades went undefeated as they shut out Stockton, Compton, Long Beach, and Valley College. They outscored Harbor College 27-12, East Los Angeles 57-6, San Diego 26-6, Santa Monica 55-8, and El Camino College 35-14. Hernández had his finest game of the season against the El Camino Warriors. He demolished the Warriors, scoring 4 touchdowns in the 35-14 victory. *The Bakersfield Californian* newspaper describes the Hernández touchdowns: "The two first-half touchdowns came just over a minute apart. Bakersfield scored first on a 36-yard pass from Ezell to Hernández . . . With three minutes remaining before the half, Hernández took a pitch-out from quarterback Ezell, turned the corner, sprinted down the sideline, stepped over a would-be tackler and went in on a 29-yard run."

"The Warrior defense just couldn't cover the speedy Hernández. On the third play after the second half kickoff, he sped down field and had a clear three-yard lead on the defense, Ezell hit him on the three yard line, the play covering 41 yards and a score . . . From the Warrior 43-yard line, Ezell sizzled a strike to Hernández cutting over the middle on the 19, Joe had them beat and the El Camino defenders didn't give chase." With this game Hernández captured the team scoring title. He completed the season by scoring a total of 11 touchdowns for 66 points.

Because Bakersfield was the Metropolitan Conference Champion in 1959, they earned the right to play in the Annual Junior Rose Bowl Classic in Pasadena, California, against the Del Mar Junior College Vikings from Corpus Christi, Texas, representing the Texas Junior College Football Federation. The game was an exciting one and it was the big plays by the Bakersfield Renegades that beat the Del Mar Vikings 36-14.

Pregame Junior Rose Bowl publicity reported that "much of Bakersfield's hope for victory will rest on the performance of a slim, will-o'-the-wisp halfback. . . . He's Jack Rabbit Joe Hernández, a hometown product who returned to Bakersfield College this year after a stint at New Mexico Military Institute at Roswell, New Mexico."

Unfortunately, Hernández was held scoreless in the game. Defensively, Hernández intercepted a Del Mar pass to end a fourth quarter threat and ensure the Renegades' victory. It was another great season for Hernández, who added another championship and an NCAA All-American Honorable Mention to his accolades.

The following year (1960) Hernández continued his gridiron exploits. He transferred to the University of Arizona, which had offered him a full athletic scholarship, and the Border Conference, where he played two outstanding seasons.

The scholarship benefited the University of Arizona in football and track. The following are narratives of Hernández's football endeavors for the 1960 season: as the *Bakersfield Californian* described a game against the University of Tulsa, "Hernández caught a Wilson pass for a 52-yard goal by grabbing the pass, which had bounced off end John Renner, and running 19 yards to the Tulsa 21." Unfortunately, Arizona lost

the contest 17-16. About the game against New Mexico the *Arizona Daily Star* wrote, "Hernández took a Wilson pass for a 42-yard touchdown with 1:41 left in the first half. . . then Hernández caught a 14-yarder from Wilson 22 seconds later for another touchdown . . . and finally, Hernández made a great leaping catch of another Wilson pass for his third touchdown of the game. It was a 24-yard play." Final score: Arizona 26, New Mexico 14.

In the game against West Texas State, "Hernández took a 20-yard pass from Wilson for the game-tying touchdown . . . Later he returned a kickoff for 42 yards to set up the winning score." Arizona 21, West Texas 14.

Against the University of Idaho, "Joe returned a kickoff for 58 yards and scored on a 53-yard run that couldn't even be stopped by an official who got in the way of the Arizona halfback . . . Last, Joe Hernández scored on a 4-yard sprint around left end." Arizona 32, Idaho 3.

In the game against Texas Western, "Hernández sped 65 yards on a draw play to score. . . . He returned a kickoff 43 yards and took a 25-yard pass to the 3 yard line to set up the Arizona third touchdown of the game." Arizona 28, Texas Western 14.

At Kansas State, Arizona's speedy halfbacks Bobby Thompson and Hernández had a great day. . . . For the second time this year Hernández scored 3 times, twice on runs of 8 and 4 yards and once on a 21-yard pass from quarterback Eddie Wilson. Arizona 35, Kansas State 16.

In the 1960 season finale, Hernández caught a 29-yard touchdown pass from Wilson, as Arizona beat Arizona State 35-7. Hernández concluded the season as the Arizona Wildcats' leading scorer with 76 total points. He was their leading receiver, punt returner, and kickoff returner, and was second in rushing yardage with 419 yards. He was also selected to the All-Border Conference Second Team for 1960. In NCAA statistics, Hernández was ranked 10th in scoring on the national level.

In 1961, Hernández's senior year at the University of Arizona, the Wildcats won 8 games, tied 1, and lost only to West Texas State 27-23. They beat Colorado State, Hardin Simmons, Oregon, New Mexico, Wyoming, Idaho, Texas Western, and Arizona State. The tie game was against the University of Nebraska.

However, it was the University of New Mexico game, described by Carlos Salazar, that was Hernández's finest: "Jack Rabbit Joe Hernández, who scored three times a year ago when Arizona bumped the Lobos here, 26-14, duplicated the feat at Tucson. Hernández's circus catches kept alive the few goalward thrusts that Wilson directed. Joe's three touchdowns, however, came via the overland route. Arizona's miracle finish culminated when quarterback Eddie Wilson speared a pass to Bobby

Lee Thompson with the 2-pointer that turned defeat into victory." The score: Arizona 22, New Mexico 21.

Hernández finished the 1961 season in grand fashion. He was 14th in the nation in pass receptions, with 27 receptions for 423 yards. Also, he finished 19th in the nation in kickoff returns, returning 12 for 286 yards. In all, Hernández finished the season with 1,007 total offensive yards for the Arizona Wildcats.

In postseason play, Hernández played starting left end on the East Team in the U.S. Bowl in Washington, DC, on January 7, 1962. Later, on June 29, 1962, Hernández also participated in the All-American Bowl game played in Buffalo, New York.

Professionally, Hernández was a second-round draft choice of the NFL's Washington Redskins. While in the AFL draft, he was the fifth-round pick of the Oakland Raiders. Hernández also received an offer from and opted to play pro football with the Toronto Argonauts of the Canadian Football League (CFL). The *Bakersfield Californian* relates the following: "The Washington Redskins have admitted they have little hope of signing their number two draft choice. Indications are the Arizona star is leaning toward the Canadian Football League. It was understood that Canada's offer of $5,000 bonus for signing and a $15,000 salary tops that of Washington by several thousand dollars."

In his only year with the Toronto Argonauts, Hernández led the team in kickoff return yardage. Against the Montreal Alouettes, the game played on October 14, 1962, "Jack Rabbit" Hernández returned kickoffs for a total of 156 yards to rank fourth in Toronto career statistics for a single game. Also, in that game he ran back a kickoff for 75 yards to rank fourth in Toronto career statistics for a single play.

As his hometown newspaper reported, the following year (1963), Toronto traded Hernández to the Edmonton Eskimos. "The Toronto Argonauts parted with five players in the deal that brought them quarterback Jackie Parker from the Edmonton Eskimos. To get the perennial all-star quarterback, the Eastern Football Conference club gave up Jon Rochner, Mike Wicklum, Joe Hernández, Zeke Smith, and one other player. Hernández, a graduate of the University of Arizona, joined Toronto at the start of the 1962 campaign."

With the Eskimos, Hernández experienced a good season. He returned 40 punts for 261 yards and 26 kickoffs for 650 yards—an average of 25 yards per kickoff return. He also rushed 73 times for 358 yards, averaging 4.9 yards per carry, and caught 27 passes for 400 yards and 5 touchdowns.

The following year, Hernández returned to the NFL to play for the Washington Redskins, who had drafted him a couple of years earlier.

Hernández's hometown newspaper had this to say: "Coach Bill McPack of the Washington Redskins

expressed complete satisfaction over the acquisitions . . . He was impressed with the speed of pass receivers Angelo Coia and Joe Hernández, who spent last season playing in Canada."

Hernández started two games for the Redskins and saw considerable action on special teams. However, Hernández recalls great frustration at Washington: "Considered too small by most NFL coaches, Hernández was rankled endlessly and always considered he got a bad deal with Washington." He wanted to play but the Redskins didn't give him the opportunity. At the end of the 1964 season, his NFL statistics included 1 pass reception, 5 punt returns, and 1 kickoff return.

In 1965 Hernández was cut by the Redskins and signed by the new Atlanta Falcons of the NFL. He went to their training camp and received some encouragement from an Atlanta newspaper: "It comes as no small surprise to Atlanta pro football fans that Joe Hernández, free agent, has established himself as No. 1 flanker of the Falcons." However, soon after Hernández arrived, the Redskins urged Hernández to go with the Annapolis Sailors of the North American Football League (NAFL) to get into shape. Once again, he was cut from the team for reasons that disturbed him. He says, "I was convinced I could play in the NFL as a wide receiver, but felt the coaches were unduly prejudiced against my size." He played with the Annapolis Sailors in 1965, and ran wild in NAFL play. His efforts were summed up in the *Mobile Register* as follows: "What is impressive about Joe is not only his speed and desire to excel but his versatility. Hernández has scored seven touchdowns in the same number of games, but he's turned the trick via end runs, punt returns, and pass catching. . . . Against the visiting Mobile, Alabama, Tarpons last October 16, 1965, the Arizona speedster did almost a one-man wrecking job on Coach Ed Backers' crew from Alabama. Hernández fooled Tarpon defenders twice on long pass patterns for touchdowns and scored a third time in returning a pitchback of a punt return from a Sailor teammate."

In postseason accolades, Hernández was among the seven Annapolis players selected for the first North American Football League All-Star Team. Additionally, Joe was selected as NAFL's number one flanker.

In 1966, Hernández rejoined the Atlanta Falcons and played one game with the Falcons, against the Los Angeles Rams before he was released. Again, coaches' prejudice was an obstacle for Joe, who returned to Canada. When I spoke to Hernández about the problems he had with the Atlanta coaches, he said it was his size that they did not like for the offense they had. In other words, he was not big enough physically for them and thus played very little. He rejoined the

Joe Hernández

Rushing

Year	Team	No.	Yds.	Avg.	Long	TDs
1962	Toronto Argonauts (CFL)	33	146	4.4	19	0
1963	Edmonton Eskimos	79	372	4.7	23	0
1966	Edmonton Eskimos	9	29	3.2	16	0
1967	Edmonton Eskimos	2	5	2.5	7	0[1]
		123	552	4.48	23	0

Passing

Year	Team	No.	Comp.	Yds.	Pct.	Long	TDs
1963	Edmonton Eskimos (CFL)	3	2	43	.666	25	0
1966	Edmonton Eskimos	1	0	00	.000	00	0[2]
		4	2	43	.500	25	0

Pass Receptions

Year	Team	No.	Yds.	Avg.	Long	TDs
1962	Toronto Argonauts (CFL)	24	328	13.6	75	3
1963	Edmonton Eskimos	30	449	14.9	57	4[3]
1964	Washington Redskins	1	18	100.	18	0[4]
1966	Edmonton Eskimos	9	223	24.7	43	1
1967	Edmonton Eskimos	4	59	14.7	21	0
1968	Edmonton Eskimos	2	20	10.0	12	0[5]
		70	1,097	15.6	75	8

Punt Returns

Year	Team	No.	Yds.	Avg.	Long	TDs
1962	Toronto Argonauts	20	125	6.25	21	0
1963	Edmonton Eskimos	40	261	6.5	28	0[6]
1964	Washington Redskins	5	49	9.8	—	0[7]
1967	Edmonton Eskimos	49	222	4.5	23	0
1968	Edmonton Eskimos	2	6	3.0	6	0
1969	Edmonton Eskimos	2	3	1.5	3	0
1970	Edmonton Eskimos	1	0	0.0	0	0[8]
		114	666	5.84	28	0

Joe Hernández, continued

Kickoff Returns

Year	Team	No.	Yds.	Avg.	Long	TDs
1962	Toronto Argonauts (CFL)	21	594	28.2	75	0
1963	Edmonton Eskimos	26	650	25.0	46	0[9]
1964	Washington Redskins	1	19	19.0	—	0[10]
1966	Edmonton Eskimos	4	117	29.2	38	0
1967	Edmonton Eskimos	20	485	24.2	39	0
1968	Edmonton Eskimos	3	65	21.6	31	0
1970	Edmonton Eskimos	23	636	27.6	45	0[11]
		98	2,566	26.1	75	0

Scoring

Year	Team	TDs	FG	PATs	Total Pts.
1962	Toronto Argonauts	3	0	0	18
1963	Edmonton Eskimos	4	0	0	24
1965	Annapolis Sailors (NAFL)	7	0	0	42[12]
1966	Edmonton Eskimos	2	0	0	12
1970	Edmonton Eskimos	2	0	0	12[13]
		18	0	0	108

Interceptions

Year	Team	No.	Yds.	Long	TDs
1967	Edmonton Eskimos	6	28	20	0
1968	Edmonton Eskimos	2	23	23	0
1969	Edmonton Eskimos	4	37	12	0
1970	Edmonton Eskimos	4	149	6	2[14]
		16	237	23	2

(Recovered own punt for touchdown in 1966)[15]

Canadian Football League All-Time Leaders in Kickoff Return Yardage

Joe Hernández
Listed #16
Returned 97 kickoffs for 2,547, average 26.3 per return, longest 75 yards vs. Montreal Alouettes, October 14, 1962.[16]

Notes

1 Canadian Football League, Individual Statistics for Joe Hernández.

2 Ibid.

3 Ibid.

4 Telephone call to Washington Redskins Public Relations Office for statistics on Joe Hernández, Monday, May 11, 1987.

5 Canadian Football League, Individual Statistics for Joe Hernández.

6 Ibid.

7 Telephone call to Washington Redskins Public Relations Office for statistics on Joe Hernández, Monday, May 11, 1987.

8 Canadian Football League, Individual Statistics for Joe Hernández.

9 Ibid.

10 Telephone call to Washington Redskins Public Relations Office for statistics on Joe Hernández, Monday, May 11, 1987.

11 Canadian Football League, Individual Statistics for Joe Hernández.

12 "Tarpon-Sailors Eye Attendance Record Wednesday," *Mobile Press,* Monday, November 22, 1965, 1-D.

13 Canadian Football League, Individual Statistics for Joe Hernández.

14 Ibid.

15 Ibid.

16 *1985 Canadian Football League Facts, Figures and Records,* 27; *Toronto Argonauts 1985 Media Guide,* 79.

Edmonton Eskimos of the CFL in midseason 1966 and saw action in 7 games. As an Eskimo player, he rushed 9 times for 29 yards, caught 9 passes for 223 yards and 2 touchdowns.

The following season (1967) Joe converted to a defensive back. An Edmonton sportswriter wrote, "Hernández is one of the meaner players in the league. Coupled with his clutch and grab tactics against rival pass receivers, and the suspicion exists that he could be the most illegal Mexican since Pancho Villa." Hernández experienced a fine season with the Eskimos. He returned 49 punts for 227 yards, 20 kick-off returns for 485 yards, and intercepted 6 passes. For his efforts, Hernández was named to the CFL Western Football Conference All-Star Team at defensive back.

Hernández continued to play with the Edmonton Eskimos through the 1970 season. However, the Edmonton relationship was not without its problems. In 1967 Joe had not signed a player's contract with Edmonton and was playing out his option clause. Edmonton had been reluctant to pay what he had asked for and he threatened to go elsewhere the following season. "It's a matter of pride with me. I'll get what I'm worth or go elsewhere," Hernández told Wayne Overland of the *Edmonton Journal*. Although a little angry over the negotiations, Hernández finally signed with Edmonton in March of 1968. "The prodigal son returned, receiving an estimated $20,000 to play for Edmonton." The 1968 season was a productive one for Hernández; he helped the Eskimos to 8 wins and 7 losses to finish third place and a return trip to the playoffs.

In 1969 Hernández had another excellent season. The game against the Ottawa Roughriders typified Joe's defensive performances throughout the 1969 Edmonton schedule. Overland wrote, "Hernández had an excellent game as the Eskimo defense somehow managed to limit the defending Grey Cup champions to one touchdown and a total of 13 points. Hernández made one diving interception in front of Margene Adkins to save a touchdown, tipped down another in the end zone and knocked down several other dangerous throws." Edmonton beat Ottawa 15-13.

At the end of the season, Hernández decided to retire from professional football. He advised the Edmonton front office about his decision and immediately he was asked to reconsider his retirement. Needing time to think, Hernández returned to his home in Phoenix, Arizona. The retirement lasted seven months before Joe decided to return to Edmonton. He said, "The only reason I didn't stay retired was because I thought the Eskimos had a chance to win the title." Back in uniform, Hernández played great defense for the Eskimos, who finished second in the conference with 9 wins and 7 losses. They went to the playoffs, losing to conclude the 1970 season. For the second time in his CFL career Hernández was selected to the Canadian All-Star squad at cornerback.

Again, Hernández contemplated his future and figured nine seasons were enough to take the aches and pains of pro football. During the off season, before he told Edmonton his plans, they traded him to the Montreal Alouettes. In turn, Joe told them they could keep all those Sunday afternoon headaches because Jackrabbit Joe was hanging it up. Then the phone rang at the Hernández residence. It was the Montreal Alouettes with a final offer Joe could not refuse. Again he packed his bags and departed for Canada. "I really thought I was quitting, but the closer it got to hanging it up, the more anxious I got. When you've got an itch, nothing is as sweet as scratching it just one more time."

Once again in Canada, Hernández showed up at the Alouettes' training camp in 1971, a little out of shape but a seasoned CFL veteran. He remained with Montreal for only a short while and then retired for good. "I was in my 10th year of professional football when I left Montreal. I probably could have played longer but it was time for me to do something else." Hernández recalls that Edmonton was probably his favorite place to play and to date relishes his football experiences.

In the CFL record book, Hernández ranks sixteenth on the all-time career kickoff return yardage with 97 returns for 2,547 yards, averaging 26.3 yards per return. Today you can find Joe Hernández and family residing in Tucson, Arizona.

Gus Gonzales
Tejano Athlete Remembered

Even though Texas colleges and universities have not actively recruited Mexicano athletes into their athletic programs, there have been exceptions to the rule and the Mexicanos who have had the opportunity to play Texas collegiate football have been stellar performers. Players such as Chico Mendoza (TCU); René Ramírez and Richard Ochoa (Texas); Robert Cortez (Texas A&M); Gabriel Rivera and Bobby Cavazos (Texas Tech); and Inés Pérez and Mike Romo (SMU) are just a few.

Once such talent who appears to have been overlooked by Texas teams in the late 1950s was 6'1", 210-pound Gus Gonzales. Gonzales hails from Wharton, Texas, a small town located southwest of Houston, where he came of age as an honor student and accomplished athlete at the local high school. Unfortunate for Texas football, Gonzales went outside the state to play for Tulane University in New Orleans, Louisiana. Hopeful for an education and the opportunity to play football, Gonzales launched his career in the state called the "Sportsman's Paradise."

In his sophomore year at Tulane, Gonzales continued to learn the ropes and with increased playing time his skills improved by leaps and bounds. He was quick for his size and played a brilliant last half of the 1959 season at offensive tackle and defensive middle guard. The young Gonzales learned rapidly that versatility was the key to success in college football and worked hard to master it. He lettered that season and was named to the All-Southeast Conference Sophomore Team.

Gonzales became a significant Tulane player in his junior year. Prior to the start of the 1960 schedule, Gonzales was named to the preseason All-Southeast Conference Team by the sportswriters of the *Birmingham News*. During the season, Gonzales played primarily on defense and was one of the dominant Green Wave defenders all year. A highlight of Gonzales's regular season play occurred against the Rice University Owls. Gonzales intercepted an Owls' pass and ran it back 67 yards to cap a sterling defensive performance. The *San Antonio Express-News* illustrates: "After Rice dominated play the first half, Tulane, triggered by a 67-yard pass interception return by Gus Gonzales, was in command most of the second half. . . . Gonzales's long third quarter interception return moved the ball to the Rice 20 and paved the way for Tulane's touchdown to tie the score 7-7."

Throughout the season, it was plays like these that brought Gonzales recognition and earned him the privilege to play in the postseason North-South All-Star and All-American Bowl games. Also, he was named to the All-Southeast Conference Third Team on defense.

In his final collegiate season, while Tulane struggled to complete a successful season, Gonzales continued to lead the defense for the Green Wave. It was one of those seasons in which, despite the efforts,

Tulane lost more than they won in 1961. Postseason kudos for Gonzales were his participation in the Senior Bowl and another selection to the All-SEC Third Team. It was a great career for Gonzales, who went to Tulane University unheralded and became one of their best players.

The next football event for Gonzales was preparing to play in the pros. The Philadelphia Eagles picked him in the sixth round of the 1962 NFL draft; the Houston Oilers of the rival AFL drafted him in the seventh round of the AFL draft; and the Toronto Argonauts of the CFL made him an offer to attend their training camp. It was good news for him to learn that Houston expressed an interest in him professionally and the prospect of playing close to home was appealing to the Wharton native. For a defensive lineman to be drafted by two pro football leagues and recruited by a third was quite a tribute to Gonzales's skills and potential as a pro football player. Of the three choices, Gonzales went with the better money offer and signed with Toronto of the CFL.

At the Argonauts' training camp, Gonzales worked diligently, but was sent to the Indianapolis Warriors of the United Football League (UFL) for some minor league experience. He performed well for the Warriors at offensive guard and rejoined Toronto

in 1963. However, the return to the Argonauts was bittersweet for Gonzales. Although he played a strong offensive guard position, he fell into disfavor with Toronto and found himself without any options.

The Argonauts released him from his contract, and before the ink on the release was dry, the Montreal Alouettes signed him to play for them in 1964. As with Toronto, the Alouettes sent Gonzales to the minors—this time to the Portland Seahawks of the UFL, where he remained until they were able to use him on offense. Determined to make the grade, Gonzales made good on his commitment to play in the CFL and demonstrated to his peers that he was a quick and sharp blocker. In 1965 Gonzales was recalled by Montreal and immediately became their starting offensive guard. That season, Montreal reached the CFL Eastern Conference semifinals. With the end of the 1965 CFL campaign, Gonzales regretfully concluded his career in professional football.

He had an outstanding collegiate experience, and was drafted by NFL/AFL teams and played in Canada. One can only speculate how different his career might have turned out if his field of play had been Philadelphia or Houston. One thing is certain: Gonzales was an exceptional athlete who did not reach his potential in the CFL.

Aztec Runner
Mario Méndez

On December 11, 1941, four days after the Japanese attack on Pearl Harbor which plunged the United States into World War II, there was born a son to the Méndez family of Los Angeles, California. It was a fateful and miraculous event which took place during a blackout on the way to the hospital. Mario Méndez was born into a world torn apart by war.

But the war would last only a few years and the young Méndez would remember the war only from the history books he read in school. He grew up in greater Los Angeles, living in the communities of Norwalk and Whittier. He prepped at Santa Fe High School and flourished in football as running back. A diamond in the rough, Méndez had a superlative high school career, and initially hoped to play at USC. Instead he was recruited and given a football scholarship to San Diego State University.

Méndez had a highly successfully career with the San Diego State Aztecs. They won the California Collegiate Athletic Association (CCAA) title in 1962 and tied for first place in 1963. During those championship years, Méndez changed from an excellent blocking back to an exceptional runner and did everything a great offensive back should do. The *1962 San Diego Aztecs Media Guide* describes Méndez as "a hard runner with good speed and excellent hands and a fine competitor."

One game in particular that lifted Méndez to stardom was the October 4, 1963, contest against the Mustangs of Cal-Poly of San Luis Obispo in the Aztec Bowl. Méndez was the Aztecs' starting halfback, but until this game was used primarily as a blocking back. It was a coming-out performance for Méndez, who raced for 5 touchdowns to lead San Diego State to a record-shattering rout of Cal-Poly San Luis Obispo, 69-0. The *San Diego Union* provides highlights of Méndez's efforts: "The five Méndez touchdowns and his 2-point conversion also gave him a single game record of 32 points. . . . For one of his touchdowns, Méndez ran 4 yards. He later scored on gallops of 5, 15, 1, and 6 yards, and powered off tackle for a 2-point conversion. . . . Méndez gained 80 yards in 11 carries and returned 2 punts for 52 yards." It was a great game for the Mexicano speedster who set the tempo for the Aztec offense for the remainder of the season.

The Aztecs continued their winning ways and earned a tie for first place in the conference. For Méndez, his career rushing record places him tenth on the San Diego All-Time list with 1,168 yards. He also holds the school record for the most 2-point conversions in a season (3) and career (5). At the end of the 1963 season, he was selected to the All-California Collegiate Athletic Association (CCAA) team at fullback and was the recipient of the John Simcox Memorial Trophy as the Aztecs' most valuable player. Recalling his collegiate career, Méndez credits coach Don Coryell for being a big motivator in his life. "While in high school and then at San Diego State,

Coach Coryell was a big influence on my athletic success." He says, "Coach Coryell kept me in school and always moving forward."

In 1964, with encouragement from Coach Coryell, Méndez successfully tried out and signed as a free agent with the San Diego Chargers of the American Football League (AFL). Although suffering from a recurring shoulder injury, Méndez turned out to be the best rookie running prospect in preseason training camp. Chargers coach Sid Gillman had this to say about the Mexicano rookie: "Mario certainly knows how to run and he knows where to run."

During the preseason, Méndez returned kickoffs and alternated at halfback with veteran star Keith Lincoln. He turned in impressive performances, helping the Chargers to win 4 of their 5 preseason games. At the start of the regular season, Méndez signed on with the team and played on their special teams throughout the 1964 schedule. It was a productive year for both Méndez and the Chargers, who became the AFL Western Conference champions. They did it in grand fashion by defeating the New York Jets 38-3 to clinch their fourth AFL West title in five years. However, injuries to stars Lance Alworth and Keith Lincoln in the AFL Championship game stopped the Chargers in their quest for the championship, as they lost to Buffalo 20-7. For Mario Méndez, his rookie year was yet another championship added to his football career. Unfortunately, it would be his only AFL season.

In 1965 the speedy but injured Méndez gave minor league football a try. He played for the Hartford Charter Oaks of the Atlantic Coast Football League (ACFL) and despite the nagging shoulder injury, gave a good account of himself in their field of glory. But the time had come for Méndez to re-evaluate his future in pro football. With the shoulder still a problem, he decided to leave football and return to his alma mater to finish his degree program at San Diego State.

Méndez turned his attention to a coaching and teaching career. Not one to be far from athletics, his first coaching job after graduation was at Monte Vista High School. He was there for three years (1966-1968) before he became an assistant coach at Grossmont College, where his teams were the conference champions. In 1971 Coach Méndez assumed the track coach responsibilities at Palo Mar Community College in San Marcos, California. At Palo Mar, Méndez found a home, and during his tenure he moved from track and field to head football coach in 1977. He developed the Palo Mar Comets football program, experiencing a very successful season in his initial coaching year. He coached football for another six years before putting his coaching days behind him. Remaining at Palo Mar College, Coach Méndez shifted gears to academics. He became a professor in physical education and nowadays commands the classroom and helps students make the best of their education. Just like the motivation he received from Coach Coryell when he too was a student in school, Professor Méndez does the same for his students. After all, what better way to learn than from those who have been successful and are winners. Today, the extraordinary Mario Méndez and his family make their home in the community of Vista, California.

The Marvelous George Mira

Possibly the strongest passing arm in collegiate football belonged to George Mira, a Latino athlete from Key West, Florida. Throughout his illustrious collegiate career and somewhat frustrating pro career, this quarterback phenom was many things to many people. His coach at the University of Miami, Andy Gustafson, was so excited by this athlete that he postponed his retirement until his quarterback's eligibility ran out. Nebraska football coach Bob Devaney called him the greatest passer he ever saw in college, while Maryland coach Tom Nugent referred to him as the most dangerous man in football when he's cornered.

Additionally, the Miami sportswriters called him the "Matador" because of his Spanish good looks and his uncanny ability to elude would-be tacklers. But whatever they chose to call him, to fans, friends, and

family he was George Ignacio Mira from the marvelous Mira clan. George I. Mira was born on January 11, 1942, in Key West, Florida. He was the second of three sons and two daughters of Jimmy and Dolores Mira. The family lived in Key West, and all three Mira sons quarterbacked the local high school football team. But it was George who springboarded into the college ranks. His brothers set football aside for golf and both of them added golf championships to the Miras' trophy case. They were a large and extended Cubano family, which included five uncles. His uncles were his best fans and followed their nephew's career fanatically. Mira was very fortunate to come from a very strong, loyal, and caring family. Throughout his playing days they supported him in good times and bad. They all knew he was destined to be great at whatever he chose to do and luckily, the University of Miami in Coral Gables was close by. Otherwise Mira might have gone elsewhere to play collegiate football.

At Miami, Mira did not require much development time. His sophomore year he was pressed into service and from that moment forward the fireworks he produced began to illuminate the Hurricanes' offense.

All through the 1961 campaign, Mira's passing gained a reputation for its velocity and propensity to break fingers and damage egos. *Sports Illustrated* writer John Underwood attests: "His complete follow-through once came down on a lineman's hand cleaving his fingers apart, requiring 12 stitches." Other times his receivers wore extra padding to minimize the bruising to the chest and other body parts when catching his passes. But in the season finale against the rival University of Florida Gators, he displayed just how amazing his athletic talent could be. Going into the final game of the season, the Hurricanes had won 6 and lost 3. (The three losses came when the nineteen-year-old Mira was injured or on part-time back-up duty.)

Played at Florida's home field, the hard-fought gridiron battle was determined by a sheer desire to win. Sportswriter Jeff Miller described Miami's march and Mira's miracle pass:

> Miami moved ahead in the third quarter, which wasn't so unbelievable in itself. It was the method, though, that had the Florida fans numb. Miami started on its 42 with a 4-yard run by Jim Vollenweider. Mira then pitched to Bill Miller, who took the ball 40 yards to the Florida 14. (Latino teammate) Sam Fernández carried 7 yards to the 7. From there Mira rolled out as if following the blocks for a sweep around left end. But he was hemmed in by Florida defenders and switched the ball to his left hand after having his right shoulder grabbed by Florida defensive end and high school friend Sam Holland. What seemed to be a lifetime took a split second for Mira to push a soft pass with his left hand toward the end zone. Mira's favorite target Nick Spinelli leaped to catch the ball for the touchdown that gave Miami the lead 12-6. Later in the fourth quarter, Miami added a field goal to seal the victory, 15-6.

Even though it was not a statistically great game for Mira, the split-second, left-handed pass was magnificent and a winner for the Hurricanes. Concluding the season with a 7-3 record, the Hurricanes were invited to play the University of Syracuse Orangemen in the third annual Liberty Bowl, held in Philadelphia. The game was advertised to be a war of the best independent teams in the country. As expected, the game lived up to its billing but Miami succumbed to a comeback effort by Syracuse. Not making any excuses, a less than healthy Mira led Miami to a first half shutout of Syracuse 14-0. However, in the second half, Syracuse regrouped behind their All-American Ernie Davis to defeat Miami 15-14.

The young Latino's time to shine was as close as the 1962 season. "Air Mira" and the Miami Hurricanes had a very successful year. He was named to several All-American teams; was fifth in the Heisman Trophy balloting (with 3,232 yards total offense and 20 touchdowns); and, for the second consecutive year, led Miami to a postseason bowl game.

This time around, Miami faced the always powerful Nebraska Cornhuskers in the Gotham Bowl. Despite the freezing weather on game day, it was an exciting clash of titans. Mira broke a school record by completing 24 of 46 passes for 321 yards and 2 touchdowns. However, this was not enough to prevent a late fourth quarter kickoff return for a touchdown by Nebraska that put them ahead of Miami 36-34. Mira was voted the "Outstanding Player of the Game" by the sportswriters—the first of 3 MVPs in postseason games he garnered during his college football days. (The only other Latino with as many all-star honors is Jim Plunkett, who played for Stanford in the late sixties.)

Compared to the previous two seasons, Mira's senior year at Miami was somewhat anticlimactic. At the start of the 1963 season, Mira appeared on the cover of *Sports Illustrated* and was appropriately called college football's best passer.

Without a doubt, he stood above his peers around the country. Statistically, he outmatched quarterbacks such as Pete Beathard at USC, Roger Staubach at Navy, Jack Concannon at Boston College, and Bill Munson at Utah State.

The 1963 Miami Hurricanes schedule was as challenging as ever and the best the Hurricanes could muster was a 3-7 record. Throughout the season, Mira continued to rip holes in opposing pass defenses and led the NCAA university division in total offense for the year. Careerwise, Mira broke all passing records at Miami and finished with a total offense of 5,130 yards and 30 touchdowns.

After a superlative collegiate career for the Cubano star, he now awaited the draft call from the NFL. However, before he moved up to the next level, there were a few calls to stardom he had to answer. The first came on December 21, 1963, in the sixteenth annual North-South All-Star game. Mira passed for 2 touchdowns and a pair of 2-point conversions to lead the South college All-Stars to a 23-14 victory over the North. For his efforts, Mira was voted the South's most valuable player.

A month later in the fifteenth annual Senior Bowl, Mira's passing game helped topple the North team by the score of 28-21. Mira threw the winning touch-down—a 15-yard pass—to Dave Parks of Texas Tech University.

In the Coaches' All-American Game in Buffalo, Mira turned in a spectacular performance by completing 21 of 40 passes to lead the East All-Americans to an 18-15 victory, and he was voted the game's most valuable player. Against the NFL champion Chicago Bears, in the Chicago All-Star game, Mira put on a superb exhibition. His passing accounted for a beautifully thrown touchdown against the NFL's toughest defense. The pro scouts who earlier said Mira was susceptible to the outside rush were grossly mistaken in their assessment. He eluded blitzing linebackers with the ease and confidence of a pro veteran.

The San Francisco 49ers of the NFL chose George Mira in the second round, while the Denver Broncos of the American Football League (AFL) claimed him in the 18th round of their draft. Mira remembers the anticipation and comments, "Being drafted by the 49ers was great but I felt I should have been the number one pick." (Instead, the 49ers drafted Dave Parks as their number one choice.) A little disappointed in not being number one, Mira nonetheless looked forward to the opportunity to play pro football in San Francisco.

His tenure at San Francisco lasted five years, during which he primarily played a back-up role to starting quarterback John Brodie. Always a fierce competitor, this backup role did not agree with Mira and he recalls, "My five years in San Francisco were good, but sometimes frustrating because of the head coach Jack Christiansen. I felt I should have been the starter many times. When I did start, I was successful."

Without a doubt, whenever he was given the opportunity, he indeed was successful. On November 8, 1964, rookie George Mira connected with the other 49ers rookie Dave Parks on a 79-yard touchdown play against the Minnesota Vikings. The super start by Mira sent a message to the coaching staff to play him more often. The following week, Mira stepped in for Brodie once again to lead San Francisco to an upset victory over the Green Bay Packers 24-14. His pass-run options plays kept the Packers off balance throughout the hard-fought contest.

However, the 49ers and the NFL would only see the marvels of Mira a few more times before his departure. On October 9, 1966, again against the Packers, Mira replaced John Brodie at quarterback and threw for 2 touchdowns, including an 8-yard toss to John David Crow, which proved to be the winning score. For the Packers, it was their first defeat of the season, losing to the 49ers, 21-20.

The following season, after a 6-game losing streak, Mira came off the bench to pace the 49ers to 2 victo-ries to salvage a 7-7 record. Starting his first game of that season, Mira passed for 294 yards and 2 touch-downs to lead San Francisco to a 34-28 win over the Atlanta Falcons. A week later, Mira threw 3 touch-down passes for a total of 239 yards to defeat the Dallas Cowboys 24-16.

Despite outstanding efforts by the underutilized Latino, Brodie remained the 49ers' número uno quar-terback. Without much choice, Mira played out his option and moved on to three other NFL teams—the Philadelphia Eagles, the Baltimore Colts, and the Miami Dolphins. As at San Francisco, the Latino quar-terback played back-up role to Norm Snead at Philadelphia; was on the taxi squad at Baltimore; and served as back-up to Bob Griese at Miami. While at Miami, Mira earned an AFC Championship ring and a trip to Super Bowl VI.

Still hoping for a starting role, Mira looked toward Canada for an opportunity. His friend J. D. Albrecht, the Montreal Alouettes' general manager, arranged for him to play in Montreal. Leaving the warmer climates, Mira went north to the frozen tundra of the CFL grid-iron. He played two seasons in Canada, 1972 and 1973. His best year was the latter, when he led the Alouettes to a 7-6 record, completing 55 percent of his passes, throwing 11 touchdowns, and leading his team to an appearance in the CFL playoffs.

Mira enjoyed playing in the CFL, but his football dream was still unfulfilled. By 1974 he was a 10-year pro football veteran, whose brief spurts of greatness in the NFL were still remembered south of the Canadian border. Meanwhile, a new pro football league, called the World Football League (WFL), was forming and it reached out for George Mira. The league recruited rookies and NFL veterans alike. Many glamourous names like Virgil Carter, John Huarte, Larry Csonka, Paul Warfield, and many others left their established teams to play in the new league.

Mira's call came when Birmingham Americans coach Jack Gotta approached him about joining Birmingham and the WFL. Accepting the challenge, Mira agreed to give the new league a try. "I wanted to finish my career in the states, and the challenge of helping a new league get off the ground was exciting," said Mira.

He signed with the Birmingham Americans and led them to the league's first and only championship game, called the "World Bowl," held on December 5, 1974. Mira and the Americans defeated the Eastern Division Champion Florida Blazers 22-21. Mira played a splen-did game, alternating at quarterback with Matthew Reed. Mira's key pass plays were the difference and he was named the World Bowl's most valuable player.

In 1975, the WFL's franchises were still struggling financially and the league's future looked uncertain.

George Mira

Passing

Year	Team	Atts.	Comp.	Yds.	Pct.	TDs	Int.
1964	San Francisco 49ers	53	23	331	43.4	2	5
1965	San Francisco 49ers	58	28	460	48.3	4	3
1966	San Francisco 49ers	53	22	284	41.5	5	2
1967	San Francisco 49ers	65	35	592	53.8	5	3
1968	San Francisco 49ers	11	4	44	36.4	1	1
1969	Philadelphia Eagles	76	25	240	32.9	1	5
1970	Baltimore Colts	(Taxi squad—no stats)					
1971	Miami Dolphins	30	11	159	36.7	1	1
1972	Montreal Alouettes (CFL)	146	61	887	41.7	8	0
1973	Montreal Alouettes (CFL)	168	92	1,356	54.8	11	8
1974	Birmingham Americans (WFL)	313	155	2,248	49.5	17	14
1975	Jacksonville Express (WFL)	254	123	1,675	48.4	12	12
1977	Toronto Argonauts (CFL)	13	4	48	32.5	0	0
		1,240	592	7,991	43.3	67	54

Rushing

Year	Team	No.	Yds.	Avg.	Long	TDs
1964	San Francisco 49ers	18	177	9.8	37	0
1965	San Francisco 49ers	5	64	12.8	25	0
1966	San Francisco 49ers	10	103	10.3	38	0
1967	San Francisco 49ers	7	23	3.3	9	0
1968	San Francisco 49ers	1	5	5.0	5	0
1969	Philadelphia Eagles	3	16	5.3	6	0
1970	Baltimore Colts	(Taxi squad—no stats)				
1971	Miami Dolphins	6	-9	-1.5	0	0
1972	Montreal Alouettes (CFL)	10	67	6.7	0	0
1973	Montreal Alouettes (CFL)	(No stats)				
1974	Birmingham Americans (WFL)	1	13	13.0	13	1
1975	Jacksonville Express (WFL)	8	38	4.8	18	0
1977	Toronto Argonauts (CFL)	1	15	15.0	15	0
		82	512	6.24	38	1

Sources: 1972 The Sporting News Football Register; 1972 Miami Dolphins Media Guide; "Birmingham Americans and Jacksonville Express Individual Statistics for George Mira," World Football League, provided by Joe Horrigan, Curator, Pro Football Hall of Fame, Canton, Ohio, October 18, 1994; "Biographical and statistical information on George Mira," provided by Louise Froggett, assistant curator, Canadian Football Hall of Fame and Museum, Hamilton, Ontario, Canada, April 4, 1994.

The Birmingham Americans became the "Vulcans" and Mira returned to Florida to sign with the WFL Jacksonville Express. Unfortunately for Mira, who continued to play a good game and to be one of the league's leading passers, the WFL folded on October 22, 1975. For the two seasons he played in the WFL, Mira recalls, "It was the most fun I had in pro football. I had a good relationship with the coaches and the team unity was exceptional.

At this juncture in his career, retirement from the game was becoming a reality. He had been away from his family for nearly a decade and his oldest son was now playing high school sports. For these reasons, Mira retired, only to return to pro football in Canada as a coach. The Toronto Argonauts solicited his services and hired him as an offensive backfield coach, but coaching proved to be too mundane for the spirited Latino. Mira also played in six games but eventually concluded his pro football career in Toronto.

Finally, after seventeen years in football, the marvelous and often magnificent George Mira said farewell to the sport he loved so much. His collegiate all-star performances, the cameo starts with the 49ers, and the World Football League Championship are just a few reminders of his football legacy. Looking back on his career, Mira offered this advice to future players: "You must have the dedication, be a hard worker, have enthusiasm, and be mentally and physically prepared. Otherwise, you won't make it. Also being able to accept praise and criticism is important to achieving success."

Mira played a great game of football and one can only speculate just how good he could have been given the full opportunity to play. Few were his moments of glory, but even with just a few, he will be remembered as one of the all-time great Latino quarterbacks.

Nowadays, the George Ignacio Mira family live and operate a seafood business in Miami, Florida, not far from the university where he once commanded national attention and excitement. Today he still evokes those fabulous football memories because those are the things legends are made of.

Purdue Great
Big Jim García

Amongst the gigantic elite of Mexicano/Latino pro football linemen, past and present, there is a midwest Latino whose speed and physical attributes made him the Cleveland Browns' first draft selection in 1965.

His name is James R. García, born on March 7, 1944, in the windy city of Chicago, Illinois. Of Filipino and German ancestry, García was the benefactor of proud, hard-working parents who nurtured and guided their talented son along.

At Lane Tech High School, García's football skills began to blossom in his senior year. That year, 1959, the Lane Tech team claimed the Illinois State Football Championship.

With the glory prep days behind him, García considered the various scholarship offers he received. The Purdue University Boilermakers in nearby West Lafayette, Indiana, expressed a serious interest in him, but García had doubts about his ability to play Big Ten Conference football. Initially he considered a smaller college but then realized, with a little encouragement from friends and family, that he could succeed as both a student and an athlete.

Awed by it all, García learned his lessons well and began to develop into a big-time collegiate football player. Overcoming his lack of confidence, he played defensive end for the years 1963-64 and, much to the coach's satisfaction, was achieving his potential. His collegiate football coach Jack Mollenkopf provided some observations on the young García after he had

been on the Purdue program a couple of years: "Jim can be just about as great as he sets his mind to be. He has the size and the speed. With two years of Big Ten play behind him, he has the necessary experience. We expect him to be outstanding and he could be an exceptional player. He was good as a sophomore and was greatly improved last fall. There seems to be no end to his potential when he wants to play."

To illustrate García's mushrooming success, assistant Boilermaker coach Dale Samuels recalls a play from García's sophomore year in the Iowa-Purdue game: "We're in a looping defense and García loops to his right . . . the wrong way, because Iowa halfback Larry Ferguson sweeps around the other end. Well, García catches him," Samuels marvells. "He must have raced 35 yards across the field and dragged him down."

García's playmaking became the key to Purdue's defense. His senior year was his best as the Boilermakers, now quarterbacked by Bob Griese, won 6 and lost 3 to place third in Big Ten Conference play. The highlight of the season was a big 21-20 victory over the University of Michigan, who eventually won the Conference Championship and a trip to the Rose Bowl.

García had such a fine 1964 season that he was often compared to former University of Minnesota star Bobby Bell. Coach Mollenkopf, who during his tenure in Big Ten football was a sideline witness of the destruction Bobby Bell wrought as he led Minnesota into two Rose Bowls, saw a lot of similarities in García. "Jim García is a lot like Bell physically, 6'4" and 218 pounds, tall and rangy and quick as a cat."[1]

During the season, García was selected as United Press International (UPI) Midwest Lineman of the Week and, at the end of the season was named to the All Big-Ten Conference First Team at defensive end. In postseason action he played in the East-West Shrine All-Star game, the Hula Bowl, and the Chicago College All-Star game.

In the East-West Shrine game, which featured future Hall of Famers Roger Staubach and Dick Butkus, García played a brilliant defensive game and sacked West's quarterback Craig Morton twice as the East team lost a closely contested battle by the score of 11-7.

In August 1965, García started at left defensive end for the College All-Stars. The August classic was played in Chicago's Soldier Field against the NFL's Cleveland Browns. It was a golden opportunity for García to display his defensive skills against the team who drafted him earlier in the NFL collegiate lottery.

Interestingly, García was also sought in the AFL and had been selected by the Denver Broncos in the seventh round of the 1965 American Football League (AFL) draft.

Not wanting to leave the Midwest, García signed with the Browns and tried out at the defensive end position. Unfortunately, he had sustained an injury in the College All-Star game and was reinjured at the Browns training camp. It hampered his chances with the Browns. He played on various specialty teams and displayed fine speed and agility, but was inactive most of the season. That year the Browns won the Eastern Conference Championship with 9 wins, 2 losses.

The following season, García was still considered a prime defensive end prospect due largely to his natural physical attributes, but he could not fully recover from his previous injuries. Cleveland traded him to the New York Giants, but with the Giants, García watched from the sidelines most of the 1966 campaign.

In 1967 as a free agent, García signed with the second-year franchise New Orleans Saints, but good health continued to elude him and García concluded his professional football career in 1968 with another new and struggling franchise, the Atlanta Falcons.

Having played sparingly through four years and four NFL teams due to persistent injuries, García never fully achieved the greatness associated with his talent and physical attributes. He was a great collegiate football player whose fame and fortune was short lived in the best of all gridirons, the NFL.

Notes

1 Bobby Bell, who was a senior when García was a sophomore, became a seventh-round draft choice of the Kansas City Chiefs in 1963. Bell had an illustrious twelve-year career with the Chiefs, including a Super Bowl IV win over Joe Kapp and the Minnesota Vikings.

Reluctant Star Emilio Vállez

In the 1968 NFL draft, the Chicago Bears made a shy but talented New Mexico native named Emilio Vállez their twelfth-round pick.

Hailing from the sun-baked town of Belen, the young Emilio overcame a shy character, and at the prompting of his older brother, got involved in sports such as track and basketball, and of course football. "I had always been a little shy, and without my brother's encouragement, I probably wouldn't have played sports at all!" Vállez said.

At Belen High School, Vállez blossomed into a three-sport athlete. In all he earned eleven varsity letters: four in football, three in basketball, and four in track. Vállez also earned All-State honors his junior and senior years in football.

Upon graduation, Vállez attracted many college recruiters, but as is true and indicative of many other Mexicanos who chose to stay close to home, he accepted a football scholarship to the nearby University of New Mexico at Albuquerque.

Vállez, like many other outstanding high school athletes, found the transition to collegiate competition somewhat difficult. Vállez only played one game as a freshman, but he was named a Western Athletic Conference (WAC) "Lineman of the Week" as a sophomore. The versatile New Mexican starred on both defense and offense. Vállez's junior year brought more accomplishments. He established school records in pass receiving, and in a game against the University of Arizona, set a single-game record for most yards in pass receiving.

In that same contest, Vállez caught an 89-yard touchdown pass to set the school record for longest pass reception. And yet another WAC "Lineman of the Week" honor was bestowed on the talented young star.

Vállez enjoyed a prosperous senior year with the Lobos. He rewrote his own records and established the single-game record for most pass receptions (17), and most yards receiving (257). Vállez was the only Lobo player named to the 1967 All-Western Athletic Conference team.

Vállez is considered one of the all-time great receivers in Lobo football history, holding career marks in several pass-receiving categories. His sisters, Daisy and Priscilla, talk proudly about their brother the football player and his accomplishments, and insist that he hasn't been recognized enough for a remarkable and illustrious collegiate career.

The Chicago Bears and the Oakland Raiders expressed interested in signing Vállez out of college. Vállez chose to sign with the Bears, who were in the established and reputable National Football League, as opposed to the Raiders of the newly formed and upstart American Football League.

Vállez reported to camp in July of 1968, and once again encountered some difficulty in dealing with the transition because of his shy nature.

The best way to describe Vállez's character in regard to his athletic ability, accomplishments, and status as a professional football player is reluctant. Reluctant to accept that he was of exceptional ability, reluctant to accept the limelight, and reluctant to believe that he did indeed deserve to be a pro football player.

Vállez says that he was most secure in the shadows. He really thought that if he made himself too visible, someone would realize that he didn't belong there and send him home. He realized later that the insecurities he felt then did in fact affect his game. Although he played two seasons (1968-1969) with the Bears, he did not display the aggression the coaches were looking for and the skills he had shown in college. Consequently, the Bears put him on waivers.

After leaving the Bears, Vállez tried out with the Edmonton Eskimos of the Canadian Football League (CFL), but the three-a-day workouts took their toll and Valléz injured the cartilage in both knees and could not play. He returned to Illinois for knee surgery and recuperation. Once recovered and back on his feet, he formed a construction company and worked a couple of years.

In 1971, Vállez returned to football one last time. He played tight end for the Rockford (Illinois) Rams of the Central States Football League (CSFL), a semi-pro football league that played their season from August through October. Vállez was an All-CSFL selection in 1971. He played two more years at Rockford, but after the 1973 season, the Rams moved their franchise to Racine, Wisconsin. Vállez did not make the move with them and retired from professional football.

Vállez has fond recollections of his precious time in the pros, including playing against all the stars of the era and with Hall of Fame teammates Gayle Sayers, Dick Butkus, and the late, great Brian Piccolo.

With a laugh, Vállez recalls the day he caught Bullet Bob Hayes of the Dallas Cowboys, who was considered the "Fastest Human Alive," and remembers quite vividly meeting Bears owner George Halas. Halas, one of the pioneers of pro football, was considered a cold and shrewd businessman. Nonetheless, he found the time to talk to his players warmly. "He shook my hand during one of the practices and said, 'Hi Emilio, glad to have you here.' "

In recounting his experiences in football, Vállez expresses the same concern that affects many other talented Mexicano athletes—lack of confidence. Vállez admits that his lack of confidence during those years was detrimental to his longevity in the NFL. However, he has lived through the experience with significant success and can reflect back on his football career with a sense of achievement and pride. Today Vállez still works in construction and lives with his family in Marengo, Illinois.

The Return of Al Gonzales

For a young Mexicano growing up in the southwest valley of Albuquerque, New Mexico, life was hard and challenging. Hard because of the poverty that prevailed in the area and challenging because of the lack of opportunity for its inhabitants. However, adversity sometimes strengthens individuals and helps them overcome their environment. One such person able to do just that was a young Chicano who survived the drugs and gangs of the neighborhood to become an All-American athlete and successful university administrator.

Albert Thomas Gonzales was born on November 25, 1945, on a ranch near the post office of Cedar Vale, New Mexico. Blessed in many ways, Gonzales came from a very traditional Catholic family, which explains why he was named after the Archbishop of New Mexico, Albert Thomas. His father was a hard-working man and his mother, he says, was the foundation of the family.

In Albert's developing years, the Gonzales family moved to Albuquerque where the transition from a rural to urban lifestyle influenced the enthusiastic Gonzales. There he learned the ways of the known world and what began as a mild interest in football became a passion for him. He recalls, "Had it not been for athletics, particularly football, I might have taken a different road and wound up in a lifestyle or situation less than positive."

Staying in school, Gonzales was an active participant in all school functions and he took to football with an eagerness unparalleled at the time. At Albuquerque Rio Grande High School, big Al Gonzales

motivated his teammates to reach their goals. The motivation paid off as Rio Grande took the high school city and state championships.

Nicknamed "Speedy," Gonzales was the fastest lineman on the team. At practice, the coaches had him run with the halfbacks instead of the linemen because they didn't want to slow him down. He had a gift for blocking opponents and running down breakaway runners.

After his glory prep days, Gonzales received three offers to play collegiate football. The University of New Mexico in his hometown of Albuquerque sought his talents, as did the University of Arizona, and New Mexico State University. He visited all three campuses and decided on New Mexico State, where he received a full four-year athletic scholarship.

Playing for coach Warren Woodson, for whom he has great respect, Gonzales began his freshman year with the Aggies as a starter on the defensive line and a tackle on the second-team offense. He was rated the fastest lineman on the squad, so Speedy kept his nickname. But Gonzales was more than just a fast lineman; he played linebacker and could also kick the football with accuracy. He became the Aggies' regular kicker in the last game of his freshman season. Career wise, Gonzales is ranked fifth in kick scoring with 124 points at NMSU.

During Gonzales's playing days at New Mexico State, the Aggies did not lose a home game in four seasons (1964-67). As a matter of fact, New Mexico State captured 14 straight victories in Aggie Memorial Stadium until the lone tie with North Texas State on October 7, 1967. After this contest, Gonzales and the Aggies added another 3 victories for a total of 17 home field wins and an impressive school record.

Also during Gonzales's tenure, the Aggies played as an independent team. Previously they had been members of the now defunct Border Conference (1932-61) and had won championships in 1938 and in 1960. After the independent years and Gonzales's four-year career, New Mexico State joined the Missouri Valley Conference and added another two conference championships in 1976 and 1978.

But independent or not, Speedy Gonzales was going to make a name for himself in the unheralded world of interior linemen. He recalls his first collegiate game against the Florida State Seminoles. Aside from the hurricane weather that befell them in Florida, the Aggies were pelted by oranges thrown by the Florida State fans. Not satisfied with being poor host to the New Mexico visitors, they also pelted them with racial remarks directed at the blacks and Mexicano players on the team. Thus began Gonzales's collegiate football career in the South.

In 1965 the Aggies posted their best record for the four years Gonzales was there, winning 8 and losing 2. Gonzales remembers the Texas Tech game and playing against their star Donny Anderson. Anderson was their All-American and by Gonzales's estimation, was the biggest factor in the Aggies' 48 to 9 loss to the Red Raiders. In other games, the Aggies had big wins over Lamar University, Wichita State, New Mexico, and North Texas State. Gonzales was now a force on the team and was their regular placekicker.

The following season (1966), Gonzales had outstanding performances against Pacific University and Wichita State. He kicked five conversions en route to a 49-23 win over the Pacific Tigers. Against Wichita State, Gonzales scored three different ways: he converted 5 extra points, kicked a field goal, and, defensively, recovered a blocked punt in the end zone for a touchdown. His 14 points helped the Aggies defeat Wichita State 45-17.

However, Gonzales's highly successful season was disrupted in the game against the University of New Mexico Lobos when, on the third play of the game, he injured his knee and did not play for the rest of the contest. Disappointed that he could not show off for his hometown fans, Gonzales had to wait until the next season to display his talents against the Lobos.

At the onset of the 1967 football campaign, Gonzales and teammate Tony Field were the New Mexico State All-American candidates in preseason polls. At season's end both of them had lived up to their billing and were key players throughout the schedule.

The Aggies continued to be winners and Al Gonzales's senior year was no different. They posted a record of 7 wins, 3 losses, and 1 tie. One distinguishing highlight of Gonzales's senior year was his kicking performance in the Northern Arizona game, when the Aggies broke three school records on their way to a 90-0 rout of the Northern Arizona Lumberjacks. The score of the game was one record; the others included a season's pass reception record set by end Howard Taylor, and a Gonzales school and NCAA record for 12 point after touchdown conversions in a single game. After 28 years, the record still stands in annals of New Mexico State University football history. (The NCAA mark was broken the very next year by University of Houston's Terry Leiweke, who converted 13 extra points playing against Tulsa University on November 23, 1968.)

Although records like those mentioned above are meant to be broken, this particular one was tied 23 years later by Fresno State's Derek Mahoney in the contest opposing the University of New Mexico on October 5, 1991. At season's end, Gonzales finished on a healthy note and received All-American Honorable Mention recognition from the Associated Press and United Press International. He had a superlative collegiate football career but because of the Aggies' independent status there would be no postseason play for the team. Gonzales was selected as an alternate to the East-West Shrine All-Star game in 1967, but was never called to make the trip.

Next the proud Gonzales awaited the annual pro draft and readied himself for a few professional football offers. For reasons unknown, he was not drafted, but Al Davis from the Oakland Raiders of the American Football League (AFL) contacted Gonzales and enticed him to come to Oakland for a tryout. The Raiders were very interested in him but according to Gonzales, "There were no other incentives for him to go to Oakland." While still thinking about the Davis offer, Gonzales received a call from the Saskatchewan Roughriders of the Canadian Football League. Coach Eagle Keys called Gonzales personally to discuss his future with the Roughriders. Keys guaranteed him a contract and money and sent him a plane ticket to the winter wonderland of Regina, Saskatchewan, Canada. Gonzales also received an offer from the Cleveland Browns, an offer similar to the one from Oakland and nothing more.

Gonzales decided to take Keys's offer and in 1968 flew to Canada to play pro football for Saskatchewan. In the two years prior to Gonzales's signing with Saskatchewan, the Roughriders won the Grey Cup Championship (CFL's equivalent to the NFL's Super Bowl). He had come to a team that had a winning tradition. Once there, he got an eyeful of the countryside that was so different from the semi-arid landscape of his native New Mexico. His acclimation continued at training camp at the University of Saskatchewan in Saskatoon. He practiced at linebacker and remembers when he first got frostbite during one of the practice sessions. After that episode, he wore more clothing under his uniform and began soaking his feet in ice water prior to practice to prevent any more frozen body parts.

With each practice, he impressed his coaches with his playing. It looked good for Gonzales to become a starter until the final exhibition game when he sustained a serious knee injury while tackling a ballcarrier. The 1968 Roughrider season began without him.

Gonzales remained under doctors' care until midseason. At that time, he underwent surgery, but efforts to rehabilitate the knee in time to finish the season were unsuccessful. Watching from the sidelines on crutches, Gonzales saw the Roughriders win the Western Football Conference title, but lose to the Calgary Stampeders in the playoffs. It was a season of disappointment for Gonzales because the knee injury kept him from reaching his potential as a professional football player.

In 1969 Gonzales tried a comeback, but the knee did not lend itself to the rigors of professional football. The Saskatchewan front office chose not to renew his contract, thus ending his pro career. Reluctantly, Gonzales returned to Las Cruces, New Mexico, to finish his college education.

His playing days now over, Gonzales began to focus on a coaching career at his alma mater. Football was still a love for him and he became a graduate assistant to football coach Jim Wood. In 1973 Gonzales was hired as the Aggies' offensive line coach and remained in that capacity for the next four years. But as fate would have it, his career at New Mexico State changed from field athletics to administration.

Always the worker his father had taught him to be, Gonzales took over the responsibilities as the assistant director of student housing. From there he went to personnel to run the school's Affirmative Action/Equal Employment Opportunity programs. His success led to an appointment as the school's personnel director. Now an established administrator, he continued to work hard and, according to this recollections, did not visualize returning to athletics. However, this would change after the university hired a new president, Jim Halligan. Also during this time, the NMSU athletic director retired, which left a vacancy to be filled by the new leader. Looking within the ranks, Halligan first asked Gonzales to fill in as the interim athletic director until a replacement could be found, but after evaluating Gonzales's credentials, Halligan appointed him the permanent athletic director. Needless to say, this surprised a lot of people, including Gonzales.

In selecting Gonzales, a Latino, Halligan had broken with tradition, and this brought clamor from the Anglo community. When I asked Gonzales about his appointment and the reactions he received, he said, "It was controversial when Mr. Halligan appointed me the athletic director because it put me into a nontraditional position. I received hate mail. Some of the letters said, 'You shouldn't be the athletic director, they should have brought someone else in'. Also, 'you should go back to picking lettuce in the field,' just to quote a few of the remarks."

Nevertheless, Gonzales put all this into perspective and said further, "You need to remember I was put into an area where the traditional white males were the choice for this job and then all of a sudden, there is a brown face sitting there. They didn't like it and the letters were also very critical of my heritage, birthright and family."

Not surprised but concerned by this behavior, Gonzales dealt with it accordingly. He had experienced this kind of racial discord before and applied strong conviction not to let it interfere with school business and him personally. As quickly as the hate mail had appeared, it also dissipated because other than race, there were no reasons to be heard. For Gonzales this was a moral and spiritual victory. His appointment was the first of its kind in the state and in the nation. It broke an old tradition and history will later show just how important this appointment has been to the Mexicanos of this country.

Since the appointment, Gonzales has been busy working with his athletic programs. Throughout his eleven-year tenure, the men's basketball teams have posted seven straight 20-victory seasons and seven consecutive postseason appearances, including five NCAA Tournament invitations. The football program has finally turned around. The Aggies have gone from last in the Big West Conference to contending for the league title in 1993. Under his guidance, New Mexico State finally posted a winning season in fourteen years with a 6-5 mark in 1992.

The women's basketball team has made two trips to the NCAA Tournament and 1 to the National Women's Invitational Tournament, and NMSU programs in baseball and golf are nationally ranked.

For over a decade since his appointment, the best term to describe his tenure as athletic director is "successful." Things have improved due to his leadership, but the road from the barrio of Albuquerque to his office in the university athletic building was a rocky one. Simply stated, Gonzales endured and succeeded by utilizing a strong work ethic, sound judgment, and the belief that virtue is its own reward.

Today when you ask Al Gonzales who and what were the big influences in his life, he will tell you his parents' work ethic and the football coaches throughout his career, who reinforced that ethic. Without it there is nothing and if there are lessons to be learned from similar experiences, what better man to learn from than Al Gonzales.

Dolphins Strongman Manny Fernández

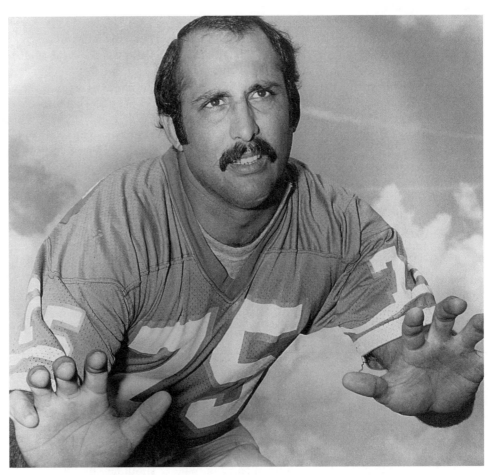

Never before in NFL history has a team been so awesome on offense and so devastating on defense as the 1972 World Champion Miami Dolphins. They are the only NFL team to go undefeated the entire season, and among the key players who contributed to that success was Manny Fernández.

By collegiate and pro football standards, Fernández was an exception. He was not big for a defensive lineman, not very fast, had poor vision, and his college coach Mike Giddings was convinced Manuel José Fernández did not have the stuff to play pro football. However, Fernández proved him wrong and went on to become the most famous free agent in Miami Dolphins history.

Born on July 3, 1946, in Oakland, California, Fernández attended San Lorenzo High School. As a prep athlete he was a state runner-up in wrestling and set a school record of 305 pounds in the bench press. This foundation in strength would later prove to be invaluable for Fernández in college and the pro ranks.

When Fernández arrived at the University of Utah in 1965, he looked forward to playing football in the Western Athletic Conference. His first season there was not very successful and the following year, Utah hired Mike Giddings as their new head coach. Under Giddings's guidance, the Utes broke even in 1966 with a 5-5 record and won 4 and lost 7 in 1967. But the Fernández experience under Giddings was less than favorable. They did not get along; and when the 1968 NFL draft took place, Fernández was not even considered. Giddings told the interested Dolphins his player couldn't make pro grade. Although Fernández had captained the Utah team, he recalls, "I wasn't hard to overlook. . . . At Utah not only was I not all-conference, I barely was all-team."

However, that would change as the Dolphins were looking for a name to appeal to the Hispanic population in Miami. Aside from the linguistic consideration, the Dolphins' scouts saw promise in Fernández's football abilities and signed him as a free agent. He would be the Hispanic gate attraction, but the Dolphins would later learn that American-born Fernández could not speak Spanish. At the time, the only other Mexicano pro prospect was Emilio Vállez, whom the Chicago Bears had selected in the twelfth round of the 1968 draft.

The Fernández language deficiency was soon forgotten as the fans' attention focused on the head-knocking, body-slamming type of football Fernández played for the next nine seasons with the Dolphins.

As a rookie, Fernández played defensive end and then switched to defensive tackle in 1969. A charter member of Miami's "No Name" defense, he became the bulwark of the middle defensive line for the Dolphins. His quickness and strength enabled him to out-maneuver bigger men. Fernández was voted the Defensive Lineman of the Year by the South Florida media for six straight years (1968-1973).

In 1971 Fernández led the Miami defense in quarterback sacks with eight and was selected to the All-AFC team. A couple of seasons later, Fernández had an All-Pro year, and received the Johnny Unitas Award, presented by the South Shore Quarterback Club of Massachusetts to an outstanding player who had come to professional football without any college fanfare.

The pinnacle of Fernández's career were the Super Bowl winning years of 1972 and 1973. In both seasons, he collected 107 and 113 tackles, respectively. His finest game was Super Bowl VII, in which he destroyed the Washington Redskins with 17 tackles. Fernández and the Miami Dolphins beat the Redskins 14-7, thereby completing the first and only perfect season in NFL history.

Defensively, Fernández disrupted Washington's offensive schemes throughout the game. Although Washington coach George Allen did not single out any Dolphin as the key to the defense, he did admit that Fernández had led the Miami charge. "The play I remember most vividly from the Redskins game," Fernández recounts, "was getting hold of Larry Brown and then [my teammate] Nick Buoniconti, having a clear shot at Brown, hit me instead. Hardest lick I ever had. I was dazed for three plays afterwards. I didn't leave the game, but they had to tell me what to do for awhile."

Fernández had missed the MVP award because, according to some newspaper reporters, they wanted a glamour name like Jake Scott instead of a sweathog.

But, this recognition did not matter to Fernández. He had played a great game and for a player who was not given much of a chance to be successful in the sport, Fernández was atop the world of professional football.

The formation of the World Football League (WFL) in 1974 disrupted the World Champion Dolphins. The rival WFL would snatch Csonka, Kiick, and Paul Warfield from the Dolphins and temporarily place Miami in a tenuous but controllable situation. Also, the Portland Storm of the WFL made Fernández their twelfth pick in the pro draft of 1974, but Fernández stayed on with the Dolphins and profited by signing a five-year contract worth $500,000. Although missing the offensive talents of Csonka and company, the Dolphins continued their winning ways.

During the 1975 season, Fernández sustained an ankle injury and missed four games. The gridiron battles were taking their toll and the ankle was now added to the list of injured body parts for Fernández. His left knee had already undergone surgery five times and had more stitching tracks than a railroad station switching area. His shoulder was questionable and it became evident that the healing powers of youth had escaped the once quick and guileful Fernández.

At the start of the 1976 training camp, injuries continued to plague Fernández, and he was placed on injured reserve for the year. He underwent knee and shoulder surgery with little success and was forced to conclude his illustrious pro football career at the end of the 1976 season.

Fernández was honored in 1981 when *The New York Times* sportswriters selected an All-Time Super Bowl team and named him as one of the defensive tackles along with Bob Lilly of the Dallas Cowboys. A fitting tribute to a great individual and one of the NFL's best defensive lineman.

Manny Fernández

Defensive Statistics

Year	Team	Games	Tackles	Asst.	Total	Opp. Fumbles	QB Sacks
1968	Miami Dolphins	13	31	15	46	1	4
1969	Miami Dolphins	14	68	22	90	1	4
1970	Miami Dolphins	13	54	17	71	-	4 ½
1971	Miami Dolphins	14	47	20	67	1	8
1972	Miami Dolphins	14	68	39	107	2	5
1973	Miami Dolphins	14	67	46	113	-	6 ½
1974	Miami Dolphins	12	38	21	59	1	3
1975	Miami Dolphins	10	10	12	22	-	-
1976	Miami Dolphins	(Injured Reserve)					
		104	383	192	575	6	35[1]

1 *Miami Dolphins 1976 Media Guide*, 37.

Other NFL/CFL Alumni

Robert Luna

One would think it unusual to find a Latino or Spanish surname individual playing football at the University of Alabama. But, unusual or not, it happened when Robert Luna entered the Crimson Tide campus and gave a good account of himself as a student/athlete.

His junior year at Alabama, Luna's name went into the Orange Bowl record book when the multitalented athlete scored a total of 19 points against the Orangemen of Syracuse. In what has been referred to as the Alabama rout of Syracuse, Luna scored two touchdowns and kicked seven consecutive extra point conversions to lead all Crimson Tide scorers, in defeating Syracuse 61-6.

In 1955 the NFL draft sent Luna to the San Francisco 49ers camp, where he made the team and played defensive back and punter. He finished his rookie season with a 40.6 yards per punt average (63 punts for 2,528 yards), and his NFL career was well on its way. However, shortly after his initial season, Luna was drafted into the military.

Having fulfilled his military obligation, Luna returned to civilian life. However, before resuming his pro football career, Luna decided to finished his college education and returned to classes at Alabama. After receiving his degree in 1959, Luna returned to the 49ers but was immediately traded to the Pittsburgh Steelers. In Pittsburgh, he played one season in the defensive secondary and punted for a 40.7 yard average. Defensively in 1959 with the Steelers, Robert Luna intercepted three passes for 43 yards, returned two punts for 13 yards, longest for 8 yards. Luna concluded his pro career after the 1959 season.

Robert Luna

Punting

Year	Team	No.	Yds.	Avg.	Long	Blk.
1955	San Francisco 49ers	63	2,558	40.6	63	3[1]
1959	Pittsburgh Steelers	62	2,528	40.7	—	—[2]
		125	5,086	40.6	63	3

Notes

1 *1983 San Francisco 49ers Media Guide,* 185.

2 Telephone call to Pittsburgh Steelers Public Relations Office for statistics on Robert Luna, Tuesday, May 19, 1987.

Robert Luna, continued

Rushing

Year	Team	No.	Yds.	Avg.	TDs
1959	Pittsburgh Steelers	3	3	1.0	0[3]

(Additional statistics: 1 pass for 55 yards.)

San Francisco 49ers Career Statistics

Robert Luna ranked #10 — Punting, 63 punts for 2,558 yards, average 40.6 per punt, longest 63 yards.[4]

Notes

3 Ibid.

4 *1983 San Francisco 49ers Media Guide,* 179.

Vernon Valdez

Photo by: Robert L. Smith—Buffalo Bills Team

The Lancaster, California-born Mexicano, Vernon Valdez, began his football career at Antelope Valley High School and continued through Antelope Valley Junior College, Cal-Poly, and University of California at San Diego. Initially a T-formation quarterback, Valdez was a successful signal caller and was selected to the Junior College All-American Team in 1957 while at Antelope Valley Junior College.

With his eye toward a higher level of collegiate football, the military draft intervened and Valdez enlisted in the United States Marines. He played for the

Marine Corps depot team and showed strong offensive and defensive talent on the military gridiron.

With his military obligation completed and football still coursing through his veins, Valdez, the civilian, went to the Los Angeles Rams training camp in Redlands, California. His speed and strength made him a strong candidate for the defensive backfield, but he was cut due to lack of experience. However, after the third game of the season, Valdez was recalled by the Rams and added to the list of players. He played the

121

Vernon Valdez

Punt Returns

Year	Team	No.	Yds.	Avg.	Lg.	TDs
1961	Buffalo Bills	1	30	30.0	30	0[1]
1962	Oakland Raiders	2	14	7.0	8	0
		3	44	18.5	30	0

Interceptions

Year	Team	No.	Yds.	Avg.	Lg.	TDs
1962	Oakland Raiders	4	47	11.8	36	0[2]

Notes

1 David S. Neft, Richard M. Cohen, and Rick Korch, *The Football Encyclopedia: The Complete, Year-by-Year History of Professional Football from 1892 to the Present* (New York: St. Martin's Press, 1994), 345.

2 *Decades of Destiny: 1960-1984 the Historic First 25 Years* (Los Angeles: CWC Sport Publications, 1985).

rest of the season, starting several games at the right cornerback position.

In 1961 Valdez played with the Buffalo Bills for one year, then in 1962 played for the Oakland Raiders. The second-year Raiders were loaded with Mexicano talent and Valdez added to that talent. In the defensive secondary for the Raiders, Valdez returned punts and intercepted four passes to close out a brief three-year pro football career.

Robert Coronado

During his football days at College of the Pacific, Robert Coronado was considered to be one of the nation's fastest collegiate ends. His skills were exemplary and his coach Jack "Moose" Meyer rated him an outstanding NFL prospect—an offensive threat each time he ran a pass pattern.

Born and raised in Vallejo, California, Coronado lettered at the College of the Pacific in 1957 and 1958. He had a very successful career that included playing with present day legends Tom Flores and Dick Bass. Back in its heyday, College of the Pacific, now renamed University of the Pacific, was well known for the football talent it produced.

In the 1959 NFL draft, the Chicago Bears selected Coronado, but his pro football debut was delayed by the military. After two years of military service, Coronado gave pro football a try.

The Bears, who had drafted him 2 years earlier, opted to forego his contract and traded him to the Pittsburgh Steelers in 1961. At Pittsburgh, with limited playing time, Coronado had 3 receptions for 32 yards for the year. At the end of his rookie season, Coronado re-evaluated his future in pro football and returned to his alma mater to finish his education in 1963.

Robert Coronado					
Pass Receptions					
Year	Team	No.	Yds.	Avg.	TDs
1961	Pittsburgh Steelers	3	32	10.6	0

Source: Phone call to the Pittsburgh Steelers Public Relations Office for statistics on Robert Coronado, May 2, 1984.

Herman Urenda

Nicknamed "squirming Herman" at Brentwood High School in the farming community of Brentwood, California, Herman Urenda was an exceptional athlete adept at many sports. At College of the Pacific, Urenda participated in four sports, but excelled as a varsity performer in football. He played halfback, quarterback, and end equally well. In one brief season he played with football greats Tom Flores and Dick Bass.

Versatility his forte, Urenda also did the punting for the Pacific Tigers and with an arsenal of many skills was invaluable to the team. For career statistics, he accumulated 688 total offensive yards, scored three touchdowns, and intercepted six passes. In 1958, Urenda received the Tully Knowles Award for the most minutes played that season.

Overlooked in the pro football drafts, Urenda went to the nearby Oakland Raiders training camp for a tryout. Before he could start the season, however, he was drafted by Uncle Sam. Like so many young men of his time, Urenda served in the military for two years before embarking on a pro football career. Urenda joined the Raiders in 1963 and played in the AFL for a single season.

John Aguirre

Although, it was rumored that John Aguirre and Redskins kicker Joe Aguirre were brothers, this was not the case. They were not related, but shared striking similarities. Both attended colleges in California; both were drafted by NFL teams from the eastern part of the country; both played pro football in Canada; and both were CFL All-Stars. Despite the football-related similarities, the two were distinctly different individuals.

John Aguirre played his collegiate football as USC. He was an extraordinary strong tackle, drafted by the Cleveland Rams of the NFL in 1944. Nick Pappas, of the Sports Information Department at USC, recalls Aguirre as a fine young man and aggressive football player. Aguirre lived in a garage apartment behind where Pappas lived in Los Angeles;

and Pappas referred to John like a son for the time he attended USC.

Unable to pursue a pro football career until the end of World War II, Aguirre awaited his opportunity and opted to play with the Calgary Stampeders of the CFL in 1948. Calgary coach Les Lear considered Aguirre a promising recruit and chose him as one of the five regular imports from the United States—a decision he would not regret. At the time, the Calgary franchise was in the rebuilding phase, and the players brought together to comprise this team were all winners.

In their first season, the Calgary defensive line, anchored by Aguirre, Rattle Matheson, and others, was impenetrable. They played magnificently throughout the 1948 season and shut down their opponents in grand style. They were victorious in each of their games, including the Grey Cup Championship, beating the Ottawa Roughriders 12-7, for a perfect 12-0 record. Aguirre was selected to the Western Conference All-Star team in his most memorable rookie pro football year.

The next season Aguirre was selected to his second consecutive Western Conference All-Star team, but the Stampeders were unable to repeat as the Grey Cup champions. In 1950 a neck injury forced Aguirre into early retirement, but he left the CFL a champion.

Greg Pérez

As a youngster growing up in Southern California, Gregory Pérez was inspired by a television college football game he watched between the USC Trojans and the University of Miami Hurricanes. At the time, Pérez was a senior in high school and was so motivated by what he saw, he hoped to one day play for Miami. Within a couple of years, Pérez's wishful thinking came true.

In the meantime, he played great football at Excelsior High School in Norwalk, California. Known as a "phantom" at intercepting passes, Pérez led the conference with ten interceptions in his final prep year. In one game, Pérez put on an All-American performance by returning a kickoff the length of the football field, intercepting two passes, throwing a

touchdown pass, and rushing for two touchdowns. It was outstanding performances like this that defined a fabulous high school career for the speedster, who was named the team's most valuable player.

After high school, Pérez played two years at nearby Cerritos Junior College in his hometown of Norwalk before he journeyed cross country to the University of Miami. He experienced two brilliant campaigns at Cerritos and like in high school, Pérez was a three-way threat, returning punts, rushing for yardage, and what became his specialty, intercepting passes. There was no limit to the football skills he displayed, and for his contributions to the Cerritos football program, he was once again given most valuable player status.

In February 1968 with Norwalk in his rearview mirror, Greg Pérez checked in at the University of Miami in Coral Gables, Florida. Basking in the Florida sun and happy to be there, it took him just one week in spring training to win the first-string defensive backfield job. Pérez did so well nobody could unseat him at cornerback, and his hopes of being a Hurricane football player were now realized.

For the next two seasons at Miami, Pérez distinguished himself on defense and improved his pass interception skills. In 1968 Pérez was tied for first place on the team with three interceptions returned for 82 yards, and was eighth among Hurricane defenders with 43 tackles. He played a great defensive game in the 1969 season, but the Hurricanes finished one win short of a .500 record.

With no postseason bowl games on the schedule and his collegiate career concluded, Pérez hoped to hear from the pro football teams. The Toronto Argonauts of the Canadian Football League (CFL) recruited him, and once again Pérez would travel cross country, this time heading north to play football. His stay in Toronto was brief, for just prior to the start of the 1970 CFL season, they traded him to the Calgary Stampeders. At Calgary, Pérez was given a serious opportunity to play, and after the fourth league game, he became their regular defensive back. In 1970 he intercepted six passes, including one in the Grey Cup Championship loss to the Montreal Alouettes. The Pérez highlights from the 1970 season were his three interceptions against the Edmonton Eskimos on Labor Day. According to the *1971 Calgary Football Media Guide,* his addition to the Stampeders defensive secondary added strength to an already strong defensive unit. True to his skills, Pérez lived up to expectations and contributed to the success of his team.

The following year, Pérez was traded to the Hamilton Tiger-Cats where he played six games. As a Tiger-Cat, he intercepted 1 pass, had 11 punt returns for 56 yards, and 2 fumble returns, 1 for a touchdown. Pérez was then traded to the Saskatchewan Roughriders where he played four games. In 1972 Pérez played one final game with Saskatchewan and finished his two-year, one-game career in the CFL.

It was a notable football journey for the Californian from Norwalk. His talent, perseverance, and hard work enabled him to fulfill a dream and play for the Hurricanes of Miami. In pro football, he became a starter, excelled on defense, and played in the Grey Cup Championship. Although his professional career did not extend beyond three seasons, Pérez was renowned for his speed and adeptness at pass interceptions.

Greg Pérez

Interceptions

Year	Team	No.	Yds.	Long	TDs
1970	Calgary Stampeders	6	69	25	0[1]
1971	Hamilton/Saskatchewan	1	31	31	0[2]
		7	100	31	0

Punt Returns

Year	Team	No.	Yds.	Avg.	TDs
1971	Hamilton/Saskatchewan	11	56	5.09	0[3]

Notes

1 *Calgary Stampeders 1971 Fact Book,* 18.

2 Telephone call to CFL office for statistics, March 28, 1994.

3 Ibid.

Complete Draft History

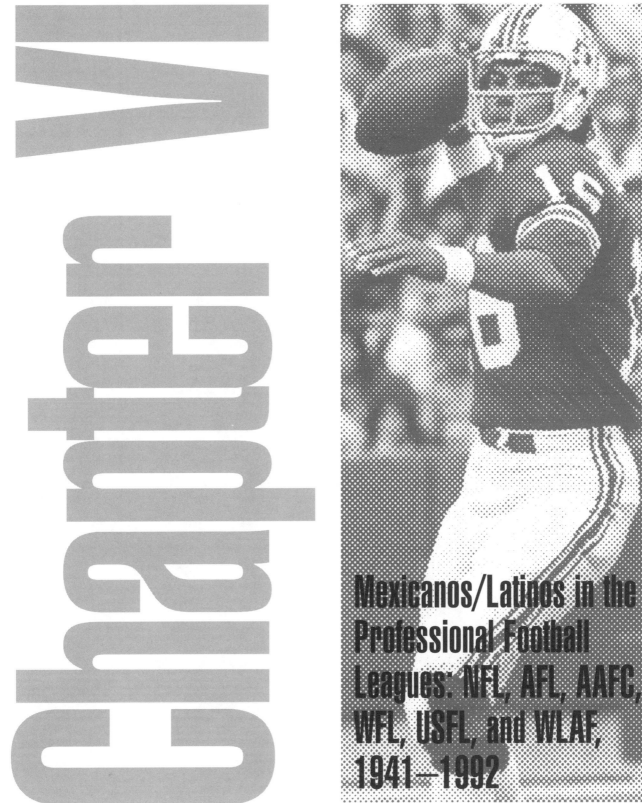

Chapter VI

Mexicanos/Latinos in the Professional Football Leagues: NFL, AFL, AAFC, WFL, USFL, and WLAF, 1941–1992

The Big Ivory Hunt

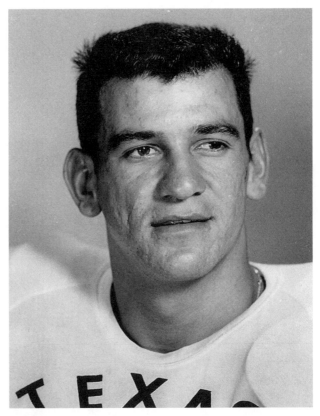

René Ramírez   *University of Texas Sports Information*

The ritual known as the NFL collegiate football draft has long been a significant part of professional football history. In 1936 the first ever collegiate player was chosen, and over the years the NFL ranks have been replenished by young and talented collegians. For Mexicanos and other Latinos, it has been over a half century of participation in the "Big Ivory Hunt" for professional football players.

Since 1941, when the Washington Redskins selected the first Latino in the history of the draft, there have been 107 Mexicanos/Latinos drafted by the various professional football franchises throughout the years.

Within the decade, Latinos regularly appeared in the annual collegiate lottery. Historically, Latinos had already entered the professional ranks as players with the Rodríguez brothers from West Virginia signing on with the Buffalo Bisons and the Frankford Yellowjackets as early as 1929. Jesse Rodríguez was the first to enter pro football as a punter/fullback with Buffalo, followed by his younger brother Kelly, who played a two-team schedule with the Frankford Yellowjackets and the Minneapolis Redjackets during the 1930 season.

The decade of the forties was significant for Mexicanos. A total of nine athletes was chosen in the lottery; most of them were drafted by NFL teams while they served in the armed forces during World War II.

Joe Aguirre, an end who doubled as a kicker from St. Mary's College of California, became the first Latino draftee. The Washington Redskins selected him in the ninth round of the 1941 draft. From the beginning Aguirre showed promise. "Big Joe Aguirre and equally husky Sam Golden stood head and shoulders above the rest figuratively as well as literally," wrote Bill Dismar of the *Washington Star*.

In the years that followed, Latino pro football draftees had big years in 1954, 1962, and 1987. Among the four Latino selections of 1954, two of them were powerful and swift running backs. Rick Casares took the NFL by storm and was known as one of the toughest players in the NFL, during football's "Fabulous Fifties." Casares, who played his collegiate ball at the University of Florida, played ten seasons with the Chicago Bears and was the NFL's leading rusher in 1956. He also played in five Pro Bowls.

California Poly speedster Alex Bravo, a 9.7 sprinter, played five years in pro football. As an offensive back in the CFL, he established a season record for the longest run from scrimmage. In the NFL/AFL, the Los Angeles Rams and Oakland Raiders utilized his speed in the defensive secondary. Bravo's claim to fame was the 1957 game against Cleveland where he caught Hall of Famer Jim Brown twice from behind on breakaway runs.

In 1960 the rival American Football League (AFL) conducted their first collegiate draft of players. Among those first selected by the Buffalo Bills expansion team was René "The Galloping Gaucho" Ramírez,

129

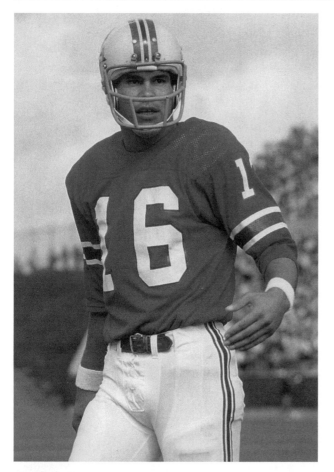

Jim Plunkett

from the University of Texas. Ramírez was a superlative running back for the Longhorns and an All-Southwestern Conference selection. However, the speedy Ramírez chose not to pursue a career in pro football. For the next several years, until 1969, the AFL held a separate collegiate draft of players. In 1970, the NFL and AFL solidified an agreement to merge the two leagues and become an expanded NFL.

The 1962 NFL draft gathered five Mexicano athletes. Notable among the talent were Hank Rivera and José Hernández. The hard-hitting Rivera used his defensive skills with the Oakland Raiders and the Buffalo Bills, while the fleet Hernández specialized in kickoff and punt returns. Although Hernández was with the Washington Redskins for a season, his gridiron success became most evident in the Canadian Football League.

Several years later, Mexicanos hit the jackpot with Heisman Trophy winner Jim Plunkett. Plunkett was the number one choice of the New England Patriots in the 1971 NFL draft. The formidable Plunkett replaced another Mexicano quarterback, Joe Kapp, at New England and forged a career with three NFL teams. A career highlight for the Mexican

American quarterback was being named the most valuable player of Super Bowl XV in 1981, while playing for the Oakland Raiders.

Other prestigious first-round draft choices include Filipino descent Roman Gabriel, Los Angeles Rams, 1962; Big Jim García from Purdue University, Cleveland Browns; future Hall of Famer and possibly the best offensive lineman in the history of the game, Anthony Muñoz, Cincinnati Bengals, 1980; Cubano Luis Sharpe, St. Louis Cardinals, 1982; Gabriel Rivera, Pittsburgh Steelers, 1983; Tony Zendejas, Washington Redskins, 1984 (supplemental draft); and Tony Casillas, Atlanta Falcons, 1986. With the exception of Casillas, the others are retired NFL players.

The 1987 NFL draft included 5 Latinos. This group of athletes included punter Rubén Rodríguez and offensive lineman Danny Villa. Interestingly, both of these Mexicano athletes attended Pac 10 schools in Arizona, the University of Arizona and Arizona State, respectively.

Rodríguez punted successfully for the Seattle Seahawks for three seasons. Danny Villa, who

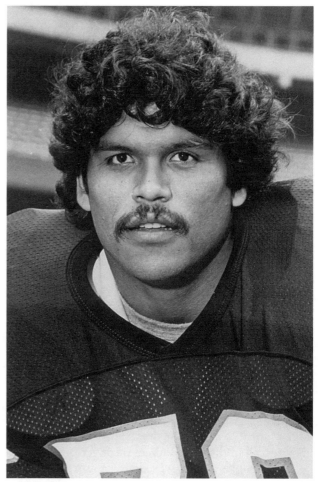

Anthony Muñoz

The 1991 NFL Mexicano/Latino draft picks were linemen who liked to throw their weight around. The 6'6", 300-pound tackle Eduardo Vega hailed from Inglewood, California, and starred at offensive tackle at Santa Monica City College before transferring to Memphis State University. The Phoenix Cardinals selected him in the sixth round. The other hefty lineman was defensive end Mike Flores who, at 6'3", 246 pounds, was notorious for quarterback sacks and led the University of Louisville Cardinals in sacks the previous two seasons. Flores was picked in the eleventh round by the Philadelphia Eagles.

Other Drafts

Historically, other pro football leagues were organized and competed with the NFL for players, gate receipts, glory. The All-American Football Conference (AAFC) operated during the years after World War II, 1946-1949, and conducted four collegiate player drafts. Their process reduced the NFL pickings by some 560 players and among those numbers was a lone Latino. Dan Garza, an end from the

Gabriel Rivera

anchored the offensive line for the New England Patriots for several campaigns, returned to Arizona by way of a trade and played for the Phoenix Cardinals. His home stay was short as another trade sent him to the Kansas City Chiefs.

The Dallas Cowboys draft record of Latinos is dismal. Next to the Tampa Bay Buccaneers, who have never drafted a Latino athlete in their short history, the Cowboys have drafted only two in their 35-year existence. The Washington Redskins have the distinction of the most Mexicano/Latino draftees—ten since 1941. The most distinguished of their draft choices are Joe Aguirre, an All-Pro in 1944; Eddie Sáenz, the 1947 NFL kickoff return leader and possibly the best all-purpose Mexicano running back of all time; "Mean" Gene Brito, a four-time All-Pro defensive end for the Redskins from 1955 to 1958, and the outstanding lineman of the 1958 Pro Bowl contest; and Joe Kapp, who went on to pro football fame in Canada by leading the British Columbia Lions to the Grey Cup Championship in 1964, then led the Minnesota Vikings to the Super Bowl in 1969.

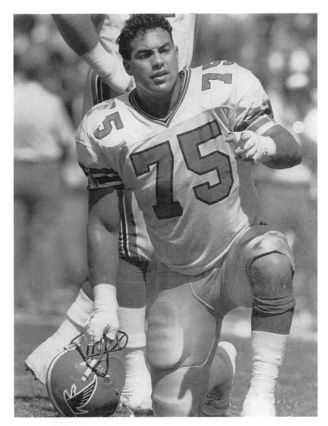

Tony Casillas

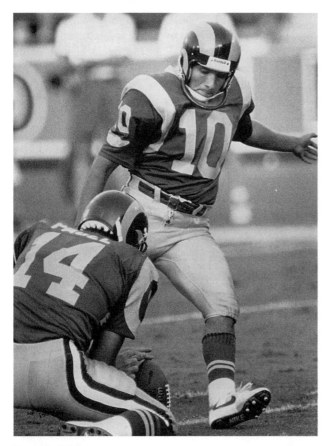

Tony Zendejas

University of Oregon, was selected in the 1949 draft by the New York Yankees.

The World Football League (WFL) appeared in 1974 and lasted two years. Their draft history was a single lottery of collegiate and professional players in 1974. Among the selectees by WFL teams were established Mexicano players such as Jim Plunkett, Manny Fernández, and Efrén Herrera.

Less than a decade later, in 1983, the United States Football League (USFL) made its debut. Like the rival leagues before them, their longevity was shortlived and after three seasons succumbed to the established NFL. The three lotteries held by the USFL resulted in 19 Mexicano/Latino athletes selected.

Unlike previous rival leagues to the NFL, the World League of American Football (WLAF), an NFL-sponsored preparatory league with teams in the United States and Europe, completed two spring seasons before folding. The WLAF conducted their only draft of collegians and free agents over the course of 4 days in February 1991. Three Mexicano quarterbacks were drafted by the Frankfurt Galaxy of the WLAF's European division. Mike Pérez, Sammy Garza, and Alex Espinoza were selected 3, 18, and 23 in the quarterback draft. Garza and Pérez had been NFL draft picks in 1987 and 1988. In all, eight Mexicanos were identified in the WLAF lottery.

NFL Draft of Mexicanos/Latinos in Pro Football, 1941–Present

Year	Name	Pos.	College/University	Team Drafted By	Rnd.
1941	Joe Aguirre	E	St. Mary's College	Washington Redskins	9th
1944	John Sánchez	T	University of San Francisco	New York Giants	9th
	John Aguirre	T	USC	Cleveland Rams	14th
	Abel Gonzales	B	SMU	Green Bay Packers	30th
1945	Edwin Sáenz	B	USC	Washington Redskins	13th
	Gonzalo Morales	B	St. Mary's College	Philadelphia Eagles	5th
1946	Russ López	B	University of West Virginia	Pittsburgh Steelers	17th
1948	Dan Garza	E	University of Oregon	New York Giants	15th
	Joe Suárez	G	St. Mary's College	Detroit Lions	24th
1951	Joe Arenas	B	University of Nebraska-Omaha	San Francisco 49ers	8th
	Gene Brito	E	Loyola University	Washington Redskins	17th
1952	Richard Ochoa	B	University of Texas	New York Giants	12th

NFL Draft of Mexicanos/Latinos in Pro Football, 1941–Present, continued

1953	Eli Romero	B	Wichita State University	Philadelphia Eagles	24th
1954	Rick Casares	B	University of Florida	Chicago Bears	2nd
	Jesús Esparza	T	New Mexico A&M	Baltimore Colts	26th
	Bobby Cavazos	B	Texas Tech University	Chicago Cardinals	3rd
	Alex Bravo	B	California Poly-San Luis Obispo	Los Angeles Rams	9th
1955	Alex Esquivel	B	Mexico City College	Baltimore Colts	24th
	George Maderos	B	California State-Chico	San Francisco 49ers	21st
	Robert Luna	B	University of Alabama	San Francisco 49ers	6th
1956	Gil Moreno	T	UCLA	Washington Redskins	12th
	Vincent González	B	LSU	Washington Redskins	20th
1957	Clem Corona	G	University of Michigan	Philadelphia Eagles	28th
1959	Robert Coronado	E	College of Pacific	Chicago Bears	10th
	Joe Kapp	QB	California-Berkeley	Washington Redskins	18th
1960	Robert Luna	DB	University of Alabama	Dallas Rangers (from Pittsburgh)	Expansion Selections
	Everisto Niño	T	East Texas State	San Francisco 49ers	9th
1962	Roman Gabriel	QB	North Carolina State University	Los Angeles Rams	1st
	José Hernández	B	University of Arizona	Washington Redskins	2nd
	Curtis Miranda	C	Florida A&M	New York Giants	5th
	Henry Rivera	DB	Oregon State University	Cleveland Browns	5th
	Gus Gonzales	G	Tulane University	Philadelphia Eagles	6th
1963	Luis Hernández	G	UTEP	Green Bay Packers	18th
1964	George Mira	QB	University of Miami	San Francisco 49ers	2nd
	Steve Barilla	T	Wichita State University	Detroit Lions	20th
1965	James García	DE	Purdue University	Cleveland Browns	1st
	Dave Estrada	B	Arizona State University	Washington Redskins	14th
1966	Stan Quintana	DB	New Mexico	Minnesota Vikings	11th
1967	Alfredo Ávila	DB	Sul Ross University	Washington Redskins	16th
	Bruce Cortez	DB	Parsons College	New Orleans Saints	16th
	Jim García	DE	California State-Chico	New Orleans Saints	Expansion Draft

NFL Draft of Mexicanos/Latinos in Pro Football, 1941–Present, continued

1968	Emilio Vállez	E	New Mexico	Chicago Bears	12th
1969	Ted Hendricks	LB	University of Miami	Baltimore Colts	2nd
1970	Manuel Barrera	LB	Kansas State University	Pittsburgh Steelers	6th
1971	Jim Plunkett	QB	Stanford University	New England Patriots	1st
1972	Jaime Núñez	E	Weber State	Los Angeles Rams	13th
	Steve Barrios	WR	Tulane University	New Orleans Saints	14th
	Carlos Álvarez	WR	University of Florida	Dallas Cowboys	15th
1973	Ron Fernandes	DE	East Michigan University	Miami Dolphins	10th
1974	Noé González	QB	Southwest Texas State	Oakland Raiders	12th
	Rod García	K	Stanford	Oakland Raiders	7th
	Efrén Herrera	K	UCLA	Detroit Lions	7th
1975	Ralph Ortega	LB	University of Florida	Atlanta Falcons	2nd
	Gene Hernández	DB	TCU	San Francisco 49ers	11th
	Les Chaves	DB	Kansas State	Detroit Lions	16th
1976	Steve Rivera	WR	California-Berkeley	San Francisco 49ers	4th
1977	Rafael Septién	K	Southwestern Louisiana	New Orleans Saints	10th
	André Herrera	B	Southern Illinois University	Kansas City Chiefs	6th
1978	Frank Corral	K	UCLA	Los Angeles Rams	3rd
1979	Max Montoya	G	UCLA	Cincinnati Bengals	7th
1980	Anthony Muñoz	T	USC	Cincinnati Bengals	1st
	James García	WR	UTEP	Kansas City Chiefs	6th
1981	Jairo A. Penaranda	B	UCLA	Los Angeles Rams	12th
1982	Luis E. Sharpe	T	UCLA	St. Louis Cardinals	1st
	Eddie García	K	SMU	Green Bay Packers	10th
1983	Gabriel Rivera	T	Texas Tech	Pittsburgh Steelers	1st
	Kiki De Ayala	LB	University of Texas	Cincinnati Bengals	6th
	Matt Hernández	T	Purdue	Seattle Seahawks	8th
	Mervyn Fernández	WR	San Jose State	Los Angeles Raiders	10th
1984	Ron Rivera	LB	California-Berkeley	Chicago Bears	2nd
	Lupe Sánchez	DB	UCLA	Kansas City Chiefs (June Supplemental Draft)	2nd

NFL Draft of Mexicanos/Latinos in Pro Football, 1941–Present, continued

1984	Tony Zendejas	K	University of Nevada-Reno	Washington Redskins (June Supplemental Draft)	1st
	Leo Barker	LB	New Mexico State	Cincinnati Bengals	7th
1985	Leon Gonzales	WR	Bethune-Cookman	Dallas Cowboys	8th
	Fuad Reveiz	K	University of Tennessee	Miami Dolphins	7th
	Louis Garza	T	New Mexico State	Cincinnati Bengals	12th
1986	Tony Casillas	NT	University of Oklahoma	Atlanta Falcons	1st
	Max Zendejas	K	University of Arizona	Dallas Cowboys	4th
1987	Danny Villa	T	Arizona State University	New England Patriots	5th
	Rubén Rodríguez	K	University of Arizona	Seattle Seahawks	5th
	Carlos Reveiz	K	University of Tennessee	New England Patriots	11th
	Jim Reynosa	DE	Arizona State University	Indianapolis Colts	11th
	Sammy Garza	QB	UTEP	Seattle Seahawks	8th
1988	Teddy García	K	Northeastern Louisiana	New England Patriots	4th
	Mike Pérez	QB	San Jose State	New York Giants	7th
1989	No Mexicano/Latino players drafted				
1990	No Mexicano/Latino players drafted				
1991	Eduardo Vega	T	Memphis State	Phoenix Cardinals	6th
	Mike Flores	DE	University of Louisville	Philadelphia Eagles	11th
	Luis Cristóbal	G	University of Miami	New York Giants	10th
1992	Chris Pérez	T	University of Kansas	Miami Dolphins	5th
	Carlos Huerta	K	University of Miami	San Diego Chargers	12th

AFL Draft of Mexicanos/Latinos, 1960–1966

Year	Name	Pos.	College/University	Team Drafted By	Rnd.
1960	René Ramírez	B	University of Texas	Buffalo Bills (First Selections)	Expansion Draft
1961	Willie Crafts	G	Texas A&I	Denver Broncos	15th
1962	Curtis Miranda	C	Florida A&M	New York Titans	11th
	Henry Rivera	DB	Oregon State	Oakland Raiders	10th
	José Hernández	B	Arizona	Oakland Raiders	7th
	Gus Gonzales	G	Tulane	Houston Oilers	7th
	Everisto Niño	T	East Texas	Dallas Texans	31st
1964	George Mira	QB	Miami	Denver Broncos	18th
1965	James García	DE	Purdue	Denver Broncos	7th
1966	Stan Quintana	DB	New Mexico	New York Jets	14th

All-American Football Conference (AAFC) Draft

Year	Name	Pos.	College/University	Team Drafted By	Rnd./Pick
1949	Dan Garza	E	University of Oregon	New York Yankees	7th/48th player taken

World Football League (WFL) Collegiate/Pro Draft History

Year	Name	Pos.	College/University	Team Drafted By	Pick
1974	Noé González	QB	Southwest Texas State	Houston Texans	10th
	Efrén Herrera	K	UCLA	Memphis Southmen	36th

Pro Draft

Year	Name	Pos.	Pro Team	Team Drafted By	Pick
1974	Jim Plunkett	QB	New England Patriots	Portland Storm	1st
	Manny Fernández	DT	Miami Dolphins	Portland Storm	12th
	Roman Gabriel	QB	Philadelphia Eagles	The Hawaiians	24th

World League of American Football (WLAF) Draft

Year	Name	Pos.	College/University	Team Drafted By	Rnd./Pick
1991	John Guerrero	T	USC	Orlando Thunder	2nd/14th
	David Díaz-Infante	G	San Jose State	Frankfurt Galaxy	3rd/24th
	Paul Yñiguez	C	Kansas State	Birmingham Fire	6th/59th
	Max Zendejas	K	University of Arizona	London Monarchs	1st/2nd
	Mike Pérez	QB	San Jose State	Frankfurt Galaxy	1st/3rd
	Sammy Garza	QB	UTEP	Frankfurt Galaxy	2nd/18th
	Alex Espinoza	QB	Iowa State	Frankfurt Galaxy	3rd/23rd
	Alfonso García	WR	Fort Lewis	Orlando Thunder	8th/78th

United States Football League (USFL) Draft History

Year	Name	Pos.	College/University	Team Drafted By	Rnd.
1983	Kiki De Ayala	LB	University of Texas	Washington Federals	11th
	Matt Hernández	T	Purdue	Chicago Blitz	15th
	Joaquín Zendejas	K	La Verne College	Boston Breakers	23rd
1984	Lupe Sánchez	DB	UCLA	Arizona Wranglers	1st
	Tony Zendejas	K	University of Nevada-Reno	Los Angeles Express	5th
	Fred Fernandes	WR	Utah State	New Orleans Breakers	12th
	Jess García	K	Northeastern Louisiana	San Antonio Gunslingers	12th
	Jeff Reyes	DE	University of Utah	New Orleans Breakers	17th
	Joel Ríos	DT	Rice University	San Antonio Gunslingers	Terr. Draft
	Rich Sánchez	B	California-Lutheran	Los Angeles Express	Terr. Draft
	Ron Rivera	LB	California-Berkeley	Oakland Invaders	Terr. Draft
1985	Leon Gonzales	WR	Bethune-Cookman	Orlando Renegades	11th
	Louis Garza	T	New Mexico State	Arizona Wranglers	9th
	Mike Mendoza	QB	Northern Arizona University	Arizona Wranglers	16th
	Luis Zendejas	K	Arizona State	Arizona Wranglers	25th
	Ralph Partida	G	Oklahoma State	Denver Gold	19th
	Jeff Sánchez	DB	University of Georgia	Jacksonville Bulls	17th
	Juan Comendeiro	G	University of Miami	Orlando Renegades	5th
	Fuad Reveiz	K	University of Tennessee	Memphis Showboats	18th

Collegiate Bowl Games

Mexicano/Latino Performances in Postseason Collegiate Bowl Games, 1936–1980

Collegiate Bowl Games, 1936-1980

Lauro Apodaca

The history of collegiate football is a rich and colorful one. Many athletes are remembered for their plays and performances in games that have earned them respect and reverence from coaches, teammates, and fans. Their rewards often times come in selections to All-Star, All-Conference, and All-America teams, and, for a successful season or conference championship, their participation in postseason Bowl games.

In numerous collegiate postseason Bowl games, Latino athletes have a history of stellar performances in these games dating to 1936. For example, in the west Texas town of El Paso, Texas, in 1936, Anastacio and Lauro Apodaca utilized a trick play to score a touchdown to tie the game in the first ever Sun Bowl. Their efforts prevented New Mexico State from losing the game and launched the Mexicano/Latino history in college postseason games. A year later (1937) in new Orleans, diminutive Manuel Gómez intercepted 2 passes, caught a touchdown pass, and threw one to lead the Santa Clara Broncos over LSU 21-14, in the 3rd annual Sugar Bowl.

Gonzalo Morales returned a kickoff 62 yards in the 1947 Oil Bowl contest between St. Mary's College of California and Georgia Tech. In the 1953 Cotton Bowl, University of Texas fullback Richard "El Toro" Ochoa, pounded the Tennessee line for 108 yards rushing, as the Longhorns won 16-0. Meanwhile, in Miami on the same day in 1953, Alabama halfback Bobby Luna scored two touchdowns and kicked 7 extra points enabline Crimson Tide scorers. Luna scored a record 19 points enabling Alabama to destroy Syracuse 61-6 in the Orange Bowl.

The following 1954 Bowl season, Texas Tech Raider and All-American halfback Bobby Cavazos ran for glory, scoring three touchdowns to beat the Auburn Tigers 35-13.

The 1961 East-West Shrine All-Star game witnessed West team's Hank Rivera put on a defensive performance unequaled in the history of the Shriner's classic. Representing Oregon State University, Rivera intercepted two passes and his bone-jarring tackles are chronicled in San Francisco newspaper accounts of the game.

Out of the University of Miami and possibly the only collegiate player in the history of the game to play in six All-Star/Bowl games is quarterback George Mira. This Latino athlete was such a devastating talent, he began his postseason All-Star play as a sophomore in the 1961 Liberty Bowl and through 1964 made six appearances, of which he was the most valuable player in three of the contests.

Beginning the decade of the seventies, Stanford's Heisman Trophy Award winner Jim Plunkett led his Stanford team to an upset victory over the heavily favored Ohio State 27-17 in the 1971 Rose Bowl game. For his leadership, the Mexicano star was named the most valuable player.

But, in the writer's opinion, the postseason immortality award goes to defensive end Chico Mendoza of

A. F. "Hookey" Apodaca

the Texas Christian University Horned Frogs. Mendoza stormed in from his end position to block football legend Jim Brown's extra point attempt that enabled TCU to beat a determined Syracuse team 28-27 in the 1957 Cotton Bowl.

Other Mexicanos/Latinos who have played in other Bowl games over the years include players such as Eddie Sáenz, Dan Garza, Primo Villanueva, Ricardo Casares, Joe Kapp, Jim García, Eddie Valdez, and Rod García. Their performances without a doubt were exciting and memorable. What follows are excerpts from newspapers, college yearbooks, and media guides that detail the Mexicano/Latino athletes' excellence in college postseason games. The chronology begins in El Paso, Texas, on January 1, 1936:

Sun Bowl, 1936

"The New Mexico Aggies and the Hardin-Simmons Cowboys of Abilene battled to a 14-14 deadlock in the Southwest's first Sun Bowl gridiron classic before a New Year's day crowd of nearly 12,000.

"A 15-yard pass from Tyler to Scroggins in the second quarter gave the Cowboys their first touchdown.

The score stood until the third period when Mark Spanogle climaxed an Aggie drive with a one-yard plunge. Anastacio "Hookey" Apodaca's kick tied the score. The cowboys immediately put over another touchdown to take the lead.

"Held apparently helpless for a time, the Aggies came to life with a tricky offensive play worth seven points. Lem Pratt flipped a pass from midfield to A. Apodaca, who lateraled to Lauro Apodaca. Untouched, Apodaca galloped 35 yards across the goal and A. Apodaca kicked the extra point, tying the score."[1]

"In those days of the 1930s and early 1940s, there were always some Apodacas on the New Mexico Aggie squads, but Lauro and his cousin 'Hookey' were competitors in a class by themselves."[2]

1 "El Paso Game Ends 14 to 14," *San Antonio Light,* Vol. 55, no. 349, San Antonio, Texas, January 2, 1936.
2 Orren Beaty, "Sportsmanship was just part of the game for Apodacas," *Las Cruces Sun-Times,* April 2, 1993.

Sugar Bowl, 1937

"Santa Clara's redshirted Broncos, flashing a spectacular passing and running attack, battered Louisiana State's Tigers into submission, 21 to 14, today in the third Sugar Bowl football battle at Tulane stadium before a capacity crowd of 41,000.

"The Broncos drove 43 yards for their initial touchdown. Don De Rosa cut around end for 12 yards and Chuck Pavelko smacked through the line for four. Nello Don Falaschi slipped back and tossed a pass down the middle to Manuel Gómez who took the ball on the 5 and continued across the goal.

"A freak play gave Santa Clara its third touchdown shortly after the start of the second half. Gómez intercepted a pass and raced 25 yards to Louisiana's 15. Falaschi then scored from the one and Gómez passed to Walter Smith for the extra point.

"Santa Clara missed a scoring opportunity midway in the second period when Gómez intercepted one of Pat Coffee's long aerials and returned it 22 yards to Louisiana's 18."[1]

1 "Santa Clara Wins from LSU, 21-14," *The New York Times,* January 2, 1937.

Rose Bowl, 1944

"Surprising even their staunchest adherents, the Southern California Trojans today passed the University of Washington dizzy and won their seventh Rose Bowl football game in as many tries, 29-0.

"The Trojans scored all four touchdowns on passes and picked up 2 points in an automatic safety in the final period."[1]

". . . runs by Eddie Sáenz . . . netted a first down to set up USC's third touchdown of the afternoon . . ."[2]

1 "So. California Tops Washington, 29-0 in Rose Bowl Upset," *The New York Times,* January 2, 1944.
2 *1944 USC Yearbook.*

Sun Bowl, 1945

"Southwestern University's Pirates did a neat job of turning the tables on the University of Mexico's Pumas New Year's Day in the 10th edition of the Sun Bowl held at Kidd Field. It was the Pumas who were expected to display all the razzle dazzle. The Pirates, who were touted as leaning toward the conservative, managed to hand the Pumas a 35-0 shellacking.

"For the first quarter it looked like the game was going to be a real fight with the Pumas stopping the Pirates on the nine-yard line. They came back with the jack-rabbit running of left halfback Omar Cardona and right halfback José Espinosa who kept the Pirates on their toes."[1]

"Touchdowns were made by Blodzinski, the Pirates acting captain who picked up a blocked punt and returned back over the Puma's goal line. Rudy Flores, a native El Pasoan, carried the pigskin over for two touchdowns while J. D. Ulrey and Robby McDonald accounted for the other two."[2]

"This game was marked by the only appearance of a foreign university in an American college bowl game. The Pumas of Mexico University were expected to display a powerful, razzle-dazzle offense while Southwestern's was extremely conservative. Exactly the opposite occurred. Initially, the Pumas were able to control the bigger, quicker Southwestern, halting an initial drive on its own 9-yard line early in the first quarter. However, that would be the only highlight for Mexico."[3]

1 Don White, "Pirates Trounce Mexico U 35-0 in Yearly Classic," *The El Paso Times,* January 2, 1945.
2 "Pirates Set Up Many Firsts in Sun Bowl," *The Williamson County Sun,* January 2, 1945.
3 Pearl Mueller, El Paso Sun Bowl Association, "1945 Game Program/Media Guide Information," and letter to Mario Longoria, May 9, 1996.

Oil Bowl, 1949

". . . Third annual Oil Bowl football game . . . fans braved freezing temperatures and cold rain . . .

"Georgia Tech cashed in on 8 pass interceptions and 3 St. Mary's Gael's fumbles to take the lead . . .

"Gonzalo Morales, substitute Gael halfback, provided the biggest thrill when midway in the final period he took a Tech kickoff on his 23 and returned it 62 yards to the Georgia Tech 15 . . ."[1]

1 "Georgia Tech Triumphs, 41 to 19, Grabbing 8 St. Mary's Forwards," *The New York Times,* January 2, 1947.

Cotton Bowl, 1949

"Oregon and Southern Methodist, two high-powered football teams that like to toss the ball around will meet in Dallas for the thirteenth annual Cotton Bowl.

"Oregon is rated stronger in the line and Southern Methodist better in the backfield. The Oregon line is big and rangy. Dan Garza, senior end, stands 6 feet 2 inches and weighs 198. Behind the Oregon line is Norman Van Brocklin who is considered up to SMU's best."[1]

"All-American Doak Walker and his brilliant running mate Kyle Rote carried SMU to victory over Oregon, 21-13.

"Oregon's Norman Van Brocklin engineered two sensational last quarter touchdowns to cap a brilliant offensive contest."[2]

1 "SMU with Doak Walker, Picked to Defeat Oregon in Dallas Battle," *The New York Times,* January 2, 1949.
2 "So. Methodist Trips Oregon as Walker and Rote Excell," *The New York Times,* January 2, 1949.

Cotton Bowl, 1953

". . . University of Texas . . . smacked down Tennessee 16-0, in the 17th renewal of the cotton Bowl Classic.

". . . But it was Dick (El Toro) Ochoa, 200 pounds of battering fullback, who carried the brunt of the crushing Texas offensive that ground out 269 yards.

". . . Ochoa carried the ball 26 times for 108 yards. . . Ochoa who also finished his college career, an overwhelming choice of the sportwriters as the outstanding back of the day."[1]

1 Dick Peebles, "Ochoa Leads Strong Steer Ground Game," *San Antonio Express-News,* January 2, 1953.

Gator Bowl, 1953

"Rick Casares got a second chance to kick a conversion because of a Tulsa penalty that gave Florida a 14-13 victory over Tulsa in the eighth annual Gator Bowl.

Richard Ochoa   *University of Texas Sports Information*

". . . Casares bulled over the one-yard line for the first score. . .In rushing statistics, . . . Casares rushed for 86 yards."[1]

1 "Florida Nips Tulsa in Gator Bowl on Conversion by Casares, 14-13," *The New York Times*, January 2, 1953.

Orange Bowl, 1953

"Alabama's Crimson Tide rolled with such force that it set records in beating Syracuse by 61-6 in the Orange Bowl football game before a gathering of 66,208, the largest ever to attend the classic.

". . . After a 42-yard run back at the start of the third period, Bobby Luna went the remaining 38 yards for the touchdown . . .

". . . Seven players accounted for the Alabama touchdowns and halfback Bobby Luna, who twice crossed the goal line, kicked seven extra points. Luna thus accounted for two of the thirteen marks that were

set. His total of 19 points and his seven conversions went into the record books."[1]

1 Lincoln A. Werden, "Alabama's Nine Touchdowns Rout Syracuse by Record Orange Bowl Score: Crimson Tide Wins at Miami, 61-6," *The New York Times*, January 2, 1953.

Gator Bowl, 1954

"Texas Tech broke Auburn's back with a 53-yard scoring pass in the third quarter and a record-breaking 59-yard touchdown run by Bobby Cavazos in the fourth quarter today and won the ninth annual Gator Bowl football game, 35-13.

"Cavazos, a second-team All-American halfback, thrilled the crowd of 32,000 by scoring three touchdowns and showing his brilliant long-distance running form. He was noted the most valuable player on the Red Raider squad by the sportswriters."[1]

1 "Texas Tech Routs Auburn, 35-13, Cavazos Registers 3 Touchdowns," *The New York Times*, January 2, 1954.

Bobby Cavazos

Blue-Gray All-Star Game, 1955

"Kentucky's brilliant passing quarterback, Bob Hardy, led the Southern College All-Stars to a thrilling 20-19 gridiron victory over a Northern team in the annual Blue-Gray game today . . . The Kentucky back outgunned Wisconsin's Jim Haluska in a spectacular aerial duel to put the South in front, 13-0, early in the game. The Yankees later gained a 19-13 edge.

"With time growing short, Mississippi State back Art Davis got loose for a 17-yard run that put the Gray [team] in scoring position. Kenneth Keller of North Carolina scored from the 2 and Vince González of Louisiana State added the extra point."[1]

1 "Grays Pass Plays Defeat Blues on Gridiron, 20-19," *The New York Times*, January 1, 1956.

Hula Bowl, 1955

"Quarterback Paul Larson of California and fullback Carroll Hardy of Colorado passed and ran the college All-Stars to a 33-13 victory over the Hawaii All-Stars in the ninth Hula Bowl game before 21,000.

"The contest is between the collegiate cream of the mainland and the local military and Hawaiian players, fortified by the presence of five pro stars . . . Otto Graham, Gordon Soltau, Elroy Hirsch, Lou Groza and Jim Clark . . .

"The collegiate line ripped big holes for Hardy, Dick Moegle, and Primo Villanueva of UCLA."

". . . Larson figured in every scoring drive and set up the final score with a 29-yard touchdown toss to Villanueva."[1]

1 "College All-Star Eleven Beats Hawaiians in Hula Bowl, 33-13," *The New York Times*, January 10, 1955.

Cotton Bowl, 1957

"A blocked conversion attempt enabled Texas Christian to score a 28-27 victory over Syracuse University in the Twenty-First annual Cotton Bowl football game today.

"Chico Mendoza, a second string TCU end, stormed in from the right side to smother Jim Brown's placement after the Orangemen's third touchdown late in the final period.

". . . this provided the Horned Frogs with the cushion they needed to hold off a determined Syracuse rally. . . ."[1]

Narciso "Chico" Mendoza

"It was the sports picture of the year (1957), Chico Mendoza blocking Jim Brown's extra point try to preserve TCU's 28-27 Cotton Bowl victory over Syracuse.

"It stole some of the thunder from Brown, who put on one of the best individual performances ever in the New Year's classic, scoring three touchdowns and kicking three extra points.

" 'Someone just barely brushed my arm, Mendoza said of his rush in a postgame interview. I didn't think it would make any difference though. I thought we had a good lead (29-20 with 5:07) at the time.'

"Syracuse coach Ben Schwartzwalder said afterwards that the game boiled down to that blocked extra point that beat us. TCU coach Abe Martin said the single thing that won the game was Mendoza blocking that kick."[2]

1 Joseph M. Sheehan. "TCU Defeats Syracuse; 68,000 See Frogs Triumph by 28-27," *The New York Times*. January 1, 1957.

2 Bill Hart. Blocked Kick Run of the Mill for Mendoza," *Abilene Reporter-News*, June 11, 1991.

Hula Bowl, 1957

"A professional All-Star squad led by Norman Van Brocklin of the Los Angeles Rams today defeated a College All-Star team, 52-21, before 24,000 fans at the eleventh annual Hula Bowl football game. Van Brocklin completed nineteen of twenty passes for 281 yards and five touchdowns.

". . . The pro scoring was led by Elroy 'crazy legs' Hirsch of the Los Angeles Rams and Joe Arenas of the San Francisco 49ers. Hirsch caught 3 touchdown passes from Van Brocklin while Arenas had a 5-yard touchdown run and an 8-yard touchdown pass from Van Brocklin . . . Arenas' teammate Bob Toneff was voted the outstanding lineman of the game. . ."[1]

1 "Pro Eleven Beats Collegians, 52-21," *The New York Times*, January 2, 1959.

Rose Bowl, 1959

"Iowa Hawkeyes, using a devastating set of running backs crushed California, 38-12 in the Rose Bowl.

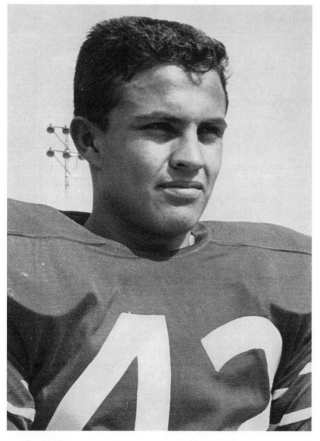

Bobby Santiago

". . . Joe Kapp, California Bear's quarterback, led his team to a touchdown after taking the second half kickoff . . . Jack Hart scoring both California touchdowns, the first from 1 yard out to end a 74-yard drive, the other on a 17-yard touchdown pass from Kapp to finish a 93-yard thrust.

". . . Kapp completed 9 of 20 passes for 130 yards."[1]

1 "Iowa Overpowers California: Hawkeye's Score on West Coast 38 to 12," *The New York Times*, January 2, 1959.

Junior Rose Bowl, 1959

"Bakersfield College, truly the Nation's best Junior College football team defeated Del Mar Vikings of Corpus Christi, Texas, 36-14 in the 14th annual Junior Rose Bowl.

"Bakersfield fans . . . expressing surprise that Renegade ace halfback pass catcher Joe Hernández had failed to catch a pass for six points. Early in the first period an incomplete pass to Joe Hernández went for a 39-yard gain when interference was called on the Viking defense . . .

". . . Late in the second quarter, Hernández was also the intended receiver on the game's other interference call resulting in a 37-yard gain . . .

". . . Defensively, in the fourth quarter, Hernández broke up a Viking threat with an interception in the end zone for a touchback . . ."[1]

1 Larry Press, "Big Plays Win Jr. Rose Bowl," *The Bakersfield Californian*, December 14, 1959.

Aviation Bowl, 1961

"New Mexico's shift backs led the way today in a 28-12 victory over Western Michigan in the first annual Aviation Bowl.

"A crowd of 3,694 watched the football game in snow, sleet and rain. The contest had been billed as a duel between New Mexico's running game and the passing of Ed Chlebek. The running game won.

"Bobby Santiago and Bobby Morgan sparked the Lobos powerful ground game, which rolled up 339 yards rushing. Santiago, a 5 foot 8 inch halfback, was named the back of the game for his first half heroics.

". . . Midway through the first period, Cummings recovered a fumble by Bob White of the Broncos. The Lobos took ten plays to negotiate 63 yards for a second touchdown, with Santiago racing over from the 10 for the score."[1]

1 "New Mexico Downs Western Michigan, 28-12 in First Aviation Bowl Bowl Game," *The New York Times*, December 10, 1961.

East-West Shrine, 1961

". . . 60,000 shivering Kezar stadium fans . . . saw an inspired West squad thunder to a 21-8 upset triumph over the East in the 37th edition of the Shrine Classic.

". . . Hank Rivera, the tough as nails safety man from Oregon State thought a major difference between East and West was that we had more offensive variation and it helped to be the underdog too, he added.

". . . Number 39 Hank Rivera was the best man on the field in defensive secondary. He did a wonderful job on passes and tackling.

"It was Rivera who jarred the teeth loose for Bob Ferguson in the fourth period and forced the great Ohio Stater to go to the bench for repairs.

"Rivera intercepted 2 passes and returned them for 7 yards . . . other players in the game included Roman Gabriel, Ernie Davis, Ron Bull, John Hadl and Merlin Olsen."[1]

1 Don Shelby, "West's Players Hail Owens; East is Baffled by 24 Bootleg," *San Francisco Examiner,* December 31, 1961; Curley Grieve, West's Defensive Might Difference," *San Francisco Examiner,* December 31, 1961.

Gotham Bowl, 1962

"Willie Ross ran 92 yards with a kick-off return and scored a second touchdown in the final period Saturday as Nebraska edged Miami 36-34, in a spectacular Gotham Bowl football game despite a dazzling passing show by George Mira, Miami's All-American quarterback.

"When Mira started firing away with his passes in the final minutes, Bob Brown, the Cornhuskers 6'5" 251-pound guard intercepted a Mira pass to stamp out the last threat of the Hurricanes with only seconds to play.

"Mira, voted the outstanding player in the game, broke a University of Miami record by completing 24 of 46 passes for 321 yards and two touchdowns.

"His scoring pitches were a 10 yarder to Ben Rizzo in the first period and a 30-yard bomb to Nick Spinelli in the second . . . Mira's favorite targets were Jim Simon, who caught six, and Bill Sparks, who grabbed four of his passes."[1]

1 "Cornhuskers Edge Hurricanes in Bowl," *San Antonio Express-News,* December 16, 1962.

North-South All-Star Game, 1963

"George Mira, the passing master of the Miami Hurricanes, rallied his Dixie eleven from a two touchdown deficit today and led the South to a 23-14 victory in the 16th annual North-South College All-Star game . . .

"Mira, voted the South's Most Valuable Player, thrilled a crowd of 19,120 in the Orange Bowl as he passed for two touchdowns, a pair of 2-point conversions and set up the clinching touchdown in the final quarter . . .

"Mira's pinpoint passes wrapped it up in the last quarter. On a 75-yard drive he hit Spinelli for 16 yards and Dellenger for 35, as the South moved to the 2. From there, Casinelli banged it over and Mira flipped a 2-point conversion to Crisson."[1]

1 "Mira Sparks South to Triumph," *The New York Times,* December 22, 1963.

All-American Football Game, 1964

"George Mira, a prodigious passer from the University of Miami who is headed for the San Francisco 49ers led the East to an 18-15 victory over the West in the annual All-American football game.

"Mira was smooth and spectacular quarterback who repeatedly thrilled a crowd of 21,112 in War Memorial Stadium. He completed 21 of 40 pass attempts as the East rallied and scored three times in the second half.

"Mira, voted the game's Most Valuable Player, set himself up to pass with the speed and precision of a Y. A. Tittle. He threw long and short but with accuracy; he was daring and deft as he went for the jugular of the West defense.

"In the first half, the East offense showed little, with no running and not much protection for Mira . . . Then Mira turned the game around in the second half. He began by completing 5 straight . . . he ran 35 yards in a zig zag manner to the 1 and Rick Leeson of Pitt scored the second East touchdown . . . Mira next had a streak of six completions, resulting in the winning touchdown . . . Mira outshined them all. It was his night and game."[1]

1 William N. Wallace, "East on Top, 18-15, on Mira's Passes," *The New York Times,* June 28, 1964.

East-West Shrine All-Star Game, 1965

". . . A six-yard scoring pass today with 1 minute 4 seconds remaining gave the West an 11-7 victory over the East in the 10th Shrine football game.

"East's team's . . . Jim García of Purdue broke through twice in the first half and threw West team's quarterback Craig Morton for long losses . . .

". . . Other players in the game included Dick Butkus of Illinois, Roger Staubach of Navy and Gayle Sayers of Kansas . . ."[1]

1 "West Takes Shrine Game," *The New York Times*, January 3, 1965.

Junior Rose Bowl, 1965

"Fullerton City College of California rallied in the final quarter to defeat previously unbeaten Henderson County College of Texas, 20-15, in the 20th annual Junior Rose Bowl football game.

". . . Dick Hough dueled with Inés Pérez, Henderson's passer . . . Pérez threw two touchdown passes to receiver Margene Adkins . . . one for 54 yards, the other for 22 yards. . ."[1]

1 "Fullerton Is Victor in Junior Rose Bowl," *The New York Times*, December 12, 1965.

Junior Rose Bowl, 1966

"Eddie Valdez threw six touchdown passes to lead Henderson County Junior College to a 40-13 rout of Pasadena City College in the 21st annual Junior Rose Bowl game.

". . . Three scoring passes to Margene Adkins . . . and the rugged defensive line anchored by Margarito Guerrero at tackle . . .

". . . In the second quarter, Valdez passed to Johnny Davis on a 73-yard play that established a game record.

"Eddie Valdez completed 21 of 29 passes for 337 yards and six touchdowns."[1]

1 "Henderson Crushes Pasadena by 40-13," *The New York Times*, December 11, 1966.

Rose Bowl, 1971

"The Stanford Indians, propelled by Jim Plunkett's professional caliber passing rallied for two touchdowns in the final period and upset favored Ohio State, 27-17 in the Rose Bowl. The victory quashed the Buckeye's national championship dreams.

"A roaring crowd of 103,839 watched the 57th Rose Bowl game which was one of the most surprising contests.

"The thrice-beaten Indians, registering their first Rose bowl success in 30 years, rode Plunkett's fine

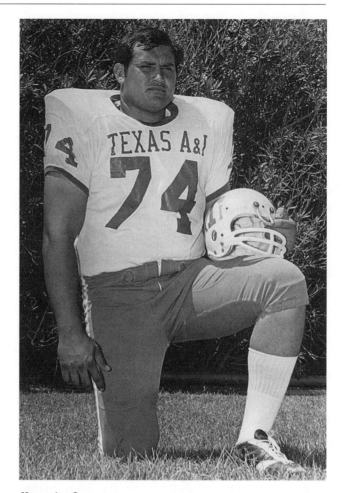

Margarito Guerrero

arm in marching 80 yards and then 25 for their decisive scores."[1]

"Plunkett had completed twenty of thirty passes for 265 yards and was named Player of the Game."[2]

1 Bill Becker, "Stanford Upsets Ohio State, by 27-17 on Late Rally," *The New York Times*, January 2, 1971.

2 Herb Michelson and Dave Newhouse, *Rose Bowl Football Since 1902* (New York: Stein and Day Publishing, 1977), 204.

Hula Bowl, 1971

"Led by Jim Plunkett, Stanford's Heisman Trophy winner, the North defeated the South, 42-32, in the 25th Hula Bowl today.

"Plunkett completed 11 of 12 passes for 131 yards and scored two touchdowns.

". . . The North team ran up five straight touchdowns, including one by Joe Theisman and two by Plunkett on runs of 5 and 1 yards.

Rod García

"Plunkett was voted the Outstanding Back and Jack Ham of Penn State earned Outstanding Lineman honors."[1]

1 "North Elevens Capture Senior and Hula Bowls; Score in Honolulu, 42-32," *The New York Times*, January 10, 1971.

Rose Bowl, 1972

"In a Rose Bowl game they'll be talking about for another 70 years, Stanford finally caught up with Michigan today . . . the Stanfords used a 31-yard field goal in the final 12 seconds by little Rod García to upset the undefeated Big Ten Champions, 13-12 . . .

"A crowd of 103,154 was treated to one of the hardest hitting of the 58 games in the Rose Bowl series . . .

"Wolverine's Dana Coin kicked a 30-yard field goal to give Michigan a 3-0 halftime lead before García tied it with a 42 yarder in the third period.

". . . On third down and 7 to go and with Steve Murray holding, García, who led the nation's field goal kickers with 14 in 1971, kicked his biggest. It was a 31-yard bull's-eye requiring only two seconds. A kick-off later, Stanford was returned a 13-12 victor."[1]

1 Bill Becker, "Michigan Is Upset; García's 31-Yard Field Goal with :12 To Go Wins Rose Bowl," *The New York Times*, January 2, 1972.

Sugar Bowl, 1974

"Florida All-American linebacker Ralph Ortega summoned up the main concern of the Gator's defense, 'I don't want to take anything away from the Nebraska running game but it's their passing that can hurt you.' "[1]

1 Marty Mule, *Sugar Bowl: The First Fifty Years* (Birmingham: Oxmoor, 1983), 193.

Other Nationally Significant Games: University of Texas vs. Texas A&M, 1920

"An unheard of crowd of 20,000 poured into old Clark Field Thanksgiving Day to watch Texas come from behind to nip the Texas Aggies 7-3 on a fourth quarter touchdown by Francisco Domínguez.

"Outplayed during half of a hotly contested game and carrying the short end of a 3 to 0 score, the Texas Longhorns came back in the final period here today and defeated their ancient rivals, the Aggies, 7-3 in one of the greatest games ever staged on Clark Field, when Francisco Domínguez, a Kerrville lad, plunged the final four yards to the Aggie goal line . . ."[1]

"Domínguez had only a yard needed for first down when he plunged three away from the goal and his huge frame plowed relentlessly over the last mark amid pandemonium of cheers. . . . But tonight, as happy Texas students render the night hideous to express their joy, they are singing the name of Francisco Domínguez, who carried the ball over."[2]

For many reasons, the story of Francisco Domínguez is actually the story of Francis Joseph Domingues, the son of a doctor whose descendants came from Spain, and a mother from Louisiana. His sister Alice Domingues Jobes from Kerrville, Texas, set the record straight on the proper spelling of the family name. Her brother, she recalls, was a superb student athlete who earned a degree in engineering from the University of Texas.[3] Significantly, the winning touchdown scored by Domingues that Thanksgiving Day earned him an honored place in the history of Texas Longhorn football. It enabled Texas to win their very first Southwest Conference Title.

1 Denn H. Freeman, *Hook'em Horns: A Story of Texas Football* (Hunstville, Alabama: Strode Publishers, 1974), 44.

2 "Longhorns Catch Aggies Near End: Farmers Outplay Texas Machine in First but Line Crumbles toward Finish," *San Antonio Express,* November 26, 1920.

3 Interview with Alice Domingues Jobes, Kerrville, Texas, April 24, 1995.

Alfredo Ávila

Sul Ross College vs. East Texas State, 1966

"Sul Ross State College Lobos had to fight from behind to gain a 14-14 tie with East Texas State before a homecoming crowd of 6,200 fans at Jackson field.

". . . Although the game was played to a tie, Sul Ross is still Texas's only undefeated college football team, the second straight year the Lobos have owned the honor . . .

". . . Sul Ross scored first Saturday afternoon after senior Alfredo Ávila made the first of his five pass interceptions of the afternoon, putting the Lobos in business on the Sul Ross 43 yard line."[1]

Ávila's five pass interceptions that game tied the Texas collegiate football single game mark of 5 interceptions held by Al Johnson of Hardin-Simmons (1946) and Byron Beaver of Houston (1962). Ávila also holds the Texas record with 14 interceptions in a single season, a record he established in 1966. Additionally, he is the national all-time career leader with 36 interceptions for the years, 1963-1966.[2]

1 "East Texas Ties Sul Ross, 14-14," *Alpine Avalanche,* October 27, 1966.

2 *Texas Sports Magazine,* July 1981, 117.

Southern Methodist University vs. Texas A&M, 1967

"While 1967 was a wonderful year for spectators, it produced a bumper crop of frustrated coaches and critics . . . the upsets came quickly. One of the most unusual happened on September 16 (Mexican Independence Day), when heavily favored Texas A&M played host to Southern Methodist University.

"The SMU Mustangs were three touchdown underdogs but they refused to believe it . . . with 43 seconds remaining, the Aggies forged ahead 17-13 . . .

"A sub quarterback came off the bench after the next kickoff. He was Inés Pérez, a tiny Mexican youth, barely 5 feet 4 inches tall, weighed 149 pounds. The crowd of 33,000 could barely read his number (16) because it was partially concealed by his pants."[1]

"They were amazed when be began hurling passes with cool precision to All-American Jerry Levias . . . Levias had returned the kickoff 24 yards to midfield, caught a 29-yard pass from Pérez, then curled into the corner of the end zone and caught a six yard pass from Pérez for the winning touchdown with four seconds left on the Kyle field clock . . . the final score, SMU 20, Texas A&M 17. Pérez had taken his team 58 yards, completing 10 of 12 passes in the winning march."[2]

For Inés Pérez, this was a great performance to an otherwise almost forgotten collegiate career at SMU.

Although lacking in size but not in heart or talent, Pérez endured the racial attitudes of the times.

He had come to SMU from Henderson County Junior College, where he quarterbacked the team to the Junior College Championship and an appearance in the Junior Rose Bowl. He was a winner all his life and despite the obstacles, Pérez forged ahead.

That eventful day before game time, when the not-so-great coach Hayden Fry introduced all the SMU seniors to the fans except him, Pérez quietly waited his turn. When it came, Fry was history and Pérez did what he did best—win football games.[3]

1 John Durant and Les Efler, *Highlights of College Football* (New York: Hastings House Publishers, 1970), 193–94.
2 Temple Pouncy, *Mustang Mania: Southern Methodist University* (Hunstville, Alabama: Strode Publishers, 1981), 211–12.
3 Telephone interview with Inés Pérez, Round Rock, Texas, August 1, 1994.

Mexicano/Latinos in Post Season Collegiate Bowl/All-Star Games, 1936-1980

Yr.	Name	College/University	Bowl/All-Star Game	Opponent	Score	
1936	Anastacio "Hookey" Apodaca	New Mexico State University	Sun Bowl	Hardin-Simmons	NMSU	14
	Lauro Apodaca				H-S	14
1937	Manuel Gómez	Santa Clara University	Sugar Bowl	LSU	Santa Clara	21
					LSU	14
1939	Joe Aguirre	St. Mary's of California	Cotton Bowl	Texas Tech	St. Mary's	20
					Texas Tech	13
1944	Eddie Sáenz	USC	Rose Bowl	Washington	USC	29
					Washington	0
	Gonzalo Morales	St. Mary's of California	East-West Shrine	East	East	13
					West	13
1945	Guillermo C. Ibarra	National University of Mexico	Sun Bowl	Southwestern University	Southwestern	35
	Fernando D. Montes				Mexico	0
	Rudy J. Flores	Southwestern University	Sun Bowl	Univ. of Mexico	Southwestern	35
					Mexico	0
1947	Gonzalo Morales	St. Mary's of California	Oil Bowl	Georgia Tech	Georgia	41
					St. Mary's	19

Mexicanos/Latinos in Post Season Collegiate Bowl/All-Star Games, 1936-1980, continued

Yr.	Name	College/University	Bowl/All-Star Game	Opponent	Score	
	Xavier Mena	UCLA	Rose Bowl	Illinois	Illinois	45
					UCLA	14
1949	Dan Garza	University of Oregon	Cotton Bowl	SMU	SMU	21
					Oregon	13
1951	Richard Ochoa	Texas	Cotton Bowl	Tennessee	Tennessee	20
					Texas	14
1952	Bobby Cavazos	Texas Tech	Sun Bowl	Pacific	Texas Tech	25
					Pacific	14
1953	Richard Ochoa	Texas	Cotton Bowl	Tenneessee	Texas	16
					Tennessee	0
	Rick Casares	Florida	Gator Bowl	Tulsa	Florida	14
					Tulsa	13
	Bobby Luna	Alabama	Orange Bowl	Syracuse	Alabama	61
					Syracuse	6
1954	Bobby Cavazos	Texas Tech	Gator Bowl	Auburn	Texas Tech	35
					Auburn	13
	Gil Moreno	UCLA	Rose Bowl	Michigan State	Michigan	28
					UCLA	20
1955	Vincent Gonzales	LSU	Blue-Gray All-Star	Blue	Gray	20
					Blue	19
	George Maderos	Chico State University	East-West Shrine	East	East	13
					West	12
	Primo Villanueva	UCLA	Hula Bowl	Hawaiian All Stars	Collegians	33
					Hawaii	13
1957	Narciso "Chico" Mendoza	TCU	Cotton Bowl	Syracuse	TCU	28
					Syracuse	27
	Joe Arenas	NFL All-Stars (San Francisco 49ers)	Hula Bowl	College All-Stars	NFL Pros	52
					Collegians	21
1958	Tom Flores	Pacific	East-West Shrine	East	East	26
					West	14
	René Ramírez	Texas	Sugar Bowl	Mississippi	Mississippi	39
					Texas	7
1959	Joe Kapp	California-Berkeley	Rose Bowl	Iowa	Iowa	38
					California	12
	José Hernández	Bakersfield JC	Jr. Rose Bowl	Del Mar JC	BJC	36
					Del Mar	14

Mexicanos/Latinos in Post Season Collegiate Bowl/All-Star Games, 1936-1980, continued

Yr.	Name	College/University	Bowl/All-Star Game	Opponent	Score	
1959	Mauricio Leal	Del Mar JC	Jr. Rose Bowl	Bakersfield JC	BJC	36
					Del Mar	14
	Danny Villanueva	New Mexico State	Sun Bowl	North Texas State	NMSU	28
					N. Texas	8
1960	René Ramírez	Texas	Cotton Bowl	Syracuse	Syracuse	23
					Texas	14
1961	Bobby Santiago	New Mexico	Aviation Bowl	Western Michigan	New Mexico	28
					W. Michigan	12
	Roman Gabriel	North Carolina	East-West Shrine	West	West	21
					East	8
	Henry Rivera	Oregon State	East-West Shrine	East	West	21
					East	8
	Steve Barilla	Wichita State	Sun Bowl	Villanova	Villanova	17
					Wichita	9
	George Mira	Miami	Liberty Bowl	Syracuse	Syracuse	15
	Sam Fernández				Miami	14
	Gus Gonzales	Tulane	North-South All-Star	North	South	35
					North	10
1962	Roman Gabriel	North Carolina State	Chicago All-Star	Green Bay Packers	Green Bay	42
					All-Stars	20
	George Mira	Miami	Gotham Bowl	Nebraska	Nebraska	36
					Miami	34
	José Hernández	Arizona	U.S. Bowl	West All-Stars	West	33
					East	19
	José Hernández	Arizona	American Bowl	West All-Stars	East	13
					West	8
	Henry Rivera	Oregon State	Senior Bowl	South All-Stars	South	42
					North	7
	Gus Gonzales	Tulane	Senior Bowl	North All-Stars	South	42
					North	7
1963	Ramsey Muñiz	Baylor	Blue Bonnet Bowl	LSU	Baylor	14
					LSU	7
	George Mira	Miami	North-South All-Stars	North All-Stars	South	23
					North	14

Mexicanos/Latinos in Post Season Collegiate Bowl/All-Star Games, 1936-1980, continued

Yr.	Name	College/University	Bowl/All-Star Game	Opponent	Score	
1964	George Mira	Miami	Senior Bowl	North All-Stars	South	28
					North	21
	George Mira	Miami	All-America Football Game	West All-Stars	East	18
					West	15
	George Mira	Miami	Chicago All-Star	Chicago Bears	Chicago	28
					All-Stars	17
1965	Inés Pérez	Henderson County JC	Jr. Rose Bowl	Fullerton	FJC	20
					Henderson	15
	Jim García	Purdue University	East-West Shrine	West All-Stars	West	11
					East	7
	Jim García	Purdue University	Chicago All-Star	Cleveland Browns	Cleveland	24
					All-Stars	16
1966	Eddie Valdez	Henderson County JC	Jr. Rose Bowl	Pasadena JC	Henderson	40
	Margarito Guerrero				Pasadena	13
	Barry Álvarez	Nebraska	Orange Bowl	Alabama	Alabama	39
					Nebraska	28
	Stan Quintana	New Mexico	Chicago All-Star	Green Bay Packers	Green Bay	35
					All-Stars	0
1967	Barry Álvarez	Nebraska	Sugar Bowl	Alabama	Alabama	34
					Nebraska	7
	Sal Olivas	New Mexico State	Blue-Gray All-Star	Gray	Blue	22
					Gray	16
	Barry Álvarez	Nebraska	Blue-Gray All-Star	Gray	Blue	22
					Gray	16
1971	Jim Plunkett	Stanford	Rose Bowl	Ohio State	Stanford	27
					Ohio St.	17
	Jim Plunkett	Stanford	Hula Bowl	South All-Stars	North	42
					South	32
	Jim Plunkett	Stanford	Chicago All-Star	Baltimore Colts	Baltimore	24
					All-Stars	17
1972	Rod García	Stanford	Rose Bowl	Michigan	Stanford	13
					Michigan	12
	Robert Guevara	Texas	Cotton Bowl	Penn State	Penn State	30
					Texas	6

Mexicanos/Latinos in Post Season Collegiate Bowl/All-Star Games, 1936-1980, continued

Yr.	Name	College/University	Bowl/All-Star Game	Opponent	Score	
1973	Ralph Ortega	Florida	Tangerine Bowl	Miami	Miami	16
					Florida	7
1974	René Amaya	Texas	Cotton Bowl	Nebraska	Nebraska	19
					Texas	3
1975	Ralph Ortega	Florida	Sugar Bowl	Nebraska	Nebraska	13
					Florida	10
	Ralph Ortega	Florida	Chicago All-Star	Pittsburgh Steelers	Pittsburgh	21
					All-Stars	14
1976	Steve Rivera	California-Berkeley	Japan Bowl	East All-Stars	West	27
					East	18
1979	Kiki De Ayala	University of Texas	Sun Bowl	University of Washington	Washington	14
					Texas	7
1980	Anthony Muñoz	USC	Rose Bowl	Ohio State	USC	17
					Ohio St.	16
	Kiki De Ayala	University of Texas	Blue Bonnet Bowl	North Carolina	North Carolina	16
					Texas	7

Appendix I

List of All-Conference, All-Pro, Super Bowl, Pro Bowl, Grey Cup Records and Awards

Jesse Rodríguez

Honorable Mention All-West Virginia Inter-Collegiate Conference Team, 1928.

All-Time West Virginia Inter-Collegiate Athletic Conference Team for the years 1925-1965, 1974.

Kelly Rodríguez

All-West Virginia Inter-Collegiate Athletic Conference First Teams, 1928-1929.

Honorable Mention *New York Telegram's* All-Eastern Teams, 1927-1929.

All-Time West Virginia Inter-Collegiate Athletic Conference Team for the years 1925-1965, 1974.

Waldo E. Don Carlos

All Missouri Valley Conference Teams, 1929 and 1930.

Knute Rockne's All Western Team, 1930.

Notre Dame All-Opponent Teams, 1929 and 1930.

1931 Green Bay Packers NFL Championship Team.

Named to Drake University's First 100 Years Football Team in 1981.

Joe Aguirre

Honorable Mention All-American, 1940.

NFL All-Pro Team, 1944.

NFL field goal leader, 1945.

All-American Football Conference (AAFC) All-Pro Second Team, 1946.

All-CFL Western Conference Team, 1950.

CFL Western Conference scoring leader with 59 points, 1950.

Dave Dryborough Memorial Trophy, 1950.

CFL Grey Cup, 1950.

CFL Western Conference scoring leader with 85 points, 1954.

Listed #13 all-time AAFC scoring with 142 points.

Listed #16 all-time AAFC pass receptions, 63 receptions for 1,040 yards.

Edwin Sáenz

NFL kickoff return leader, 29 returns for 797 yards, 1947.

John C. Sánchez

All-Metropolitan Conference Team, 1940.

All-Southern California Junior College Team, 1940.

Small College All-American Team, 1942.

All-Pacific Coast Football Team, 1942.

San Francisco Examiner All-Coast Eleven Team, 1942.

All-Northern California Football Team, 1942.

Inducted into University of San Francisco Sports Hall of Fame, 1975.

Gonzalo Morales

All-Northern California Football Second Team, 1942.

San Francisco Examiner All-Coast Eleven Team, 1942.

All-Coast Guard Service Team, 1944.

John Aguirre

All-CFL Western Conference Team, 1948-1949.

Daniel Garza

All-Pacific Coast Conference Team, 1948.

All-American Team, 1948.

Inducted into State of Oregon Sports Hall of Fame, 1990.

Inducted into University of Oregon Sports Hall of Fame, 1990.

Ray Romero

All-Big Seven Conference Team Honorable Mention, 1950.

Army Times All-Army Football Team, 1952.

Army Times All-Service Football Team, 1952.

National Hispanic Heritage Leadership Award, 1993.

Joe Arenas

Most Valuable Player/Athlete of the Year, University of Nebraska-Omaha, 1950.

University of Nebraska Outstanding Alumnus, 1953.

NFL kickoff return yardage leader, 16 returns for 551 yards, 1953.

Elected to the Nebraska Football Hall of Fame, 1977.

Listed #6 All-Time NFL kickoff returners with 3,798 yards.

Helms Athletic Foundation Hall of Fame Award.

Gene Brito

All-Coast Independent Colleges Football Team, 1950.

All-CFL Western Conference Team, 1954.

NFL All-Pro Teams, 1955-1958.

Washington Redskins MVP, 1955 & 1957.

Pro Bowls, 1956-1959.

Pro Bowl Outstanding Lineman, 1958.

Inducted into Washington Hall of Stars, Washington, D.C., 1982.

Inducted into National Italian-American Sports Hall of Fame, 1988.

George Maderos

UPI Little All-Coast Team, 1953.

Little All-America Team, 1953.

Rick Casares

Army Times All-Army Football Team, 1954.

Army Times All-Service Football Team, 1954.

NFL All-Pro Team, 1956.

NFL rushing yardage leader with 1,126 yards, 1956.

Pro Bowls, 1956-1960.

Inducted into Chicago Sports Hall of Fame.

Alex Bravo

UPI All-Coast Little Teams, 1951-1953.

All-California Collegiate Athletic Conference (CCAC) Teams, 1951-1953.

UPI All-Southern California Small College Team, 1953.

Primo Villanueva

UPI National Collegiate Football Champion, 1954.

All-Pacific Coast Conference Team, 1954.

UCLA Captain Don Brown Memorial Trophy for Most Improved Player, 1954.

UCLA Bruin Bench Award to Outstanding Senior, 1954.

Joe Kapp

All-Pacific Coast Conference Team Honorable Mention, 1956.

All-Pacific Coast Conference Second Team, 1957.

All-Pacific Coast Conference Team, 1958.

Football Writers/*Time* All America Team, 1958.

Pop Warner/Voit Awards for Top Player on the West Coast, 1958.

All-CFL Western Conference Teams, 1963-1964.

Schenley Award for Most Outstanding Playing in the CFL, Runner-up, 1963.

CFL Grey Cup Championship, 1963.

CFL Western Conference Jeff Nicklin Memorial Trophy for MVP, 1964.

Super Bowl IV, 1970.

Pro Bowl, 1970.

Pacific Coast Conference-Ten Coach of the Year, 1982.

Elected as a Player into the CFL Hall of Fame, April 10, 1984.

Vernon Valdez

National Junior College Athletic Association All-American, 1957.

Danny Villanueva

NFL All-Time co-record holder for most points after touchdown, no misses in a season 56, 1966.

Listed #12 All-Time NFL punters, 488 punts for 20,862 yards and a 42.8 average.

Inducted into New Mexico State University Intercollegiate Athletic Hall of Fame.

Tom Flores

National Junior College Athletic Association All-American Honorable Mention, 1955.

Scholastic All-American, 1956.

All-Pacific Coast Team, 1956.

Amos Alonzo Stagg Award, 1958.

Oakland Raiders MVP, 1966.

All-AFL Second Team, 1966.

Pro Bowl, 1967.

Super Bowls IV, XI, XV, XVIII Champion.

Assistant Coach of the Year-Milwaukee 1000 Yard Club, 1978.

NFL Coach of the Year, 1982.

Sugar Ray Robinson Youth Foundation "Man of the Year," 1984.

Nosotros "Golden Eagle Award," 1985.

Vincent González

All-Southeast Conference Second Team, 1955.

Inducted into the Redemtoris High School Hall of Fame as a coach, 1988.

Alan Valdés(z)

Calgary Stampeder Player of the Year, 1957.

Henry Rivera

All-Metropolitan Conference Teams, 1957-1958.

Gus Gonzales

All-Southeast Conference Sophomore Team, 1959.

All-Southeast Conference Third Team, 1961.

Willie Crafts

AP Little All-American, 1960.

All-Lone Star Conference First Team, 1960.

NAIA Football Champion, Texas A&I University, player, 1959.

NAIA Football Champions, Texas A&I University, assistant coach, 1970.

TransAmerica Football League All-Star, 1970.

Southwestern Football League All-Star, 1971.

Chon Gallegos

All-Pacific Coast Team, 1961.

Pop Warner Award for the Most Valuable Senior Football Player on the West Coast, 1961.

Sam Fernández

CFL Grey Cup, 1962.

Mario Méndez

All-California Collegiate Athletic Association Team, 1963.

John Simcox Memorial Trophy for MVP, 1963.

Joe Hernández

National Junior College Athletic Association All-American, 1958.

National Junior College Athletic Association All-American Honorable Mention, 1959.

All-Border Conference Second Team, 1960.

All-North American Football League (NAFL), 1965.

All CFL Western Conference Teams, 1967 and 1970.

Listed #16 in CFL career kickoff return yardage with 97 returns for 2,547 yards.

Inducted into Kern County Sports Hall of Fame, 1979.

Inducted into University of Arizona Sports Hall of Fame, 1981.

Jim García

All-Big Ten Conference Team, 1964.

George Mira

All-America Teams, 1962 and 1963.

Led the NCAA University Division in Total Offense, 1963.

MVP in the Gotham Bowl game, 1962.

MVP in the North-South College All-Star game, 1963.

MVP in the Coaches All-America game, 1964.

World Football League Champion/MVP in the World Bowl, 1974.

Emilio Vállez

All Western Athletic Conference Team, 1967.

Al Gonzales

UPI & AP Honorable Mention All America, 1967.

Manny Fernández

South Florida Media Dolphins Defensive Lineman of the Year(s), 1968-1973.

All NFC, 1971.

NFL All-Pro Second Team, 1973.

South Shore Quarterback Club of Massachusetts Johnny Unitas Award, 1973.

Super Bowl VI.

Super Bowls VII, VIII Champions.

New York Times All-Time Super Bowl Team, 1981.

Greg Pérez

CFL Grey Cup, 1970.

Appendix II

Mexicanos/Latinos in World Championship Football Games					
National Football League (NFL) Super Bowl:					
Super Bowl	**Year**	**Player**	**Pos.**	**Team**	
IV	1970	Joe Kapp	QB	Minnesota Vikings	
		Tom Flores	QB	Kansas City Chiefs	Champion
V	1971	Ted Hendricks	LB	Baltimore Colts	Champion
VI	1972	Manny Fernández	DT	Miami Dolphins	
		George Mira	QB	Miami Dolphins	
VII	1973	Manny Fernández	DT	Miami Dolphins	Champion
VIII	1974	Manny Fernández	DT	Miami Dolphins	Champion
XI	1977	Tom Flores	Asst. Coach	Oakland Raiders	Champion
XI	1977	Ted Hendricks	LB	Oakland Raiders	Champion
XII	1978	Efrén Herrera	K	Dallas Cowboys	Champion
XIII	1979	Rafael Septién	K	Dallas Cowboys	
XIV	1980	Frank Corral	K	Los Angeles Rams	
XV	1981	Tom Flores	Head Coach	Oakland Raiders	Champion
		Jim Plunkett (MVP)	QB	Oakland Raiders	Champion
		Ted Hendricks	LB	Oakland Raiders	Champion
XVI	1982	Anthony Muñoz	OT	Cincinnati Bengals	
		Max Montoya	G	Cincinnati Bengals	
XVIII	1984	Tom Flores	Head Coach	Los Angeles Raiders	Champion
		Jim Plunkett	QB	Los Angeles Raiders	Champion
		Ted Hendricks	LB	Los Angeles Raiders	Champion
XX	1986	Ron Rivera	LB	Chicago Bears	Champion
XXI	1987	Raúl Allegre	K	New York Giants	Champion
XXIII	1989	Anthony Muñoz	OT	Cincinnati Bengals	
		Max Montoya	G	Cincinnati Bengals	
		Leo Barker	LB	Cincinnati Bengals	
XXVII	1993	Tony Casillas	NT	Dallas Cowboys	Champion
XXVIII	1994	Tony Casillas	NT	Dallas Cowboys	Champion

Mexicanos/Latinos in Championship/World Championship Football Games

Canadian Football League (CFL) Grey Cup Championship:

Year	Player	Pos.	Team	
1948	John Aguirre	T	Calgary Stampeders	Champion
1949	John Aguirre	T	Calgary Stampeders	
1950	Joe Aguirre	K	Winnipeg Blue Bombers	
1962	Sam Fernández	B	Hamilton Tiger-Cats	
1963	Joe Kapp	QB	British Columbia Lions	
1964	Joe Kapp	QB	British Columbia Lions	Champion
1970	Greg Pérez	DB	Calgary Stampeders	
1983	Mervyn Fernández	WR	British Columbia Lions	
1985	Mervyn Fernández	WR	British Columbia Lions	Champion
1990	Sammy Garza	QB	Winnipeg Blue Bombers	Champion
1992	Sammy Garza	QB	Winnipeg Blue Bombers	
1993	Sammy Garza	QB	Winnipeg Blue Bombers	
	Tom Porras	QB	Winnipeg Blue Bombers	

World Football League (WFL) World Bowl:

Year	Player	Pos.	Team	
1974	George Mira (MVP)	QB	Birmingham Americans	Champion

United States Football League (USFL) Championships:

Year	Player	Pos.	Team	
1983	Pete Rodríguez	Asst. Coach	Michigan Panthers	Champion
	Rich Garza	G	Philadelphia Stars	
1984	Frank Corral	K	Arizona Wranglers	
	Lupe Sánchez	DB	Arizona Wranglers	
	Tom Porras	QB	Arizona Wranglers	

Sources: Joe Marshall, "World Bowl in Crisis," *Sports Illustrated,* December 16, 1974, vol. 41, no. 25, 20–23.

David S. Neft, Richard M. Cohen, and Rick Korch, *The Football Encyclopedia: The Complete History of Professional Football from 1892 to Present* (New York: St. Martin's Press, 1994), 473, 513, 531, 549, 567, 621, 639, 659, 723, 743, 785, 825, 845, 913, 979, 1001.

1985 Canadian Football League Facts, Figures & Records, Chapter 5, 2.

1994 Winnipeg Blue Bombers Media Guide, 97–98, 104.

The Official National Football League 1991 Record & Fact Book, 271–76.

The Sporting News Official USFL Guide and Register—1985, 121–25.

Winnipeg Blue Bombers Public Relations Office. Telephone call for information on the Grey Cup, February 11, 1995.

Bibliography

Letters

Balkovec, Lynne (Pittsburgh Steelers Publicity Department). Letter to Mario Longoria, May 20, 1987. (Gonzalo Morales)

Boatright, Brenda (Administrative Assistant, Public Relations, Kansas City Chiefs). Letter to Mario Longoria, March 12, 1982. (Tom Flores)

Bonnell, Lori (Canadian Football Hall of Fame & Museum). Letter to Mario Longoria, December 17, 1982. (Joe Kapp)

Brewer, Kara (Director of Alumni Programs, Pacific Alumni Association/University of the Pacific). Letter to Mario Longoria, June 20, 1984. (Robert Coronado)

Burnette, Brenda (Sports Information Office, University of Alabama). Information Letter to Mario Longoria, March 29, 1984. (Robert Luna)

Clower, Clem (Baseball coach at Salem College). Letter to Mario Longoria, October 8, 1982. (Jesse Rodríguez)

Corona, Al (for Gonzalo Morales). Letter to Mario Longoria, August 12, 1983.

Cowie, Cam (Director of Public Relations, Saskatchewan Roughrider Football Club). Letter to Mario Longoria, January 5, 1983. (Alex Bravo)

Davis, Edward T. (Coach and Director of Athletics, Salem College, Salem, West Virginia, 1923-1941). Letter to Mario Longoria, December 8, 1982. (Jesse and Kelly Rodríguez)

———. Letter to Mario Longoria, November 9, 1982. (Jesse Rodríguez)

———. Letter to Mario Longoria, January 4, 1985. (Jesse Rodríguez)

Dayton, Charlie (Director of Public Relations and Promotions, Atlanta Falcons Football Club). Letter to Mario Longoria, September 6, 1982. (Jim García)

Dennis, Brother L. (Archivist, Saint Mary's College, Office of the Librarian). Letter to Mario Longoria, including programs and press reporters handbook (1940), January 21, 1983. (Joe Aguirre and Gonzalo Morales)

———. Letter to Mario Longoria, February 23, 1989. (Joe Aguirre)

Don Carlos, W. E. Letter to Mario Longoria, June 27, 1996.

Fan, Lawrence (Sports Information Director, San José State University). Letter to Mario Longoria, September 20, 1982. (Chon Gallegos)

———. Letter to Mario Longoria, December 21, 1982.

Flores, Tom (Head Coach Oakland Raiders). Letter/Questionnaire to Mario Longoria, June 30, 1982.

Gallagher, Jim (Director of Public Relations, Philadelphia Eagles Football Club). Letter to Mario Longoria, December 5, 1985. (Ray Romero)

Gates, Victoria (Statistician, Canadian Football League). Letter to Mario Longoria, January 28, 1983. (Alex Bravo and Gene Brito)

———. Letter to Mario Longoria, April 11, 1983. (Joe Aguirre)

Goldchien, Art (Friend and former teammate of Jesse Rodríguez). Letter to Mario Longoria, January 18, 1985.

Green, Jerry (New Mexico Military Institute, Roswell, New Mexico). Letter to Mario Longoria, September 3, 1987. (José Hernández)

Haines, Robert B. (Manager, Frankford Athletic Association Yellowjackets). Letter to Kelly Rodríguez, April 26, 1930.

Hansen, Tim (Public Relations, Calgary Stampeder Football Club). Letter to Mario Longoria, December 20, 1982. (Gene Brito and Joe Kapp)

Hernández, Joe (Paul Revere Companies, Tucson, Arizona). Letter to Mario Longoria, September 12, 1987.

Hurney, Tom (Past President of the Touchdown Club of Washington). Letter and information on Gene Brito Award to Mario Longoria, April 5, 1991.

Johnson, Kristin (Sports Information Office, University of Illinois, Champaign). Letter to Mario Longoria, September 9, 1982. (Peter Pérez)

Kapp, Joe (Head Coach, University of California Golden Bear Football). Letter to Mario Longoria, December 9, 1982.

Kassen, Tex (Athletic Department, Southwestern University, Georgetown, Texas). Letter to Mario Longoria, May 26, 1996. (Rudy J. Flores)

Keller, Josh (Director Public Relations, British Columbia Lions). Letter to Mario Longoria, September 10, 1987. (Primo Villanueva)

Kordiala, Ray E. (Director of Public Relations, Winnipeg Blue Bombers Football Club). Letter to Mario Longoria, April 27, 1983. (Joe Aguirre)

Kuhn, Dave (Sports Information Office, San Diego State University News, Information). Letter to Mario Longoria, September 23, 1982. (Mario Méndez)

Loney, Francine (Public Relations, Cleveland Browns). Letter to Mario Longoria, December 26, 1984. (Joe Kapp)

Lubera, Francine (Public Relations, Cleveland Browns). Letter to Mario Longoria, December 26, 1984. (Henry Rivera)

Maderos, George. Letter to Mario Longoria, January 9, 1985.

Mansean, L. E. (President, California Professional Football League). Letter to Kelly Rodríguez, June 6, 1936.

McCaskey, Patrick (Director of Community Involvement, Chicago Bears Football Club). Letter to Mario Longoria, January 9, 1985. (Robert Coronado)

McElrone, Chick (Philadelphia Eagles Public Relations). Letter to Mario Longoria, May 18, 1983. (Gonzalo Morales)

Meighen, Mark A. (Graduate Assistant, Buffalo Bills). Letter to Mario Longoria, November 8, 1988. (Henry Rivera)

Mira, George. Letter/Questionnaire to Mario Longoria, April 4, 1995.

Morrison, Paul (Department of Intercollegiate Athletics, Drake University). Memorandum about Waldo Don Carlos, July 16, 1996.

Rodgers, Pat (Public Relations Office, San Diego Chargers Football Club). Memorandum to Mario Longoria, June 3, 1982. (Mario Méndez)

Rodríguez, Jesse. Letter to Mario Longoria, December 27, 1982.

———. Letter to Mario Longoria, January 18, 1983.

———. Letter to Mario Longoria, February, 9, 1983.

———. Letter to Mario Longoria, August 12, 1984.

———. Letter to Mario Longoria, September 29, 1984.

———. Letter to Mario Longoria, November 20, 1984.

———. Letter to Mario Longoria, April 5, 1985.

Rodríguez, Palmira. Letter to Mario Longoria, August 3, 1984. (Kelly Rodríguez)

Romero, Kippie T. (Account Executive, KXLK FM 105 Radio Station, Wichita, Kansas). Letter and information on her father Ray Romero to Mario Longoria, September 6, 1988.

Romero, Ray. Letter to Mario Longoria, November 14, 1986.

———. Letter to Mario Longoria, November 24, 1986.

———. Letter to Mario Longoria, September 17, 1989.

Sáenz, Edward D. Letter to Mario Longoria, October 31, 1984.

———. Letter to Mario Longoria, January 24, 1985.

Sánchez, John C. Letter to Mario Longoria, September 21, 1983.

Stechman, Dorothy J. (Library Assistant, California Polytechnic, San Luis Obispo). Letter to Mario Longoria, June 29, 1983. (Alex Bravo)

Watkins, David (Toronto Argonauts Football Club). Letter to Mario Longoria, August 21, 1985. (Gus Gonzales)

Weaver, Robert (Tulane University Sports Information). Letter to Mario Longoria, December 5, 1985. (Gus Gonzales)

Wells, Jeffrey (University of New Mexico Sports Information). Letter to Mario Longoria, September 5, 1985. (Emilio Vállez)

Williams, Dave (Marketing Manager, Edmonton Eskimo Football Club). Letter to Mario Longoria, October 18, 1982. (José Hernández)

Zusman, Dan (University of Oregon Department of Intercollegiate Athletics). Letter to Mario Longoria. (Dan Garza)

Books

Balzer, Howard, ed. *The Sporting News Football Register 1981*. St. Louis: The Sporting News Publishing Company, 1981. (Tom Flores)

Berger, Phil. *Great Moments in Pro Football*. New York: Julian Messer Publishing, 1969. (Tom Flores)

Canadian Football League Facts, Figures & Records. Toronto: Methuen Publications, 1985. (Joe Kapp, Al Gonzales, and Willie Crafts)

Canadian Football League 1982 Official Record Manual. (José Hernández and Joe Kapp)

Carroll, Bob. *When the Grass Was Real*. New York: Simon & Schuster, 1993. (José Hernández)

Clary, Jack. *Pro Footballs' Great Moments*. New York: Bonanza Books, 1983. (Manny Fernández)

Cohen, Richard M., Jordan A. Deutsch, Roland T. Johnson, and David S. Neft. *The Scrapbook History of Pro Football*. New York: Bobbs-Merrill Company, 1976. (Rick Casares and Joe Kapp)

Decades of Destiny: 1960–1984. The Historic First 25 Years. Los Angeles: CWC Sport Publications, 1985. (Alex Bravo, Tom Flores, and Vernon Valdez)

Dirigo (Salem College yearbook), 1928. (Jesse Rodríguez)

Flores, Tom with Frank Cooney. *Fire in the Iceman*. Chicago: Bonus Books, 1992.

Fox, Larry. *The New England Patriots: Triumph and Tragedy*. New York: Athenaeum, 1979. (Joe Kapp)

Goodwin, Lou, ed. *Fall Madness: A History of Senior and Professional Football in Calgary, Alberta, 1908-1978*. Calgary: Calgary Stampeder Football Club, 1979. (Joe Kapp and John Aguirre)

Green, Lee. *Sportswit*. New York: Ballantine Books, 1984. (Joe Kapp)

Kessler, Kent. *Hail West Virginians!* Pakersburg, West Virginia: Park Press, 1959. (Jesse and Kelly Rodríguez)

The Lair (Loyola University of Los Angeles yearbook). 1951 (Gene Brito)

McCallum, John D. *Pac-10 Football: The Rose Bowl Conference.* Seattle: Writing Works, 1982. (Dan Garza and Primo Villanueva)

Mendell, Ronald L., and Timothy B. Phares. *Who's Who in Pro Football.* New Rochelle: Arlington House, 1974. (Joe Kapp)

Michaelson, Herb, and Dave Newhouse. *Rose Bowl Football since 1902.* New York: Stein and Day Publishers, 1977. (Primo Villanueva)

Miller, Jeff. *Florida—Florida State—Miami: Sunshine Shootouts.* Atlanta: Longstreet Press, 1992. (George Mira)

Morín, Raúl. *Among the Valiant: Mexican Americans in WW II and Korea.* Alhambra: Borden Publishing Company, 1966. (Joe Arenas)

Neft, David S., Richard M. Cohen, and Rick Korch. *The Football Encyclopedia: The Complete Year-by-Year History of Professional Football From 1892 to the Present.* New York: St. Martin's Press, 1994.

Newlon, Clarke. *Famous Mexican Americans.* New York: Dodd, Mead and Company, 1972. (Joe Kapp)

The NFL's Official Encyclopedia History of Professional Football. New York: MacMillan, 1977.

Official 1981 National Football League Record Manual.

The Official National Football League 1991 Record & Factbook. New York: Workman Publishing Company, 1991. (Danny Villanueva)

Plunkett, Jim and Dave Newhouse. *The Jim Plunkett Story: The Saga of a Man Who Came Back.* New York: Dell Publishing Company, 1981. (Jim Plunkett and Chon Gallegos)

Quax (Drake University yearbook), 1930. (Waldo Don Carlos)

Resciniti, Angelo G. *Super Bowl Victories.* Worthington, Ohio: Willowisp Press, 1985. (Manny Fernández)

Riffenburgh, Beau. *The Official NFL Encyclopedia.* New York: New American Library, 1986.

Smith, Don. *Y. A. Tittle: I Pass.* New York: Franklin Watts, 1964. (Joe Arenas)

Smith, Loran. *Fifty Years on the Fifty: The Orange Bowl Story.* Charlotte: Fast and MacMillan Publishers, 1983. (Robert Luna)

The Sporting News Football Register 1972. St. Louis: Sporting News Publishing Company, 1972. (George Mira)

Stowers, Carlton. *Journey to Triumph: 110 Dallas Cowboys Tell Their Stories.* Dallas: Taylor Publishing Company, 1982. (Danny Villanueva)

Sullivan, Jack. *The Grey Cup Story: The Dramatic History of Football's Most Coveted Award.* Toronto: Pagerian Press, 1970. (Joe Kapp)

Treat, Roger. *The Encyclopedia of Football.* London: A. S. Barnes and Company, 1979.

University of Omaha Yearbook, 1949, 1950, 1951. (Joe Arenas)

University of Southern California Yearbook, 1944. (Eddie Sáenz)

West Virginia Wesleyan College Yearbook, 1930. (Kelly Rodríguez)

Whittingham, Richard. *The Dallas Cowboys: An Illustrated History.* New York: Harper and Row, 1981. (Danny Villanueva)

Media Guides

NFL

Boston Redskins 1935 Media Guide. (Kelly Rodríguez)

1949 Brooklyn—New York Football Sketch Book. (Dan Garza)

Buffalo Bills 1982 Media Guide. (Henry Rívera and Vernon Valdez)

Chicago Bears 1945 Media Guide. (Peter Pérez)

1956 Chicago Bears Media Guide. (Rick Casares)

1959 Chicago Bears Media Guide. (Robert Coronado)

Chicago Bears 1969 Media Guide. (Emilio Vállez)

Official Chicago Bears 1982 Media Guide. (Peter Pérez, Rick Casares, and Emilio Vállez)

1965 Cleveland Browns Media Guide. (Jim García)

1966 Cleveland Browns Media Guide. (Jim García)

Cleveland Browns 1983 Media Guide. (Henry Rivera)

1967 Dallas Cowboys Media Guide. (Danny Villanueva)

1983 Green Bay Packers Media Guide. (Waldo Don Carlos)

1983 Houston Oilers Media Guide. (Gus Gonzales)

Kansas City Chiefs 1970 Media Guide. (Tom Flores)

1947 Los Angeles Dons Players Profiles. (Joe Aquirre)

1958 Los Angeles Rams Media Guide. (Alex Bravo)

1960 Los Angeles Rams Media Guide. (Gene Brito)

1961 Los Angeles Rams Media Guide. (Danny Villanueva and Vernon Valdez)

1964 Los Angeles Rams Media Guide. (Danny Villanueva)

1982 Los Angeles Rams Media Guide. (Danny Villanueva)

1966 Miami Dolphins Media Guide. (Rick Casares)

1972 Miami Dolphins Media Guide. (George Mira)

1976 Miami Dolphins Media Guide. (Manny Fernández)

1977 Miami Dolphins Media Guide. (Manny Fernández)

1970 Minnesota Viking Media Guide. (Joe Kapp)

1950 Sketches of the Giants Media Information. (John Sánchez)

1951 New York Yanks Press–Radio–TV Guide. (Dan Garza)

1983 New York Giants Media Guide. (John Sánchez)

1961 Oakland Raiders Media Guide. (Alex Bravo and Herman Urenda)

The Oakland Raiders 1981 Media Guide. (Tom Flores and Vernon Valdez)

Philadelphia Eagles 1947 Media Guide. (Gonzalo Morales)

1951 Philadelphia Eagles Media Guide. (Ray Romero)

1983 Philadelphia Eagles Media Guide. (Ray Romero)

Pittsburgh Steelers 1948 Media Guide. (Gonzalo Morales)

1959 Pittsburgh Steelers Media Guide. (Robert Luna)

San Diego Chargers 1983 Media Guide. (Mario Méndez)

1955 San Francisco 49ers Media Guide. (Joe Arenas)

1956 San Francisco 49ers Media Guide. (George Maderos)

1983 San Francisco 49ers Media Guide. (Joe Arenas and Robert Luna)

1946 Washington Redskins Media Guide. (Eddie Sáenz)

1948 Washington Redskins Media Guide. (John Sánchez)

1951 Washington Redskins Media Guide. (Eddie Sáenz)

1958 Washington Redskins Media Guide. (Gene Brito)

1959 Washington Redskins Media Guide. (Gene Brito)

1964 Washington Redskins Media Guide. (José Hernández)

CFL

1987 British Columbia Lions Fact Book. (Primo Villanueva and Joe Kapp)

Calgary Stampeders 1971 Fact Book. (Gregory Pérez)

Calgary Stampeders 1987 Fact Book. (John Aguirre and Gregory Pérez)

Edmonton Eskimos 1962 Press Guide. (Willie Crafts)

1967 Edmonton Eskimos Media Guide. (José Hernández)

1968 Edmonton Eskimos Media Guide. (José Hernández)

1970 Edmonton Eskimos Media Guide. (José Hernández)

Edmonton Eskimos Grey Cup Champions 1982 Media Guide. (Joe Aguirre and Willie Crafts)

1987 Hamilton Tiger–Cats Grey Cup Champions Fact Book. (Vincent González and Gregory Pérez)

1965 Montreal Alouette Football Handbook. (Gus Gonzales)

Montreal Concordes 1985 Fact Book. (George Mira)

Saskatchewan Roughriders 1987 Fact Book. (Al Gonzales)

Toronto Argonauts 1985 Media Guides. (José Hernández)

Winnipeg Football Fact Book 1982. (Joe Aguirre)

Colleges

1982 California Football Centennial Media Guide. (Joe Kapp)

1986 California Football Media Guide. (Joe Kapp)

1993 California Football Media Guide. (Joe Kapp)

1981 University of Florida Football Media Guide. (Rick Casares)

1986 University of Houston Football Media Guide. (Joe Arenas)

The Main Event: Kansas State 1985 Media Guide. (Ray Romero)

1962 University of Miami Football Media Guide. (George Mira)

1969 University of Miami Football Media Guide. (Gregory Pérez)

1965 University of New Mexico Lobo Sketch Pad. (Emilio Vállez)

1966 University of New Mexico Lobo Sketch Pad. (Emilio Vállez)

1967 University of New Mexico Lobo Sketch Pad. (Emilio Vállez)

1965 New Mexico State University Aggie Press, Radio, and TV Guide. (Al Gonzales)

1967 New Mexico State University Aggie Press, Radio, and TV Guide. (Al Gonzales)

1995 New Mexico State University Aggie Football Media Guide. (Al Gonzales)

1961 Oregon State University Football Media Guide. (Henry Rivera)

1962 Oregon State University Football Media Guide. (Henry Rivera)

1963 Purdue Football Media Guide. (Jim García)

1964 Purdue Football Media Guide. (Jim García)

1961 San Jose State University Football Media Guide. (Chon Gallegos)

1986 Texas A&I University Football Media Guide. (Willie Crafts)

1960 Tulane University Football Media Guide. (Gus Gonzales)

1961 Tulane University Football Media Guide. (Gus Gonzales)

1992 University of Utah Football Media Guide. (Manny Fernández)

Author Interviews

Arenas, Joe. Telephone interview. Galveston, Texas, November 11, 1994.

———. Interview at his home. Galveston, Texas, July 20, 1995.

Bravo, Alex. Telephone interview. Manhattan Beach, California, August 12, 1983.

California State University. Telephone call for statistics and information on George Maderos. Sports Information Department, Chico, California, April 23, 1991.

Casares, Rick. Telephone interview. Tampa, Florida, May 10 and June 16, 1995.

CFL. Telephone call for statistics on Gregory Pérez. Toronto, Ontario, March 28, 1994.

Crafts, Willie. Interview. San Antonio, Texas, July 30, 1994.

Flores, Tom. Interview. Alice, Texas, at high school sports banquet, January 26, 1989.

Gallegos, Chon. Telephone interview. San Jose, California, October 11, 1983.

Garza, Dan. Telephone interview. Warrenton, Oregon, January 31 and February 2,1996.

Gonzales, Al. Telephone interview. Las Cruces, New Mexico, September 14, 1995.

Gonzales, Vincent J. Telephone interview. Baton Rouge, Louisiana, April 8 and 24, 1994.

Henderson, Pat. Telephone call for information on Jim García. Sports Information Department, Purdue University, September 29, 1982.

Hernández, José M. Telephone interview. Tucson, Arizona, August 21, 1987.

Hum, Lillian. Telephone call for information on Joe Kapp. British Columbia Lions Public Relations Office, March 4, 1994.

Maderos, George. Telephone interview. Chico, California, February 8, 1984.

Mello, Rick. Telephone interview about Herman Urenda. Sports Information Office, University of the Pacific, Stockton, California, July 15, 1983.

———. Telephone interview about Robert Coronado. Sports Information Office, University of the Pacific, Stockton, California, June 14, 1984.

Méndez, Mario. Telephone interview. Palo Mar College, San Marcos, California, April 8, 1994.

Mira, George I. Telephone interview. Miami, Florida, Feburary, March 4, and April 2, 1995.

NCAA. Telephone call for information on records and statistics. Overland Park, Kansas, October 6, 1995. (Al Gonzales)

Pappas, Nick. Telephone interview about John Aguirre. USC Sports Information Office, Los Angeles, California, October 13, 1993.

Pérez, Peter. Telephone interview. Aurora, Illinois, September 4, 1983.

Porter, Colonel, and Jerry Green. Telephone interview about José Hernández and the 1958 NMMI Broncos football team. New Mexico Institute Alumni Office, September 3, 1987.

Prieur, Richard. Telephone interview about Gus Gonzales and the 1965 Montreal Alouettes team. Media Information Coordinator, Montreal Concordes Football Club, January 29, 1986.

Rice, Tom. Telephone interview about John Sánchez. University of San Francisco Alumni Relations, San Francisco, California, September 22, 1983.

Robertson, Larry (CFL statistician). Telephone call for information on Primo Villanueva. October 9, 1987.

Rockford, Illinois, City Library. Telephone call for information on the Rockford Rams, July 2, 1990. (Emilio Vállez)

Romero, Ray. Interview at his restaurant Taco Romero. Miami, Florida, August 21, 1988.

Sánchez, John. Telephone interview. Danville, California, September 25, 1983.

———. Interview at his home. Danville, California, May 14, 1988.

Shutt, Steve. Assistant Director for Media Relations. Telephone interview for information on Al Gonzales, Anastacio and Lauro Apodaca, and Sal Olivas. New Mexico State University, Las Cruces, September 12, 1995.

Vállez, Emilio. Telephone interview. Marengo, Illinois, June 29, 1990.

Villanueva, Danny. Telephone interview. Los Angeles, California, August 20, 1984.

Villanueva, Primo. Telephone interview. Surrey British Columbia, Canada, September 1, 1987.

Programs

The Bob Elias Kern County Sports Hall of Fame Banquet Program, Bakersfield, California, February 5, 1979. (José Hernández)

Frankford Yellowjackets Game Program, November 1930. Provided by Joe Horrigan, Curator, Pro Football Hall of Fame. (Kelly Rodríguez)

Frankford Yellowjackets Game Programs, September 9, 1930; November 15, 1930. Provided by Joe Horrigan, Curator, Pro Football Hall of Fame. (Kelly Rodríguez)

Frankford Yellowjackets Game Program, October 12, 1930. Provided by Joe Horrigan, Pro Football Hall of Fame. (Kelly Rodríguez)

San Francisco Forty Niners vs. Los Angeles Rams Football Program, September 25, 1955. (George Maderos)

"Tom Flores: 50 Victories," Gameday Program Raiders vs. Chargers, 25, no. 4, Los Angeles Coliseum, September 24, 1984. (Tom Flores)

University of New Mexico Lobos vs. UTEP Miners Game Program, October 27, 1967. (Emilio Vállez)

Press Information/Releases

"NFL Draft for 1945; Draft selections of the Washington Redskins for the years 1936-1973," provided by Joe Horrigan, Curator, Pro Football Hall of Fame, April 1984.

"Primo Villanueva," Press Release by Vic Kelley, ASUCLA News Bureau, University of California at Los Angeles, May 31, 1956.

"B.C. Football Club Regular Season Results and Information Sheet for the Years 1956-58," provided by Josh Keller, Public Relations Director, British Columbia Lions Football Club, September 10, 1987.

"Statistics and National Rating of the NMMI Broncos— 1958 Football Season," (on José Hernández) Williamson's Rating System, News Release, Houston, Texas, December 2, 1959.

"1960 Thumbnail Sketches of Beavers," (on Henry Rivera) Sports information office, Oregon State University.

"NFL Draft Selection List of Philadelphia Eagles, December 4, 1961, for 1962," provided by Joe Horrigan, Curator, Pro Football Hall of Fame, April 24, 1984.

"1962 Profile of Joseph M. Hernández," University of Arizona Sports Information Department, Tucson, Arizona.

"1962 Oakland Raiders Profile information on Hank Rivera."

"1963 Oakland Raiders Profile/Statistics Information on Chon Gallegos."

Press Release, by Charles Callahan, Public Relations Director, Miami Dolphins Ltd., June 19, 1966.

"World Football League College/Pro Draft Lists, June 15, 1974," provided by Joe Horrigan, Curator, Pro Football Hall of Fame, May 12, 1987.

"Seven Are Inducted into 1975 Athletic Hall of Fame," *USF Alumnus: The Official Publication of the University of San Francisco Alumni Association.* University of San Francisco, California, 94117, vol. 2, no. 2, November 21, 1975.

"Washington Hall of Stars Elects 5 D.C. Sports Greats," (Press Release, on Gene Brito), Washington, D.C., September 9, 1982.

"All-Time Rankings," (on Emilio Vállez) University of New Mexico Sports Information Department, 1985.

"Canadian Football League—Individual Statistical Record for Gus Gonzales," provided by Larry Robertson, Statistician for the CFL, Toronto, Ontario, Canada, June 16, 1986.

"Tom Flores Retires from Football Coaching," Raiders Release, January 20, 1988.

"Biographical Information on Vince Gonzales," Louisiana State University Sports Information office, April 6. 1994.

Player Information on George Mira, provided by Louise Froggett, Assistant Curator, Canadian Football League Hall of Fame, April 4, 1994.

Public Records

California State Board of Health, Bureau of Vital Statistics, standard certificate of birth for Genaro G. Brito, County of Los Angeles, Registrar/Recorder, County Clerk, local registration no. 937/6943, filed 10/28, 1925, and no. 10, 1925, obtained August 25, 1995, (19-005186).

Certificate of death for Genaro Herman Brito, State of California, Department of Public Health, County of Los Angeles, Registrar/Recorder, County Clerk, local registration district and certificate number 7026/23123, filed July 2, 1965, obtained August 25, 1995, (19-006014).

Television Programs/Films

"The Fabulous Fifties." Television program, narrated by Harry Kalas, about the teams and players in the NFL during the decade of the 1950s, produced by NFL Films, n.d. (Rick Casares)

La NFL en Telemundo, (Spanish-language TV football show), Hialeah, Florida. Ray Romero interview, October 23, 1993.

"1953 Forty Niners Highlights Film." Bud Foster, narrator, Sports Reel Production, Berkeley, California. (Joe Arenas)

"Where Are They Now?" *Inside the NFL,* HBO sports program. Joe Kapp television interview, November 1993.

"Where Are They Now?" *Inside the NFL,* HBO sports program. Manny Fernández television interview, September 29, 1995.

Newspaper Articles

Addie, Bob. "Redskins Get John Sánchez, Detroit Tackle." N. p., November 17, 1947. From John C. Sánchez personal scrapbook. (John Sánchez)

Anderson, Dave. "NFL Best of the Best: The All-Time Super Team." *New York Times,* January 1981. (Manny Fernández)

Barker, Chris. "Cal Beats Stanford and Its Band on Last Play." *Los Angeles Times,* November 21, 1982. (Joe Kapp)

Barker, Herb. "Sánchez, Pacewic on Little All-America." *San Francisco Examiner,* December 9, 1942. (John Sánchez)

Brachman, Bob. "Arenas' Runbacks Tip Colts; 43,791 See Pro Finale." *San Francisco Examiner,* December 17, 1956. (Joe Arenas)

Burnett, Bill. "Baugh Takes Pass Lead Once Again." *Washington Post,* November 13, 1947. (John Sánchez)

Burton, Lewis. "NYU Defeats Wesleyan, 26-7." *New York Herald Tribune,* October 7, 1928. (Kelly Rodríguez)

Carmazzi, Rinaldo A. "From the Press Box—Sánchez Great Tackle." *San Francisco Foghorn,* October 23, 1942. (John Sánchez)

Childs, Kingsley. "Redskins Beat Brooklyn, 3 to 0, on Aguirre's Third Period Boot." *New York Times,* October 6, 1941. (Joe Aguirre)

Cote, Greg. "Hispanics Honor a Life of Learning." *Miami Herald,* September 14, 1993. (Ric Romero)

Culver, Harry. "Shy Primo Now Bull on Grid: Villanueva Hero to Undefeated Bruins." *Los Angeles Herald Express,* November 4, 1954. (Primo Villanueva)

Daly, Arthur. *New York Times,* October 1971, Sports section.

Dickey, Glenn. "Cal Program Has Reached a Plateau." *San Francisco Chronicle,* September 25, 1984. (Joe Kapp)

Effrat, Louis. "Groza Field Goals Topple Giants, 8-3." *New York Times,* December 18, 1950. (John Sánchez)

Finch, Frank. "Contract Sidestepped, Bravo Ignores Rams to Play in Canada." *Los Angeles Times,* February 18, 1956. (Alex Bravo)

Florence, Mal. "Illness Forces Brito to Quit Pro Football." *Los Angeles Times,* August 30, 1961. (Gene Brito)

———. "Ex-Pro Grid Star Gene Brito Dies: Former Loyola, Redskins, Ram Player Succumbs after Four Year Paralysis." *Los Angeles Times,* June 9, 1965. (Gene Brito)

Flores, David. "Brack Graduate Ready for Overdue Visit to Cotton Bowl." *San Antonio Express-News,* December 21, 1995. (Dan Garza)

Geyer, Jack. "Rams Charge Canadian Team Has Stolen Halfback Bravo." *Los Angeles Times,* July 24, 1956. (Alex Bravo)

Grieve, Curley. "West's Defensive Might Difference." *San Francisco Examiner,* December 31, 1961. (Henry Rivera)

Hagen, Howard. "Aztecs Wallop Poly, 69-0, Méndez Scores Five Times." *San Diego Union,* October 6, 1963. (Mario Méndez)

Hardman, A. L. "Rodríguez Will Help, Herman Hoskins Feels." *Charleston Gazette,* November 13, 1970. (Jesse Rodríguez)

Hartman, Steve. "Tom Flores: L.A. Raiders." *Los Angeles Sports Profiles,* spring issue, 1987. (Tom Flores)

Harton, Bruce. "Jesse Rodríguez, Clarksburg's Own Star at Salem College, Will Have Greatest Year of His Life in 1927." *Clarksburg Exponent,* September 23, 1927. (Jesse Rodríguez)

Hoffman, Jeane. "Classes Ended When Rams Blew Horn for Teacher Villanueva." *Los Angeles Times,* September 12, 1961. (Danny Villanueva)

Hyland, Dick. "Hyland Fling." *Los Angeles Times,* September 2, 1954. (Primo Villanueva)

Jauss, Bill. "Will García Get Message? Purdue Light Threat." *Lafayette Journal,* September 1963. (Jim García)

Keisser, Bob. "The Fabled Life of Joe Kapp." *Los Angeles Herald-Examiner,* October 22, 1982. (Joe Kapp)

Laing, Jack. "Hornets Show Resourceful Varied Attack, Punish Line and Pass over Bison Heads." *Buffalo Courier Express,* October 7, 1929. (Jesse Rodríguez)

———. "Galloping Ghost Aids Mate in Scoring 2 Touchdowns: Locals Threaten at Close." *Buffalo Courier Express,* October 14, 1929, p. 15. (Jesse Rodríguez)

———. "McDonnell's Great Sprint Breaks 3-3 Tie at Stadium: Weimer Boots Bison Points." *Buffalo Courier Express,* September 30, 1929. (Jesse Rodríguez)

Leiser, Bill. "Crow Flies 98 Yards to Gael Triumph." *San Francisco Chronicle,* December 2, 1942. (John Sánchez)

Lewis, "Spud" L. D. "Northern California All Stars Selected," N. p., from John C. Sánchez personal scrapbook, dated December 1942. (John Sánchez)

Libman, Gary. "He Gets His Kicks Serving Latino Community." *Los Angeles Times,* September 29, 1985. (Danny Villanueva)

Long, Gary. "Fernández Taking His Lumps in Dolphin Comeback Attempt." *Miami Herald,* July 14, 1977. (Manny Fernández)

Magee, Jerry. "Sharp Scrimmage for Chargers." *San Diego Union,* August 30, 1964. (Mario Méndez)

Minter, Jim. "The Unknown Falcon: Hernández? Who's He?" *Atlanta Journal,* August 20, 1966. (José Hernández)

Newhall, Bob. "Rodríguez, Bullington Stars of Bobcat Win." *Clarksburg Telegram,* September 1928. (Kelly Rodríguez)

Newland, Russ. "Sánchez Makes 1st Team." *San Francisco Chronicle,* December 10, 1942. (John Sánchez)

Oates, Bob. "Reaping the Harvest: Once a Fruit Picker, Tom Flores Worked His Way to Coach of Oakland Raiders." *Los Angeles Times,* September 1, 1979. (Tom Flores)

Olderman, Murray. "The Hungriest Bear." *San Francisco Sunday Examiner & Chronicle,* July 24, 1983. (Joe Kapp)

Overland, Wayne. "Joe Hernández' Signature Worth More Each Game." *Edmonton Journal,* September 12, 1967. (José Hernández)

———. "Jack Rabbit Hops Again." *Edmonton Journal,* February 3, 1971. (José Hernández)

———. "Hernández Decides to Quit Esks and Play Elsewhere Next Season." *Edmonton Journal,* September 26, 1967. (José Hernández)

———. "Prodigal Son Returns to Esks," *Edmonton Journal,* March 21, 1968. (José Hernández)

———. "Hernández Was Busy Putting Out Fires." *Edmonton Journal,* July 15, 1969. (José Hernández)

———. "Jauch Welcomes Hernández Back." *Edmonton Journal,* July 14 1970. (José Hernández)

Peebles, Dick. "Texas Rolls Over LSU 20-6." *San Antonio Express-News,* September 19, 1954. (Vincent González)

Perilman, Abe J. "Aggies Rob Wichita State Blind: Intercept Six Passes in 45-17 Victory." *Las Cruces Sun-News,* October 16, 1966. (Al Gonzales)

———. "Aggies Aerial, Gunnery Blasts Lobos, 47-12: Olivas' Passes Tally Four TDs, Reaps 238 Yards." *Las Cruces Sun-News,* November 13, 1966. (Al Gonzales)

———. "Aggies Humiliate Axers in One-Sided 90-0 Victory." *Las Cruces Sun-News,* November 12, 1967. (Al Gonzales)

Pope, Edwin. "A Super Bowl Hero Re-Enters Reality." *Miami Herald,* January 6, 1978. (Manny Fernández)

Press, Larry. "Big Plays Win Jr. Rose Bowl." *Bakersfield Californian,* December 14, 1959. (José Hernández)

———. "Hernández's 4 Touchdowns Top Warriors." *Bakersfield Californian,* November 22, 1959. (José Hernández)

Salazar, Carlos. "Prairie Wolfpack Lineman; Air Force Here Next Week." *Albuquerque Tribune,* October 23, 1961. (José Hernández)

Selby, Don. "West Player Hail Owens; East Is Baffled by 24 Bootleg." *San Francisco Examiner,* December 3, 1961. (Henry Rivera)

Sheehan, Joseph M. "Baugh and Sáenz Pace 28-20 Victory." *New York Times,* October 13, 1947. (Eddie Sáenz)

———. "Last Period Drive for 23 Points Gives Green Bay 29-27 Triumph." *New York Times,* October 29, 1951. (Dan Garza)

———. "Syracuse Eleven Choice over Miami Today in Liberty Bowl; Less Than 20,000 Will See Contest." *New York Times,* December 16, 1961. (George Mira)

———. "Syracuse Defeats Miami in Liberty Bowl, 15-14, with Davis Leading Rally." *New York Times,* December 17, 1961. (George Mira)

Smith, Seymour S. "Former Eagle Grid Star to Play Here." *Army Times,* December 1951. (Ray Romero)

Smith, Jim. "Big John Hits Limelight." *Redlands Daily Register,* September 1943. (John Sánchez)

Stiles, Maxwell. "Styles in Sports: Why Did Rams Pass Goux, Primo?" *Los Angeles Herald Express,* February 1, 1955. (Primo Villanueva)

Stirling, Scotty. "Raiders Nip Oilers, 52-49." *Oakland Tribune,* December 23, 1963. (Tom Flores)

———. "Charger On Slaught Shatters Raiders." *Oakland Tribune,* October 1, 1962. (Chon Gallegos)

Strauss, Michael. "Bears Over-Power Yanks' Squad, 45-21." *New York Times,* December 10, 1951. (Dan Garza)

Sullivan, Prescott. "Offside Costs 49ers Upset Victory! Lions Win, 17-13; Arenas Returns Kickoff 90 Yards." *San Francisco Examiner,* November 5, 1956. (Joe Arenas)

Templeton, Dink. *Palo Alto Times,* December 12, 1951, Sports section. (Joe Arenas)

Tobin, Jack. "Redskin Star Once Roughed Up Locals." *Los Angeles Times,* August 27, 1948. (John Sánchez)

———. "Primo Almost Gave Up." *Los Angeles Times,* October 6, 1954. (Primo Villanueva)

Vaughan, Irving. "Great Lakes Triumphs 40-12 over Wisconsin." *Chicago Tribune,* October 29, 1944. (Eddie Sáenz)

Wallace, William. "East on Top, 18-15, on Mira's Passes." *New York Times,* June 28, 1964. (George Mira)

———. "Bears Score 21 Points in Second Half and Defeat All-Stars; Passing of Mira Thrills 65,000." *New York Times,* August 8, 1964. (George Mira)

Werden, Lincoln A. "Alabama's Nine Touchdowns Rout Syracuse by Record Orange Bowl Score; Crimson Tide Wins at Miami, 61-6." *New York Times,* January 2, 1953. (Robert Luna)

White, Gordon S. "Bears Rate Slight Favorites over Steelers in Game at Pittsburgh Today; Chicago to Play without Casares." *New York Times,* November 1963. (Rick Casares)

Whorton, Cal. "McElenny, Brito Get Grid Awards." *Los Angeles Times,* January 9, 1959. (Gene Brito)

———. "33-Year-Old Veteran to Put Off Retirement." *Los Angeles Times*, March 5, 1959. (Gene Brito)

Wolf, Al. "Brito May End Grid Career in Pro Bowl." *Los Angeles Times*, January 7, 1958. (Gene Brito)

———. "Danny Boy's Now a Cowboy." *Los Angeles Times*, July 31, 1965. (Danny Villanueva)

Zimmerman, Paul. "Washington Redskins Sign Eddie Sáenz." *Los Angeles Times*, June 4, 1946. (Eddie Sáenz)

———. "Villanueva Has Itchy Toe, Views Big Season." *Los Angeles Times*, June 17, 1964. (Danny Villanueva)

Anonymous Newspaper Articles

(in chronological order)

"Here, Today, Rodríguez's Kelly and Jess, Two Brothers, Pitted One against the Other, Score Both Touchdowns of Game." *Clarksburg Telegram*, October 8, 1927. (Jesse and Kelly Rodríguez)

"Rodríguez Scores Two Touchdowns on Philippi Baptist." *Clarksburg Exponent*, November 18, 1927. (Jesse Rodríguez)

"Wesleyan Has Easy Time in First Battle." *Clarksburg Telegram*, September 21, 1928. (Kelly Rodríguez)

"Rodríguez and Kistler Lead Salem's Attack Throughout." *Clarksburg Exponent*, October 1928. (Jesse Rodríguez)

"Salem Is Winner at Marietta College, 12-0." *Clarksburg Exponent*, October 13, 1928. (Jesse Rodríguez)

"Wesleyan Wins over Concord, Rodríguez Plows Through for Two Scores, Final Count, 18 to 0." *Clarksburg Telegram*, October 13, 1928. (Kelly Rodríguez)

"Kelly Dashes 50 Yards for Lone Scores; Rodríguez's Punting Only Feature of the Wesleyan Play against Georgetown." *Clarksburg Telegram*, October 20, 1928. (Kelly Rodríguez)

"Bobcats in Decisive Win by 34-0 Tally; Thirty Seconds after Game Opens Rodríguez Runs 76 Yards to Score." *Clarksburg Telegram*, October 27, 1928. (Kelly Rodríguez)

"Jesse Rodríguez Star of Salem College Backfield." *Clarksburg Exponent*, October 31, 1928. (Jesse Rodríguez)

"Battles and Spanish Lad Are Scorers." *Clarksburg Telegram*, November 10, 1928. (Kelly Rodríguez)

"Navy Swamps Bobcat Eleven." *Clarksburg Telegram*, November 13, 1928. (Kelly Rodríguez)

"Davis and Elkins Twice Cross Wesleyan Goal." *Clarksburg Telegram*, November 17, 1928. (Kelly Rodríguez)

"Three West Virginia Boys among Ten Leading Eastern Grid Scorers." *Clarksburg Telegram*, November 30, 1928. (Kelly Rodríguez)

"Bison Pros Open Season Today with Chicago Cards: Chief Elkins with Rivals." *Buffalo Courier Express*, September 29, 1929. (Jesse Rodríguez)

"Buffalo Pros Hold Hornets Three Points." *Buffalo Courier Express*, October 6, 1929. (Jesse Rodríguez)

"Ties Steam Rollers, 7-7 Buffalo Comes from Behind to Knot Count in Pro Football." *New York Times*, October 12, 1929. (Jesse Rodríguez)

"Hagsberg the Buffalo Star in Tough Game." *Buffalo Courier Express*, October 21, 1929. (Jesse Rodríguez)

"Notre Dame Rally Downs Drake, 19-7." *New York Times*, November 10, 1929. (Waldo Don Carlos)

"Bears Misplays Present Bisons with 19-7 Win, Fumbles and Intercepted Passes." *Chicago Daily Tribune*, November 25, 1929. (Jesse Rodríguez)

"Notre Dame Repels Drake by 28 to 7." *New York Times*, November 16, 1930. (Waldo Don Carlos)

"Drake Air Game Beats Iowa State." *New York Times*, November 23, 1930. (Waldo Don Carlos)

"Packers Whip Frankford; Regain Lead." *Green Bay Press-Gazette*, November 28, 1930. (Kelly Rodríguez)

"Rodríguez's Pro Team Loses to Portsmouth by the Score of 42-0." *Clarksburg Telegram*, December 7, 1930. (Kelly Rodríguez)

"Packers Are Upset by Cardinals, 21-13." *New York Times*, November 16, 1931. (Waldo Don Carlos)

"Kelly Rodríguez Signs: Will Be upon the Same Team as 'Gyp' Battles." *Clarksburg Telegram*, May 1935. (Kelly Rodríguez)

"St. Mary's Triumphs 20 to 13, Withstanding Texas to Tech Rally." *New York Times*, January 3, 1939. (Joe Aguirre)

"Big John Sánchez Leads Tackle Choices for All Conference Honors." *Compton (Los Angeles) Tartar Shield*, September 1940. (John Sánchez)

"USF Soph Awarded Grid Honor." *San Francisco Examiner*, May 22, 1942. (John Sánchez)

"One-Man Elevens Blast Opposition." *San Francisco Examiner*, October 25, 1942. (John Sánchez)

"Dons Score 47-27 Win over Fresno." *San Francisco News*, November 4, 1942. (John Sánchez)

"Ex-San Diego High Gridder to Captain Redlands Eleven." *San Diego Union*, September 24, 1943. (John Sánchez)

"Wisconsin Upset by Illinois, 25-7" *New York Times*, October 7, 1943. (Peter Pérez)

"Illinois Topples Pitt Eleven, 35-25." *New York Times,* October 16, 1943. (Peter Pérez)

"Sánchez No. 71 Retired: Redlands Honor Ex-Hill To Gridiron Star." *San Diego Union,* October 19, 1943. (John Sánchez)

"Outgained Illinois Checks Iowa, 19-0." *New York Times,* November 6, 1943. (Peter Pérez)

"Ohio State Kick Subdues Illinois by 29-26, 12 Minutes after Game Apparently Ends." *New York Times,* November 14, 1943. (Peter Pérez)

"East-West Teams Play to a 13-13 Draw." *San Francisco Examiner,* January 2, 1944. (Gonzalo Morales)

"Ft. Sheridan First Opponent for Great Lakes." *Great Lakes Bulletin,* August 25, 1944. (Eddie Sáenz)

"Great Lakes Clashes with Ohio State at Columbus." *Great Lakes Bulletin,* October 20, 1944. (Eddie Sáenz)

"Great Lakes Routs Wisconsin by 40-12." *New York Times,* October 29, 1944. (Eddie Sáenz)

"Great Lakes, Marquette Tangle at Milwaukee." *Great Lakes Bulletin,* November 3, 1944. (Eddie Sáenz)

"Sáenz Splurges against Badgers." *Great Lakes Bulletin,* November 3, 1944. (Eddie Sáenz)

"Sailors Meet Ft. Warren in Final Home Game." *Great Lakes Bulletin,* November, 24, 1944. (Eddie Sáenz)

"Aguirre, Redskins, Best Cards, 24-21." *New York Times,* November 5, 1945. (Joe Aguirre)

"Bears Defeat Green Bay by 28-24, as Running Game Thrills 45,527." *New York Times,* November 5, 1945. (Peter Pérez)

"Bears Turn Back Steelers by 28-7." *New York Times,* November 26, 1945. (Peter Pérez)

"Bears Turn Cardinal, 28-20." *New York Times,* December 3, 1945. (Peter Pérez)

"Dons, Bisons Even at Buffalo, 21-21, Aguirre Takes O'Rourke Pass Four Minutes from End to Tie for Los Angeles." *New York Times,* September 30, 1946. (Joe Aguirre)

"Steelers Late Rush Surprises Redskins for a Tie at 14-14." *New York Times,* September 30, 1946. (Eddie Sáenz)

"Aguirre's Field Goal for Dons in Last 20 Seconds Tops Browns." *New York Times,* November 4, 1946. (Joe Aguirre)

"Sánchez, USF Tackle Joins Clippers for Tilt Tomorrow." *San Francisco Examiner,* December 1946. (John Sánchez)

"Dons Crush Bisons with Record 62-14." *New York Times,* December 2, 1946. (Joe Aguirre)

"Georgia Tech Triumphs, 41-19, Grabbing 8 St. Mary's Forwards." *New York Times,* January 2, 1947. (Gonzalo Morales)

"87-Point Total Sets a New Mark as Eagles Top Redskins, 45-42." *New York Times,* September 29, 1947. (Eddie Sáenz)

"Battered Tribe Breaks Three League Marks, Baugh Snaps Two." Detroit newspaper, December 15, 1947. (John Sánchez)

"Steelers Conquer Giants, 38-28, despite Conerly's Record Passing." *New York Times,* December 6, 1948. (Gonzalo Morales)

"SMU, with Doak Walker, Picked to Defeat Oregon in Dallas Battle." *New York Times,* January 1, 1949. (Dan Garza)

"So. Methodist Trips Oregon as Walker and Rote Excel." *New York Times,* January 2, 1949. (Dan Garza)

"Football Yankees Topple Buffalo on Johnson's Field Goal, 17-14." *New York Times,* September 12, 1949. (Dan Garza)

"37,697 See Bears Triumph by 24-21." *New York Times,* October 15, 1951. (Dan Garza)

"Bravo Breaks Two Poly Running Marks." *San Luis Obispo, California, Telegram-Tribune,* October 22, 1951. (Alex Bravo)

"Celeri's Aerial Wizardry Brings 24-24 Deadlock in Detroit Game." *New York Times,* October 22, 1951. (Dan Garza)

"Bravo Scores Twice, Mustangs Stab Gauchos, 14-7." San Luis Obispo, *California, Telegram-Tribune,* November 12, 1951. (Alex Bravo)

"Yanks Tie, Phelans Team Gains 10-10 Draw with Forty Niners on Late Goal." *New York Times,* November 26, 1951. (Dan Garza)

"Celeri's Passes Overcome Packers for Yanks First Victory, 31-28." *New York Times,* December 3, 1951. (Dan Garza)

"Service Team to Oppose Cardinal Eleven Today." *Army Times,* September 1952. (Ray Romero)

"Mustangs Beaten by Texans, 28-7." *San Luis Obispo, California, Telegram-Tribune,* September 22, 1952. (Alex Bravo)

"Local Eleven to Meet 'Red Devils' in Grid Clash This Saturday Afternoon." *Army Times,* October 1952. (Ray Romero)

"Mustangs Upset Aztecs, 20-18, in League Game." *San Luis Obispo, California, Telegram-Tribune,* October 6, 1952. (Alex Bravo)

"Bravo, Lawson, Neal Spark 34-26 Poly Win over Gators." *San Luis Obispo, California, Telegram-Tribune,* October 20, 1952. (Alex Bravo)

"Most Valuable Race Proves Close Fight." *Army Times,* November 1952. (Ray Romero)

"Who's Who among All-Army Leaders." *Army Times,* November 1952. (Ray Romero)

"Mustangs Beat Diablos 32-7, for First CCAA Title." *San Luis Obispo, California, Telegram-Tribune,* November 10, 1952. (Alex Bravo)

"Ray Romero Retains Lead in All-Army Team Voting." *Army Times,* December 1952. (Ray Romero)

"Bravo Claims Three Mustang Records, Speedy Halfback Big Factor in Poly CCAA Climb." *San Luis Obispo, California, Telegram-Tribune,* November 23, 1953. (Alex Bravo)

"Poly Dominates Mythical Team." *San Luis Obispo, California, Telegram-Tribune,* November 25, 1953. (Alex Bravo)

"Little All-Coast Team." *San Luis Obispo, California, Telegram-Tribune,* November 27, 1953. (George Maderos)

"Little All-American Honors to Three Mustang Gridders." *San Luis Obispo, California, Telegram-Tribune,* December 3, 1953. (Alex Bravo)

"UCLA Defeats Washington, 21-20" *New York Times,* October 10, 1954. (Primo Villanueva)

"UCLA Overwhelms Stanford on Coast." *New York Times,* October 17, 1954. (Primo Villanueva)

"UCLA Subdues California: Villanueva Stars as Bruins Win, 27-6." *New York Times,* October 31, 1954. (Primo Villanueva)

"46,435 See UCLA Rout Oregon by 41-0." *New York Times,* November 7, 1954. (Primo Villanueva)

"UCLA Keeps Title, Routing USC, 34-0." *New York Times,* November 21, 1954. (Primo Villanueva)

"College All-Star Eleven Beats Hawaiians in Hula Bowl, 33-13." *New York Times,* January 10, 1955. (Primo Villanueva)

"Brito Named Pro Player of the Year." *Los Angeles Times,* December 13, 1955. (Gene Brito)

"Gray's Pass Play Defeat Blues on Gridiron, 20-19." *New York Times,* January 1, 1956. (Vincent González)

"Nixon Praises Brito in Last Skins Game." *Los Angeles Times,* December 15, 1958. (Gene Brito)

"Joey Weaving Tale of Pigskin Fantasy." *Bakersfield Californian,* December 9, 1959. (José Hernández)

"Joey Picks Arizona." *Bakersfield Californian,* February 1, 1960. (José Hernández)

"UA Touchdown Twins Rejuvenate Wildcats." *Arizona Daily Star,* November 1960. (José Hernández)

"Joe Hernández Leads Arizona." *Fresno California Sun,* November 20, 1960. (José Hernández)

"Rams Field Goal Top Packers, 33-31." *New York Times,* November 21, 1960. (Danny Villanueva)

"Mira Will Start in Liberty Bowl." *New York Times,* December 15, 1961. (George Mira)

"San Jose QB Wins Pop Warner Award." *San Francisco Examiner,* December 29, 1961. (Chon Gallegos)

"South Team Choice to Set Back North." *New York Times,* January 6, 1962. (Henry Rivera)

"Canadian Loop Offers Hernández $20,000." *Bakersfield Californian,* June 18, 1962. (José Hernández)

"Cornhuskers Edge by Hurricanes in Bowl." *San Antonio Express-News,* December 16, 1962. (George Mira)

"Hernández Traded to Edmonton Club." *Bakersfield Californian,* February 19, 1963. (José Hernández)

"Rams Upset Vikings on Late Kick, 27-24." *New York Times,* October 21, 1963. (Danny Villanueva)

"Rams Defeat Colts on Field Goal, 17-16." *New York Times,* November 25, 1963. (Danny Villanueva)

"Mira Sparks South to Triumph, North Loses, 23-14." *New York Times,* December 22, 1963. (George Mira)

"South Seniors Top North, 28-21, as Burrell Stars." *New York Times,* January 5, 1964. (George Mira)

"Sports-O-Rama, The 'Remembered' Art of Punting." *Clarksburg Exponent,* August 12, 1964. (Jesse Rodríguez)

"Jesse Rodríguez on Football—Then and Now." *Clarksburg Exponent,* August 14, 1964. (Jesse Rodríguez)

"Washington Coach Likes Hernández." *Bakersfield Californian,* September 8, 1964. (José Hernández)

"West Takes Shrine Game." *New York Times,* Janaury 3, 1965. (Jim García)

"Annapolis' Joe Hernández among NAFL's Best Flankers." *Mobile Register,* November 23, 1965. (José Hernández)

"Annapolis Places Seven on NAFL All-Star Club." *Washington Post,* December 26, 1965. (José Hernández)

"Aggies Skin Pacific Tigers, 49-23: Carroll Scores Three Times, Bohl Gains 195." *Las Cruces Sun-News,* October 9, 1966. (Al Gonzales)

"Mira Substitute, Engineers Upset." *New York Times,* October 10, 1966. (George Mira)

"Cowboys Defeat Redskins, 31-30; Kick by Villanueva with 15 seconds to Play Wins." *New York Times,* November 14, 1966. (Danny Villanueva)

"Field Goal Saved Season for Danny." *Los Angeles Times,* November 18, 1966. (Danny Villaneuva)

"Villanueva Rates Soccer Style Place Kicking as Best Method." *Los Angeles Times,* December 3, 1966. (Danny Villanueva)

"Mira Paces 49ers to 43-28 Triumph." *New York Times,* December 11, 1967. (George Mira)

"49ers Aerials Top Cowboys by 24-16; Mira Playing Out Option, Connects for 3 Scores." *New York Times,* December 17, 1967. (George Mira)

"Kapp Passes for 7 Touchdowns as Vikings Crush Colts, 52-14." *New York Times,* September 29, 1969. (Joe Kapp)

"Happy Kapp Is Looking for 2 More." *San Antonio Express-News,* December 28, 1969. (Joe Kapp)

"Vikings Rally to Edge Rams, 23-20." *San Antonio Express-News,* December 28, 1969. (Joe Kapp)

"Eddie Sáenz, Ex-Trojan Dies." *Los Angeles Times,* April 29, 1971. (Eddie Sáenz)

"Nixon Nominates Gene Brito for Football Hall of Fame." *Highland Park News Herald and Journal,* October 3, 1971. (Gene Brito)

"Flashback of a Fullback." Tampa newspaper, 1977 (article provided by Rick Casares, July 20, 1995). (Rick Casares)

"Tom Flores, Longtime Raider Is Named Coach." *Los Angeles Times,* February 9, 1979. (Tom Flores)

"Kapp Comes Home." *Cal Athletic News: Special Edition,* Sports Information Office, University of California, Berkeley, August 1982, pp. 1, 4. (Joe Kapp)

"Romero Honored as NFL Pioneer." *Miami Herald,* September 15, 1993. (Ray Romero)

Magazine Articles

Anderson, Dave. "Miami's Immovable Object Meets Miami's Irrestible Force." *Sport* 57, no. 1, January 1974. (Manny Fernández)

Boyd, Denny. "It Was the Biggest Deal since Sam and Hall. A Pair of Touchdown Experts Give Their Opinions on That." *Touchdown: The All-Canadian Sports Magazine,* August 31, 1961, 24. (Joe Kapp)

Bryan Jimmy. "Center Arena for the Matador." *Football World: The Official Magazine of the World Football League* (Sun vs Birmingham Americans game program), October 16, 1974. (George Mira)

Chapin, Dwight. "Dos de la misma clase," *Pro! The Magazine of the National Football League* 1, no. 1, August 1981, 49. (Tom Flores)

Fimrite, Ron. "Surprise Marriage of the Year: Joe Kapp and Cal." *Sports Illustrated* 57, no. 10, September 1, 1982, 104-6, 108-16, 125. (Joe Kapp)

Forbes, Gordon. "Matador from Miami." *Pro-Football Guide,* October 7, 1969. (George Mira)

Hooper, Al. "Think Big." *Touchdown: The All-Canadian Sports Magazine,* November 15, 1963, 20. (Joe Kapp)

Kapp, Joe, with Jack Olsen. "A Man of Machismo." *Sports Illustrated* 33, no. 3, July 20, 1970, 29-31. (Joe Kapp)

———. "A Misfit Who Lives to Win." *Sports Illustrated* 33, no. 4, July 27, 1970, 30, 32-37. (Joe Kapp)

———. "We Were Just a Bunch of Party Poopers." *Sports Illustrated* 22, no. 5, August 3, 1970, 20-25. (Joe Kapp)

Longoria, Mario. "Jess Rodríguez: First Latino in Pro-Football." *NUESTRO* 8, no. 1, Jan./Feb. 1984, 51. (Jesse Rodríguez)

Marshall, John. "World Bowl in Crisis." *Sports Illustrated* 41, no. 25, December 16, 1974, 20-23. (George Mira)

Olsen, Jack. "He Goes Where the Trouble Is." *Sports Illustrated* 33, no. 16, October 19, 1970, 22-24, 27. (Joe Kapp)

Underwood, John. "One Wonderful Conch Is This Mira." *Sports Illustrated* 19, no. 13, September 23, 1963, 98-102, 105-6, 108, 111-12, 114. (George Mira)

Index